Roman Conquests: Gaul

For Laura

Roman Conquests: Gaul

Michael M. Sage

Pen & Sword
MILITARY

First published in Great Britain in 2011 by
PEN & SWORD MILITARY
An imprint of
Pen & Sword Books Ltd
47 Church Street
Barnsley
South Yorkshire
S70 2AS

ISBN 978-1-84884-144-4

A CIP catalogue record for this book is
available from the British Library.

Typeset by Concept, Huddersfield, West Yorkshire.
Printed and bound in England by CPI UK.

Pen & Sword Books Ltd incorporates the Imprints of Pen & Sword Aviation, Pen &
Sword Family History, Pen & Sword Maritime, Pen & Sword Military, Pen & Sword
Discovery, Wharncliffe Local History, Wharncliffe True Crime, Wharncliffe Transport,
Pen & Sword Select, Pen & Sword Military Classics, Leo Cooper, The Praetorian Press,
Remember When, Seaforth Publishing and Frontline Publishing.

For a complete list of Pen & Sword titles please contact
PEN & SWORD BOOKS LIMITED
47 Church Street, Barnsley, South Yorkshire, S70 2AS, England
E-mail: enquiries@pen-and-sword.co.uk
Website: www.pen-and-sword.co.uk

Contents

Acknowledgements

I would especially like to thank my editor Philip Sidnell for suggesting the subject of this book and for all of his help in seeing it through the press. Thanks are also due to Ian Hughes for his help with maps and to Graham Sumner and Franck Mathieu for the illustrations.

A year's leave from the Classics Department at the University of Cincinnati and the generous support provided by the Louise Taft Semple Classics Fund were instrumental in giving me the time to complete my research and to begin writing. As always any errors or omissions are the responsibility of the author.

List of Plates

Maps

List of Maps

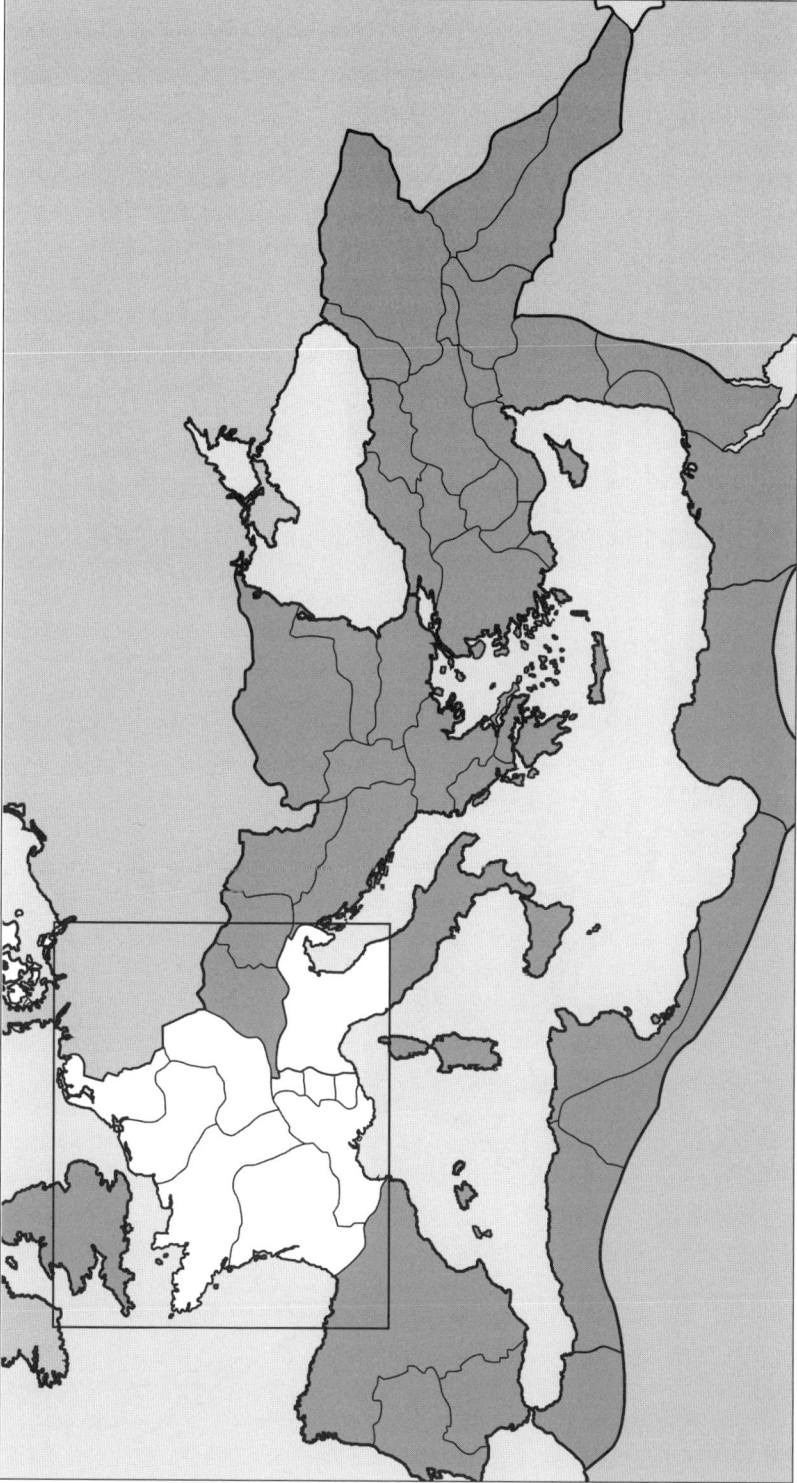

Map 1: The Roman Empire at its greatest extent with the area covered by this volume highlighted

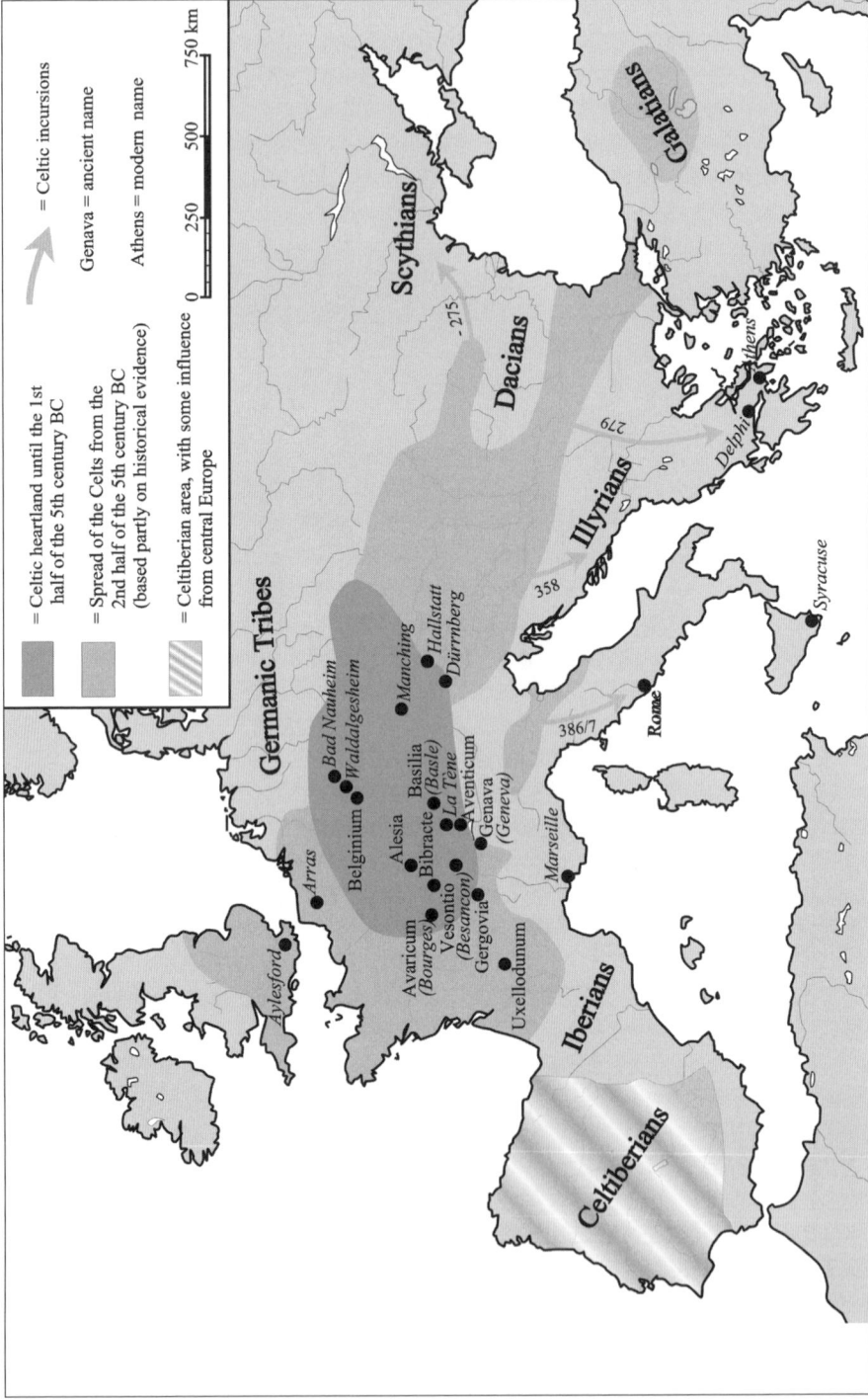

Map 2: Celtic Settlement until 150

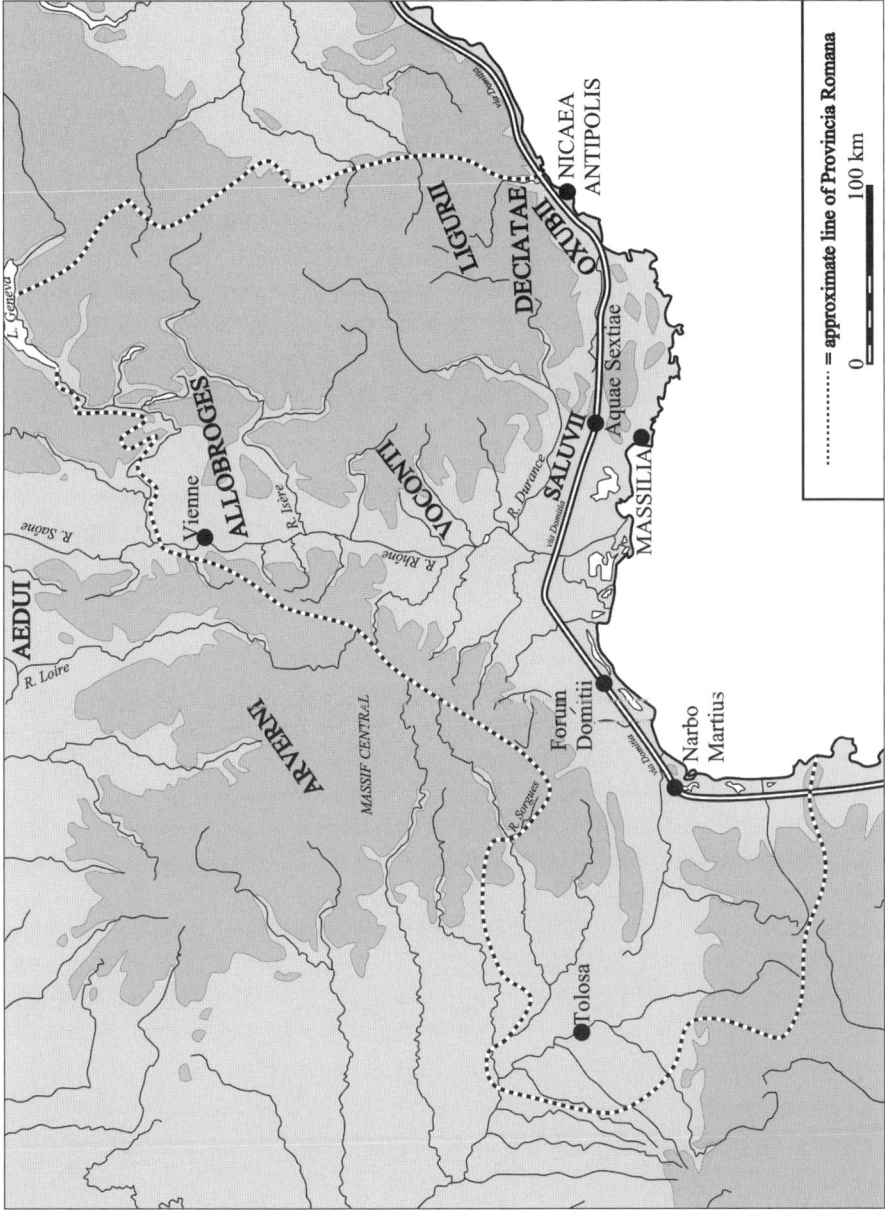

Map 3 Transalpine Gaul in the Late-Second Century BC

.... = approximate line of Provincia Romana

0   100 km

Map 4 Gaul in the Time of Caesar

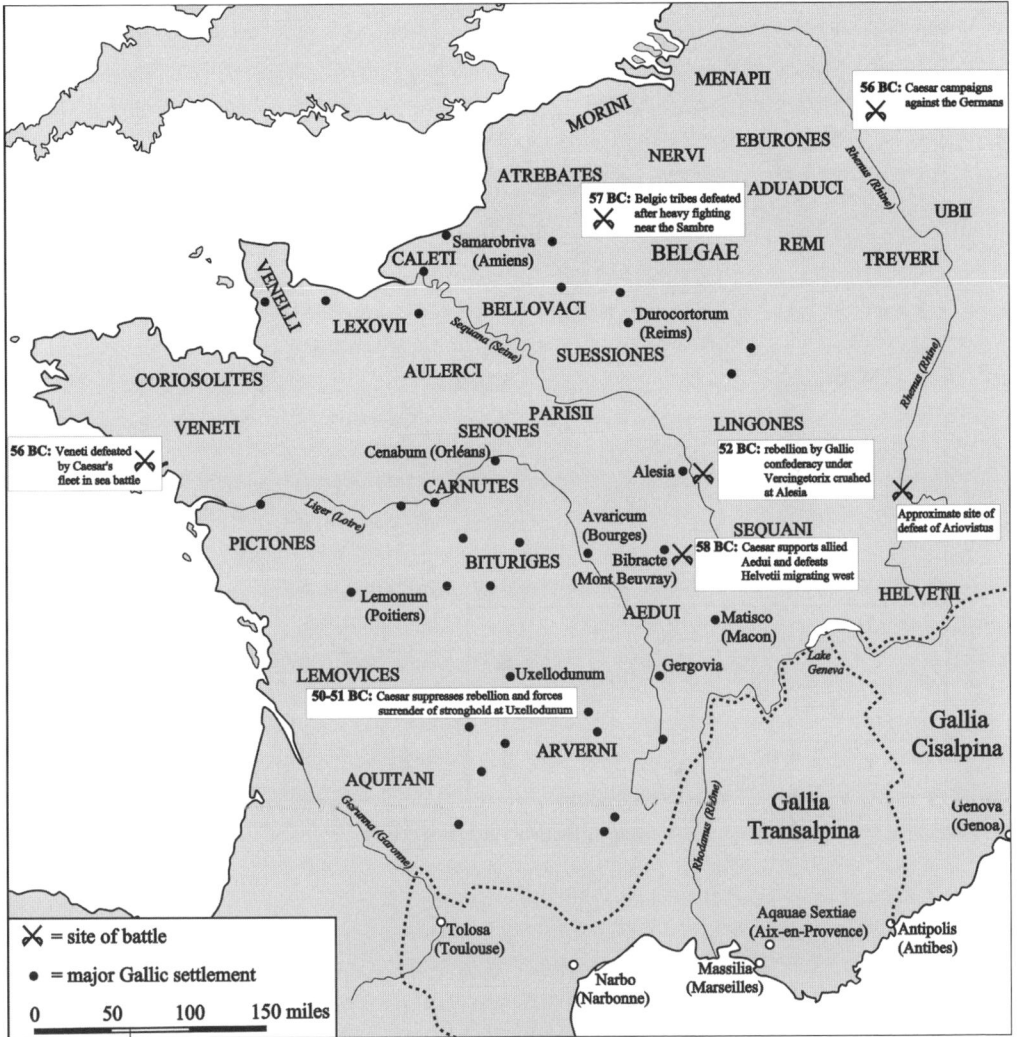

MENAPII

56 BC: Caesar campaigns against the Germans

MORINI

NERVI   EBURONES

ATREBATES   ADUADUCI

57 BC: Belgic tribes defeated after heavy fighting near the Sambre

UBII

Rhenus (Rhine)

Samarobriva   REMI

CALETI   (Amiens)   BELGAE   TREVERI

VENELLI

LEXOVII   BELLOVACI

Sequana (Seine)   Durocortorum (Reims)

CORIOSOLITES   AULERCI   SUESSIONES

Rhenus (Rhine)

VENETI   PARISII

SENONES   LINGONES

56 BC: Veneti defeated by Caesar's fleet in sea battle

Cenabum (Orléans)   Alesia   52 BC: rebellion by Gallic confederacy under Vercingetorix crushed at Alesia

CARNUTES

Liger (Loire)

Avaricum (Bourges)   SEQUANI   Approximate site of defeat of Ariovistus

PICTONES   BITURIGES   Bibracte (Mont Beuvray)   58 BC: Caesar supports allied Aedui and defeats Helvetii migrating west

Lemonum (Poitiers)   AEDUI   HELVETII

Matisco (Macon)

LEMOVICES   Uxellodunum   Gergovia   Lake Geneva

50-51 BC: Caesar suppresses rebellion and forces surrender of stronghold at Uxellodunum

Gallia Cisalpina

AQUITANI   ARVERNI

Gallia Transalpina   Genova (Genoa)

Garumna (Garonne)

Rhodanus (Rhône)

Aqauae Sextiae (Aix-en-Provence)   Antipolis (Antibes)

Tolosa (Toulouse)

X = site of battle

• = major Gallic settlement

Narbo (Narbonne)   Massilia (Marseilles)

0   50   100   150 miles

Map 5 Caesar's Campaigns

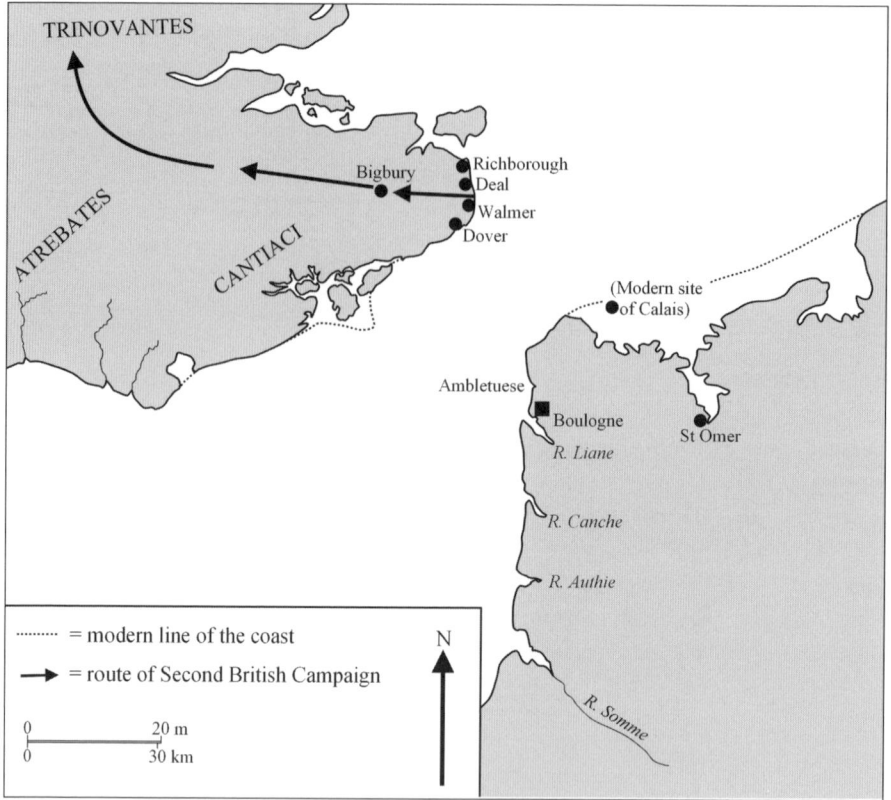

Map 6 British Invasions 55-54

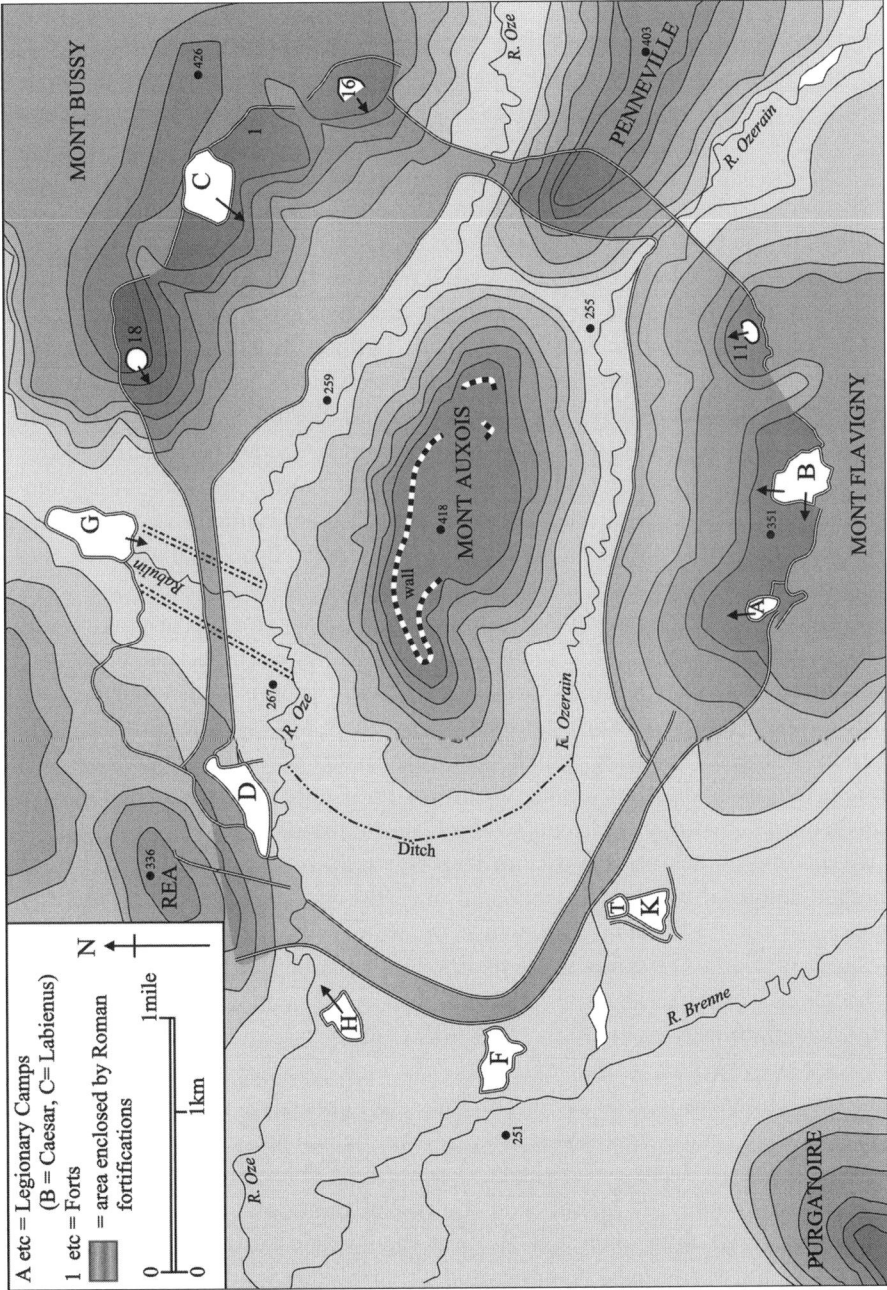

Map 7 Alesia

A etc = Legionary Camps
(B = Caesar, C= Labienus)
1 etc = Forts
= area enclosed by Roman
fortifications

N

0   1km

0   1mile

MONT BUSSY

•426

16

1

C

18

PENNEVILLE •403

R. Oze

R. Ozerain

255

259

11

MONT AUXOIS

•418

wall

•351

B

A

MONT FLAVIGNY

G

Rabutin

•267

R. Oze

R. Ozerain

Ditch

REA •336

D

K

T

H

F

•251

R. Oze

R. Brenne

PURGATOIRE

Introduction

In September of 46 BC* Julius Caesar celebrated a fourfold triumph for his victories in the Roman civil war and his conquest of Gaul north of the Alps. Vercingetorix, who led most of the Gallic tribes in their final struggle against Caesar in 52, was paraded in the triumph and then executed as a rebel.[1]

The geographical area that the Romans defined as Gaul (Latin: *Gallia*) included much of Western Europe. It comprised that part of Italy that lay north of the Apennine Mountains as far as the foothills of the Alps. It then extended across the Alps, with its principal boundaries on the Atlantic to the west, the Pyrenees and the Mediterranean to the south, and the Rhine and North Sea as its eastern and northern limits. The Romans distinguished Cisalpine Gaul, or Gaul on the Italian side of the Alps, from Transalpine Gaul north of the mountains.

In both areas the predominant population was Celtic. The origins of the Celts, whom the Romans called Gauls (Latin: *Galli*), lay as far back as the second millennium BC. By the sixth century BC Celtic groups were recognizable through their shared culture, and especially their artistic traditions as well as their common language which occupied much of Europe north of the Mediterranean lands. By the fourth century BC Celtic cultures extended in a wide arc from Spain and Britain to the Danube basin.[2]

By the mid-eighth century BC an Iron Age culture known as Hallstatt had emerged among the Celts, which lasted until the mid-fifth century. This was replaced by the La Tène culture, which the Romans encountered during their conquest of Gaul. Our knowledge of this last stage of Celtic culture rests on archaeological discoveries and references to the Celts in Greek and Roman authors beginning as early as the mid-fifth century.

Caesar provides our fullest description of Celtic society in Gaul although there are references to it in earlier authors.[3] On his arrival as governor in 58, Caesar found a highly stratified society in Gaul, which archaeological evidence shows had already been established for centuries. Three groups are attested; the great aristocrats, the Druids and the rest of the population.

The aristocrats drew their wealth from their vast estates as well as profits from trade, but their social standing and personal authority depended on the

---

* All dates are BC unless specified otherwise.

possession of a large group of clients. Caesar provides us with the example of the Helvetian noble Orgetorix, who could muster 10,000 clients when put on trial for aiming at the kingship.[4] These clients were bound to their elite patrons by various ties of which the most important was a social obligation binding a superior to an inferior through a mutual exchange of favours. Clients might be in debt to their noble patron, or workers on his estates, or they might be young warriors looking for booty and the social prestige that came from success in war. Aristocrats' political influence was based on their wealth, the number of their clients and, above all, their success as war leaders.

Druids constituted the other elite group in Celtic society.[5] They were drawn from the same group as the nobles. Caesar makes repeated reference to the druid Diviciacus whose brother Dumnorix was one of the leading nobles of the important tribe of the Aedui. The ancient sources provide a distorted picture of them, assimilating them to philosophers, which makes it difficult to understand their role. Above all, they seem to have been religious specialists who controlled all sacrifices both public and private, and issued rulings on religious matters. They also served as judges in criminal cases in various disputes, perhaps as a consequence of their religious powers since they were able to ban anyone from participating in communal sacrifices. They formed the only cohesive group that linked all of the Gallic tribes together through their yearly meetings and the election of a presiding Druid for all of Gaul. Despite their important role in Celtic society, there is no evidence that they played a significant part in organizing resistance to Roman penetration, although a century later they helped organize resistance to the Romans in Gaul and Britain.[6]

The common people who formed the majority of the population were in a state of dependence on the nobles and drew their livelihood from the land, living in scattered homesteads and villages within tribal territory. Trade, especially with the Mediterranean world, created opportunities for merchants and craftsmen but they must have formed a relatively small group. Caesar stresses the common people's complete lack of political influence.

From the beginning of the second century BC there is evidence in Gaul for the emergence of comparatively large native settlements, which the Romans called an *oppidum* (plural *oppida*).[7] They are generally located on hilltops for defensive purposes and had fortified walls. Tribes often had multiple *oppida* but the largest ones, such as Bibracte among the Aedui, often served as political and administrative centres. These sites had an important role in long-distance trade and craft production and so were often located on navigable rivers or close to mining sites. Luxury goods imported from the Mediterranean bear witness to their important role in trade. The main items imported from the Mediterranean, and more particularly from Italy, appear to be wine and pottery in addition to luxury goods. Mediterranean trade and cultural influences led to the development of coinage among the Gallic tribes. It began on a limited scale in gold around 300 and was based on Macedonian models. This coinage seems to have had more to do with gift exchange among the elite than as a medium of economic exchange. By the second century BC, silver coins were also being struck and the tribes using coinage multiplied.[8]

Gallic tribes were at various stages of political development. In the second century many tribes still had kings. When the Romans first began large-scale military operations in Gaul the major opposition came from Bituitus, king of the Arverni in the modern Auvergne. By Caesar's time kingship had been replaced in central Gaul among many of these peoples by a form of aristocratic government, although we occasionally hear of kings in the less-developed northeast.[9]

Some of the Gallic tribes that adopted aristocratic government developed formal political institutions. The best known system is that of the Aedui, the tribe in central Gaul that had the longest relationship with Rome. They had an annually-elected magistrate, the *vergobret*, chosen from the aristocracy and given extensive judicial powers including that of life and death. In addition to the *vergobret* there was an aristocratic council. Popular assemblies do not seem to have been a common feature.

Relations among the tribes were often marked by endemic warfare. In part this was a result of the need of aristocrats to maintain or enhance their prestige through success in war and to provide booty for their followers. Powerful tribes emerged, such as the Arverni, the Aedui, and the Allobroges in south-eastern France, but no tribe possessed the resources to establish an empire on a large scale. The sources mention an empire controlled by the Arverni but it seems to have been a collection of clients that extended from the Seine around Paris to the Mediterranean and collapsed as the Romans expanded in the late-second century.[10] A number of major tribes such as the Aedui, or the Treveri in the northeast, had smaller and weaker tribes as their clients and could call on them for military help. In both relations with client tribes and in relations between the major tribes, various methods were used to create and secure alliances. These agreements were based on the development of ties between the tribal aristocracies. Aristocratic intermarriage played a key role in cementing such alliances. Hostages were also routinely exchanged as a guarantee for the faithful implementation of agreements. Shortly before Caesar's arrival in Gaul, the Aedui were defeated by a neighbouring tribe, the Sequani, and were forced to give hostages as security for their good behaviour.[11]

Despite attempts at alliances and the subjugation of lesser tribes, the situation in Gaul never achieved stability and no tribe was able to establish an overall dominance. This disunity proved attractive to outsiders. Besides the Romans the most important threat was posed by the Germans living to the east of the

Rhine. Although some have argued that the distinction at this point is artificial, and there certainly was intermarriage between German tribes and the peoples of north-eastern Gaul, there is no reason to doubt that linguistic and cultural differences separated the Celtic and Germanic peoples. German settlement west of the Rhine had been going on for some time before the mid-first century; but at the time of Caesar's arrival in Gaul, the German threat had increased substantially with the arrival of the tribe of the Suebi who, at first employed as mercenaries in wars between the Gallic tribes, had seized substantial territory in modern Franche-Comté and were attempting to expand further into Gallic territory.[12]

The most comprehensive description of Celtic weaponry comes from Diodorus Siculus, a Greek author writing in the middle of the first century BC.[13] In addition, archaeological evidence also provides information on military equipment.[14] The most important piece of defensive equipment for the infantry was the man-sized shield. It was about 3.5 feet (1m) long and 2 feet (0.6m) wide. It was constructed of wooden planks fastened together and then often covered with hide and provided with a central handgrip protected by a boss. There is evidence for body armour among the elite. The mass of Gallic infantry must have had little other protection than their shield. There is evidence of the use of mail armour and it was probably from contact with the Celts that such armour was introduced into Italy, but its expense meant that its use was limited to the elite. Celtic helmets also influenced Italian and Roman types. Unlike the later Roman helmets, they tended to be made of bronze and were often adorned with animal decoration to create a more imposing and terrifying appearance. The archaeological evidence indicates that, like mail armour, helmet use was restricted to elite groups.

The majority of Celtic infantry must have fought with little protection beyond what their shields could offer. There was also a class of warriors called Gaesati living in the Alps and near the Rhône who made a strong impression on Greek and Roman writers. They went into battle naked except for their arms. It may be that their nakedness had a ritual significance. They appear at the decisive Roman victory over the Gauls at Telamon in 225 in northern Italy, but are never mentioned in accounts of the Roman campaigns in Gaul.[15]

The main Celtic offensive weapon was the sword. It was an iron weapon with a blade between 2.5 feet (0.8m) and 3 feet (0.9m) in length, far longer than Roman models. It was designed for slashing rather than stabbing. Classical sources claim it was easily bent but examples that have been found are often of high quality and there is no easy explanation for the bending mentioned in these sources.[16]

In addition to the sword Celtic warriors used thrusting spears and javelins. They occur frequently in burials and some are up to 8 feet (2.5m) in length.

More commonly mentioned in the sources is the use of javelins. Caesar mentions their frequent use by the Gauls during the siege of Alesia in 52.

The Romans were especially struck by the strength of the initial charge, which attempted to overwhelm the enemy. This was probably their most effective tactic against the densely-packed mass formations they found in Mediterranean armies. However, such a charge meant that it was impossible for Celtic warriors to maintain formation and if it failed, it must have put them at a severe disadvantage against better-organized enemies.

The Romans were most impressed by Celtic heavy cavalry.[17] After the conquest of Gaul, Celtic cavalry units were drafted into the Roman army and were considered elite troopers. The cavalry as elsewhere was restricted to the wealthy and their retainers, and it is revealing that Caesar uses the Latin word for a cavalryman (*eques*) for an aristocrat. The Celts developed an effective saddle, which allowed the cavalryman to fight from horseback and which was later adopted by the Romans. It is hard to identify equipment that belonged specifically to the cavalry but some of the longer Celtic sword finds probably belonged to cavalrymen. As was the case in other ancient armies, cavalry fought with javelins and the sword. In close combat the Celts dismounted and fought hand-to-hand. It is surprising that despite the high reputation of the Gauls as cavalry, on several occasions during the Gallic War Caesar reports that much smaller formations of German cavalry were able to defeat them.

Celtic armies that included several tribes could be quite large, although there is always uncertainty when dealing with the numbers preserved in ancient sources. At the great battle of Telamon against the Romans in 225 mentioned earlier, the sources claim that the army drawn from four tribes settled in northern Italy numbered 150,000 foot and 20,000 cavalry. Caesar records equally large numbers. He claims the Belgic tribes from north-eastern Gaul who had gathered to meet his invasion numbered close to 300,000. Numbers of the same scale reoccur in the crucial siege of Alesia in 52, when Caesar claims that the allied Gallic army sent to relieve Alesia included 8,000 cavalry and 240,000 infantry. This was in addition to the 80,000 warriors trapped within the town. Such huge numbers, if accurate, created serious logistical problems. There is no evidence for an organized supply system and several times Caesar describes logistical difficulties that caused large Gallic armies to disband.

Command was exercised by kings or specially-chosen war leaders. When armies were composed of a number of tribes a commander would be selected by the tribal leaders. But there does not seem to have been any institutional arrangements. Tribes could and did refuse to join armies or leave such forces at will. In the great rising in Gaul in 52 against Caesar, the Belgic tribe of the Bellovaci refused an invitation to join the rebel army, stating that they preferred to fight on their own.[18] From Caesar's account it appears that such coalition armies shared out commands among various nobles from different tribes that sometimes resulted in severe rivalries between them. Even in such coalition armies complex tactical plans were developed and executed. In their confrontations with the Romans it was the lack of organization and the failure to present a unified front that were the greatest weaknesses of Gallic armies.

Greek and Roman attitudes towards the Gauls had been shaped by a long history of violent confrontation.[19] Gallic tribes and war bands had invaded the Mediterranean periphery and served as mercenaries in the service of various Greek employers. This often-hostile interaction had created a stereotype, which extended in varying degrees to all of the peoples of north-western Europe.

The ancient sources were struck by the physical differences between Gauls and Mediterranean peoples. They emphasize the large size, white bodies and fair hair of both the Gauls and the Germans. Despite these physical differences the modern notion of racial difference was absent. Once Gauls adopted Roman practices there was no bar to their becoming Roman citizens and, in the first century AD, of reaching senatorial status. It was the cultural differences, particularly the opposition between the civilized and the barbarian, that were crucial. The Gauls were measured against the cultural standards of the Greco-Roman world and naturally found wanting. It was the absence of the classical city and its institutions that was perhaps the key difference.

The Gauls were characterized as warlike, cruel, superstitious drunkards and as unreliable. They were said to be prone to sudden emotional shifts moving from exultation to despair with astonishing rapidity. Their cruelty in Greco-Roman eyes was in part the result of some of their military customs. The sources are particularly struck by the Gallic practice of head-hunting. Diodorus Siculus mentions the Celtic practice of cutting off the heads of their slain enemies after battle and attaching them to the necks of their horses. These trophies were then nailed to the walls of their houses as proof of the owners' prowess.[20] It is clear that this was less a product of cruelty than a reflection of the importance of the head in Gallic culture. In possessing the head the warrior controlled the power of the deceased.

The standard Roman view of the Gauls as warriors is summed up in a speech by the Roman consul Gaius Manlius Vulso when his troops were about to face Gallic tribes in Asia Minor (modern Turkey) in battle:

> Their large bodies, their long red hair, their large shields, long swords and their battle cry as they begin fighting, their howling, leaping and the banging of their shields are all purposely designed to inspire terror ... From experience it is clear that if you stand up to their first attack in which they pour out their raging passion and blind anger their limbs begin to go limp with sweat and exhaustion;

their weapons go slack in their hands. Their soft bodies and weak spirits fade as their anger subsides. The sun, dust and thirst drain them so that you have no need of weapons.[21]

This picture of Gallic tactics as simply dependent on a wild rush to overwhelm the enemy is belied by the sources themselves. On many occasions, especially during the uprising of 52, Gallic commanders displayed an understanding of complicated tactics and were able to implement them even if they failed in their aims. Caesar's long experience in Gaul produced a more nuanced picture. Even though he shared many of the prejudices of his fellow Romans he was on occasion capable of praising Gallic courage in war. After his victory over the Belgic Nervii Caesar paid tribute to their courage in engaging Roman forces in spite of formidable natural obstacles and unfavourable ground.[22]

The first military encounter between Romans and Gauls took place in 387/6 BC. At the Battle of the Allia, a tributary flowing into the Tiber a little north of Rome, the Gauls scattered a Roman army and then moved on to pillage the city itself. Archaeology has uncovered cultural affinities in parts of northern Italy that have clear ties to those in eastern France and southern Germany as early as the sixth and fifth centuries. Presumably, some Gallic tribes had already crossed the Alps and established themselves in northern Italy in this period.[23]

Large-scale migration to Mediterranean Europe began about 400. In Italy Gallic tribes settled between the Alps and the northern rim of the Apennines. These migrations were not limited to Italy. Celtic groups also penetrated parts of Eastern Europe and the Balkans in the same period. By the first third of the third century Celtic tribes had settled parts of Asia Minor (Galatia). The reasons for these widespread movements of peoples are difficult to reconstruct. The ancient sources cite overpopulation and the riches of the Mediterranean lands as the prime motives behind the migrations. Overpopulation is thought to have played a part as it led to a lack of available agricultural land. Climatic change also adversely affected agriculture. Another factor may have been the importance of raiding and the accumulation of booty in Celtic society. As pointed out above, aristocratic status and power depended in part on the noble's success as a war leader and a provider of booty. The comparative wealth of the Mediterranean area was an attractive lure. It has been plausibly suggested that war bands played an important role in serving as leaders of these migrations. Gauls serving as mercenaries in the Mediterranean area must also have been a factor. By the beginning of the fourth century, Gallic mercenaries are found in the service of Dionysius I, the tyrant of Syracuse. In the third century, Gallic mercenaries are found in the armies of all of the major Hellenistic kingdoms.[24]

The Roman defeat at the Allia and the subsequent sacking of the city seem to have been the work of a mercenary band rather than a tribal migration. Gallic settlers never penetrated south of the Apennines in any numbers. The Roman tradition has exaggerated the effects of the city's sack. The sources paint a picture of widespread devastation, with those Romans still in the city valiantly holding out on the citadel on the Capitoline Hill against a long and difficult siege by the Gauls. The largely imaginative account from the historian Livy is typical:

> The Romans in the citadel saw the city full of the enemy who was wandering through all of the city's streets. In one place after another a new disaster appeared. Their minds and senses were unable to grasp what was happening. In their fear their attention turned to wherever there was a shout of the enemy, the cries of women and children, and the sound of the flames and the crash of falling walls as if fortune had made them spectators of their country's ruin.[25]

Despite the sources it appears that the sack was not a serious blow to the city. Archaeologists have yet to find any destruction layer that can be correlated with it. In addition, the sources make clear the quick Roman recovery. Within a decade of the sack Rome had recovered and was once again expanding. Patriotic fabrications were invented to mitigate the defeat. But it is clear that this first encounter with the Gauls left a legacy of fear. 18 July, the supposed day of the defeat at the Allia, became an ill-omened day in the Roman religious calendar.

Our knowledge of Rome's relations with the Gauls over the next thirty years is poor. The most reliable source, the Greek historian Polybius writing in the mid-second century BC, claims that there were no Gallic attacks during this period while the Roman historian Livy has a series of battles in the 360s, some or all of which may be inventions. More certainty attaches to a Gallic incursion into Latium in 350/349, which the Romans defeated despite problems on other fronts. None of these conflicts seems to have seriously affected the expansion of Roman power in Italy. The scale of these Gallic incursions is unclear. It is impossible to decide if they were full-scale invasions or raids by marauding war bands.[26]

The third century opened with a far more serious challenge to Rome's position in Italy. It began with a further movement of new Gallic tribes over the Alps. Perhaps new population pressure as well as the additional manpower persuaded the Gauls to confront Rome. The Gauls quite rightly saw the Romans as a serious threat. For the previous thirty years, Roman power had steadily advanced in central Italy. They had subdued most of Etruria to their north and were on the verge of defeating their most powerful adversary in central Italy, the Samnites, in the south. Once Rome secured central Italy she would be poised to cross the Apennines and expand into the Gauls' home territory in the Po valley. The Gauls entered into alliance with other peoples threatened by Rome's growing power. Over a period of several years a grand coalition was formed consisting of Gallic tribes, Etruscans, Umbrians and Samnites to confront the Romans.

The year 295 saw the decisive confrontation. At Sentinum in Umbria an army of Gauls and Samnites faced the Romans.[27] The Romans had mounted an unprecedented effort, fielding an army of four legions and an equal number of allies, totalling about 36,000 men. The size of the combined Gallic and Samnite armies is unknown but it was probably the greatest battle fought in Italy up to that time. The encounter was hard-fought but ended in a Roman victory which secured Rome's dominance in central Italy and prepared the way for its eventual control of the Italian peninsula. The Romans set about consolidating their position in both Etruria and Samnium. The Gallic defeat was clearly serious. For a decade the Gauls disappear from the sources. Then in 284 the Gallic tribe of the Senones crossed the Apennines and penetrated Etruria, where they besieged the important Etruscan city of Arretium. A Roman relief force was defeated with heavy losses. The defeat encouraged revolts among several important Etruscan cities and also among the Samnites to the south. In retaliation, the Romans invaded and confiscated part of the Senones' territory, the *ager Gallicus* which lay north of the Apennines along the Adriatic coast. The colony of Sena Gallica was founded in 283 to guard the new acquisition.[28]

The same year another Gallic tribe, the Boii, who were settled south of the Po and in league with Etruscan cities chaffing at Roman domination, mounted an invasion that reached as far as Lake Vadimon in Etruria, about 50 miles (80km) north of Rome.[29] There they confronted the Romans with all of their forces, along with their Etruscan allies, and were defeated. Apparently the defeat was not catastrophic as in the following year they fought the Romans again at Populonia in northern Etruria and finally made their submission; concluding a truce. In addition, in 268 the Romans founded a colony at Arminium (modern Rimini) where the Apennines come closest to the Adriatic coast. Arminium and Sena Gallica together firmly established Roman control in the *ager Gallicus*.

After Lake Vadimon, Rome's attention turned elsewhere and it was only at the end of the 230s that the stage was set for another confrontation with the Gauls. Its cause is to be sought in Roman domestic politics. Gaius Flaminius, one of the tribunes of the plebs for 232, brought forward a bill in the popular assembly to distribute the land between Sena Gallica and Ravenna in the *ager Gallicus* to individual Roman citizens. Despite fierce senatorial opposition the bill passed. Our sources about the event are dominated by the views of Flaminius's enemies so that it is hard to disentangle truth from partisan attack. It seems likely that Flaminius had multiple motives, including the provision of fertile land to citizens who lacked it and establishing a strong military bulwark in Gallic territory. The area would also be useful later as a staging point for further penetration of Gallic territory.

The combination of the earlier colonies and this land distribution must have made it clear to the Gauls that the Romans were now firmly established in their territory and would never leave, and also that further Roman advances were only a matter of time. Later Roman campaigns in the area proved that their fears were well-founded. Finally, in 225 the Gauls assembled an army that seemed capable of decisively defeating the Romans and ending any further threat to their territory. Four major tribes from the Po valley together with mercenary troops drawn from southern France moved south into Etruria. The sources claim the Gallic army numbered 50,000 foot and 20,000 horse including chariots. The Roman response was swift. Ten legions were levied with four to garrison Rome while another four were raised for the consuls, with the normal complement of two to each of them, and supplies were brought in. With the addition of allies Roman forces at least matched the Gauls in infantry, although they were greatly inferior in cavalry.

The Gallic army marched swiftly south into Etruria and severely mauled an army commanded by the praetor stationed there. One consul, who had been stationed at Arminium awaiting the expected attack, learned of the defeat and marched his army up to the Gallic encampment as a demonstration. The Roman army's arrival decided the Gallic leaders to retreat up the west coast. They were too heavily burdened with booty to fight effectively. The other consul, who had been fighting in Sardinia, rapidly brought his army up and occupied Pisa to the Gauls' north. Caught between the two consular armies they were forced to give battle at Telamon in southern Etruria. The encounter was probably the bloodiest battle so far fought in Italy. The sources claim that 40,000 Gauls were killed and a further 10,000 captured, almost the entire force.[30] The blow was devastating. Never again would the north-Italian Gauls field an army of this size. The initiative in the north had now decisively passed to Rome. In 224 the Romans campaigned against the Boii. This was followed by a further campaign against the Insubres. Both tribes had fought at Telamon. In 218 two colonies, Placentia (Piacenza) and Cremona, were founded on the territory of the Cenomani who had remained friendly with Rome.[31]

Hannibal's invasion of Italy, which he reached in the late autumn of 218, temporarily altered the balance of power. Two quick victories over Roman forces at the Ticinus and Trebia rivers in the Po valley in the same year opened the possibility that Hannibal and the Carthaginians offered a way for the Gauls to liberate themselves from the Roman control. But it was an uncertain possibility and the Gallic tribes did not immediately rally to the invader. Hannibal first approached the Taurini, who lived at the foot of the Alps and whose capital was probably at the site of modern Turin. They refused his request for support. After a three-day siege their chief town was taken and the inhabitants massacred as an object lesson. The lesson was effective and Hannibal received the submission of the neighbouring tribes. Hannibal's initial success impressed the Gauls sufficiently so that by the second battle at the Trebia only one Gallic tribe remained loyal to the Romans and 14,000 Gauls fought on the Carthaginian side. Despite this, Hannibal could never be sure where the loyalties of his Gallic allies lay. Celts fought in most of the major battles in Italy as well as in the climactic battle at Zama in North Africa in 202 that ended the Second Punic War, but support for the Carthaginians varied with their fortunes and was never universal among the tribes.[32]

As the war ended the Romans resumed operations against the Gauls in the Po valley. In 201 the Boii defeated a Roman detachment. Encouraged by the victory, in 200 or 199, with support from the Insubres and Cenomani they attacked and captured the strategically-located Roman colony of Placentia (modern Piacenza). A similar attempt made on its nearby neighbour Cremona failed when the Insubres were defeated. In 197 a large-scale campaign was undertaken by the Romans with both consuls converging on the area from the east and the west. The Cenomani acknowledged Roman authority and the Insubres were once again defeated. Despite these successes the campaign was indecisive and in 196 both consuls again took the field. A victory over the Insubres ended conflict south of the Po and a treaty was concluded with them that forbade any member of the tribe from becoming a Roman citizen. Rome asserted control in their territory by occupying the Insubrian capital of Mediolanum (Milan), which later became a colony.

The Boii were the only major tribe still resisting. Minor engagements marked the next few years until a major victory over them in 191 led to the loss of half of their territory. An invasion by Gauls over the Carnic Alps in 186 was ended when they were defeated in 183 and forced back over the mountains. This marked the end of major campaigning against the Gauls in Italy. It was followed by a series of colonies and the creation of a road network. The Romans were now free to turn their attention to the Ligurian tribes of the west coast and the Istrian peoples on the Adriatic.

When Hannibal crossed the Alps into Italy in 218, Rome's struggle with Carthage was almost a half-century old. In 264 Roman intervention in Sicily had led to a quarter-century of conflict, mostly at sea, that ended in a Roman naval victory in 241 at the Aegates Islands off Sicily's west coast. Rome annexed Sicily and Sardinia along with Corsica, which became Rome's first two overseas provinces in 227. The loss of these overseas possessions and the financial burdens imposed by the war meant that the Carthaginians were either unwilling or unable to pay their mercenaries. Refusing to forfeit their pay the mercenaries revolted. In the Truceless War of 240–238, which the historian Polybius calls the cruellest of wars that he knew, the mercenaries were literarily exterminated.[33] The most successful commander in that war had been Hamilcar Barca, from a leading family; he had also been the most successful Carthaginian general in Sicily and had then been entrusted by Carthage with negotiating the treaty that ended the war. In 237, having resigned his command in Africa, he arrived in Spain with his ten-year-old son Hannibal and his son-in-law Hasdrubal, determined to expand Carthaginian control in Spain.

Carthage had long had a presence in southern Spain. From the sixth century the Carthaginians had controlled much of the southern coast. The control of trade was not the only attraction. Spain was rich in metals and Spaniards provided needed manpower for Carthaginian armies. It may be that before Hamilcar's arrival Carthage's control in the area had weakened. From 237, Hamilcar began a deliberate attempt to expand direct Carthaginian control. Until his death on campaign in 229, he subjugated much of southern and south-eastern Spain. His motives have been much debated and the ancient pro-Roman tradition is almost uniformly hostile to him. It seems unlikely that he was from the first aiming to build up Carthage's power for a second war with Rome. With the loss of Sardinia, Corsica and especially Sicily, Carthaginian trade and revenues must have suffered. Spain offered an attractive alternative. It is true that there is no reason to doubt his hostility towards Rome. The Romans had during the Truceless War seized Sardinia and Corsica after accepting an appeal from disgruntled Carthaginian mercenaries. However, there is no evidence that he planned to use Spain as a base to attack the Romans. It was the expansion of Carthaginian rule and the aggrandizement of his family, not hatred of Rome that drove him.

Carthaginian control was consolidated and expanded by Hamilcar's son-in-law Hasdrubal, who succeeded him. He had probably not established control as far north as the Ebro River when he was assassinated by a disgruntled Celt in 221. Of some importance was the treaty he concluded with Rome in 226, which established the northern boundary of Carthaginian influence at the Ebro, the largest of Spanish rivers. The only known clause was a promise by the Carthaginian not to cross the river under arms.[34] This provision raises several problems. The Romans seem to have had little interest in Spain at this point. They were focused on their campaigns in northern Italy and on their newly acquired provinces in the Mediterranean. The first indication of any interest is a supposed embassy to Hamilcar five years before the Ebro treaty inquiring into his activities in Spain, but the reference is uncertain and even if it took place it seems to have no direct link to the later treaty. Nevertheless, two considerations may explain the embassy and the later treaty. After the First Punic War and the seizure of Sardinia and Corsica, the Romans may have been a little uneasy about Carthage's expansion in Spain and the growth in the city's power that resulted from it. Another factor may have been Rome's long-standing relationship with the Greek city of Massalia (Marseilles), which lay just east of the Rhône and was an important trading centre. Massalia had trading posts on the north-east coast of Spain at Rhode (Rosas) and Emporion (Ampurias). It may be that the Ebro was chosen to protect them against further Carthaginian encroachment.

Hamilcar's twenty-five year old son Hannibal succeeded to command in Spain on his death. He campaigned far more actively than Hasdrubal had. He conquered much of central Spain, which opened up huge new reserves of manpower and wealth to Carthaginian exploitation. Hannibal's success drew Rome's attention. An embassy was sent in 220 that warned Hannibal to keep his hands off Saguntum (Sagunto, near Valencia) and to observe the terms of the Ebro treaty. Saguntum was a native settlement which had trade contacts with Massalia. Rome seems to have had an alliance with Saguntum of uncertain date. What is particularly striking was that Saguntum lay some 100 miles (160km) south of the Ebro so that it lay in the Carthaginian sphere of influence. Why the Romans suddenly decided to make an issue of it is less clear. Internal problems at Saguntum had led to an appeal by the pro-Roman faction to Rome and so it may have provided an opportunity for Rome to send a signal that even south of the Ebro she could control the limits of Carthage's expansion. Hannibal reacted, perhaps with Roman actions in Sardinia and future Roman demands in mind, claiming that the Saguntines had attacked a tribe under Carthaginian protection, and he laid siege to the city. The siege lasted for eight months before the city fell at the end of 219. Its fall made war certain although the Romans took no action to help their ally. Finally, in the spring of 218, Rome issued an ultimatum to Carthage that was bound to be refused and Hannibal began his march north – if he had not already done so before.

Hannibal's strategy was determined by a fundamental fact: Carthage's weakness at sea. Given this any attack on Italy by sea was impractical and it would be impossible once he was in Italy to receive reinforcements by ship. A land route to Italy dependent on Spanish resources was the only available option. He might be able to win allies while in Italy, but Spain remained the only secure source for reinforcements.

It may be that at first the Romans thought the war would be for the most part fought in Spain. One of the consuls of 218, Publius Scipio, was sent with two legions (9,000 men) and 14,000 allies, as well as cavalry and a small fleet. By the time Scipio put in to a port at the mouth of the Rhône, he learned that Hannibal had already crossed and was on his way to Italy. He sent the major part of his forces to Spain under his brother Gnaeus and returned to defend Italy along with the other consul. In 217 he joined his brother in Spain and the two waged an extremely successful campaign until 211. The result was to drive the Carthaginians out of most of Spain. More importantly, they prevented supplies and reinforcements from reaching Hannibal in Italy who, despite his successes in the field, had great difficulty in finding reliable allies. In 211 disaster struck both brothers. Their armies were defeated and they themselves were killed. The Roman position in Spain was severely damaged. The arrival as commander of Publius's son, the later Scipio Africanus, completely reversed the situation. A string of impressive victories, starting with his capture of Nova Carthago (Cartagena) in 209, the main Carthaginian supply base in Spain, had by 206 succeeded in driving the Carthaginians entirely out of Spain.

The war in Spain had persuaded the Romans of the importance of the Iberian Peninsula. The richness of its resources, especially its mines, and the need to deny it to any other power led to a decision to establish a permanent presence, taken perhaps as early as 205. In 197 the Roman area of control was divided into Nearer and Further Spain. The former comprised the east coast and the latter the south-east coast along with the valley of the Baetis (Guadalquivir) River. The need to supply and reinforce armies operating in Spain underlined the importance of the coast of southern Gaul as the only practical land route, although occasionally it could be difficult.[35]

East of the Rhône River southern Gaul was controlled by Massalia, and its possible role in the Ebro treaty has already been mentioned.[36] It was a colony founded by eastern Greeks from Asia Minor around 600. The site must have been chosen for it location near the River Rhône and its excellent harbour at Lacydon. The city's economy developed rapidly with no near competitors and a fertile territory. It established a number of trading posts along the coast of the Mediterranean and inland stretching from north-eastern Spain to the French Alps, including Antipolis (Antibes) and Nicaea (Nice). These advantages allowed Massalia to serve as a transit point between the Mediterranean and the interior of Gaul and to directly control a sizeable territory extending north from the coast. The widespread diffusion of Massalia's coinage attests to her predominant role in trade along the Rhône and in the interior of Gaul.

Rome's relationship with Massalia dated back to the beginning of the fourth century. The reasons for the friendly relations between the two can only be guessed at. Massalia was primarily a commercial state while Rome was not. In that sense they complemented each other and more importantly were no direct threat to one another. They shared certain common enemies such as the Gauls and the Ligurian peoples, who had intermarried with various Celtic tribes and occupied an area stretching from the Rhône in the west into northern Italy in the east. Little is known about cooperation between Rome and Massalia until the Second Punic War when Massalia on at least one occasion contributed to a significant Roman naval victory over the Carthaginians. At some point a formal treaty was made between the two, probably during or after this war. During the early-second century Massalia seems to have been under pressure from neighbouring Gallic and Ligurian tribes, as evidenced by the construction of new and more massive fortifications. The city was primarily a commercial power and it is not clear how effectively it controlled its hinterland. Appeals to Rome for help against these tribes in the second century point to Massalia's weakness on land and sea.

Control of the western section of the route between the Rhône and the Pyrenees seems to have been in the hands of some of the Gallic tribes, in particular the Volcae. By the second century they occupied an extensive territory bounded by the Rhône, the Pyrenees, the Cevennes and the Garonne. This section of the land route seems have been less insecure than the portion east of the Rhône. [37] Even when the Romans finally intervened in force towards the end of the second century there is no evidence for any campaigning west of the Rhône. However, the route from Italy to Spain was not totally safe. In 189 the praetor Lucius Baebius, while on his way to his province of Further Spain, was set upon by a force of Ligurians and died of his wounds after reaching Massalia.[38] Eight years later Gaius Matienus, one of the two Roman naval commanders (*duoviri navales*), was assigned a command that extended from the Bay of Naples to Massalia in response to complaints by Massiliots about Ligurian pirates.[39]

In 154 the Romans intervened on a much larger scale. Once again they received an appeal for help from Massalia. The city was hemmed in and its trading posts at Antipolis and Nicaea were under siege by the Ligurian tribes of the Oxybii and Deciates, whose territories lay to the east and north-east of Massalia, between the Rivers Argens and Var. In response, the Roman Senate sent a prestigious delegation of senators to warn them off. One member of the delegation had already been put ashore when the others were prevented from landing by the Oxybii. Flaminius, the member who had already landed, refused to leave and he and his entourage were attacked. Flaminius was wounded and barely escaped with his life. He was carried to Massilia where he was nursed back to health.[40]

The attack on the embassy led to a declaration of war against both the Deciates and the Oxybii. Quintus Opimius, one of the consuls of 154, was put in charge of the campaign. He collected his forces – most likely the normal consular army of two legions and allies – and marched into the territory of the Oxybii. He took the town where Flaminius had been attacked, razed it to the ground and sold the inhabitants into slavery. Meanwhile, the Oxybii, without waiting for the Deciates, had gathered an army of 4,000 men, which must have been significantly smaller than the Roman force. Despite the odds they launched a fierce attack. The Romans routed them, killing many and turning the rest to flight. After this victory, the Deciates now arrived and, together with the surviving Oxybii, attacked the Romans with equally disastrous results. The tribes surrendered unconditionally and the consul gave some of their territory to Massilia, as well as forcing the tribes to surrender hostages to them.

Rome seems to have had no interest in maintaining a permanent presence in the area at this point. Cicero in his work on the Roman constitution mentions a prohibition on wine and olive cultivation by tribes on the other side of the Alps.[41] The dramatic date of the dialogue puts it before 129. Since there was no permanent Roman military or administrative presence in Gaul, how such a ban would be enforced is hard to understand. One attractive possibility is that the ban refers to the territory of Massalia and that it belongs to this campaign in 154. It would benefit the city's agricultural economy by removing local competition.

Such a move fits with economic developments in this period. Massalia's commerce seems to have been declining from the end of the third century. Italian wine and pottery exports began to replace those of Massalia and by 200 form the overwhelming bulk of Gallic wine and pottery imports.[42] Wine was a particular favourite:

> The Gauls are extremely addicted to wine and sate themselves with the wine that merchants bring into the country. They drink it unmixed and without moderation as they have a limitless craving for it and they then fall into a stupor or state of madness. As a result the Italian traders driven by their love of profit consider this love of wine by the Gauls as a heaven-sent opportunity. They transport the wine by boat on the navigable rivers and by wagons across the plains. The price they receive for it is incredible; for a jar of wine they are given a slave.[43]

This was in no way state-supported economic development. The trade was the product of the actions of Italian and Roman merchants and had nothing to do with Roman policy. Nevertheless, it must have had the effect of weakening Massalia and so increasing the need for further Roman intervention. The wine and olive prohibition was perhaps designed to allow Massalia to maintain its position in its local market. But its waning military and economic strength were to have important consequences for the future.

Chapter One

First Steps

In 125 BC Massalia once again appealed to Rome for help. This time she was under pressure from the Saluvii, and perhaps also the Vocontii, who lived between the Rhône and the Isère rivers.[1] The exact course of the campaign or its effects are extremely difficult to reconstruct as the sources for this period are few and at times contradictory. The consul Marcus Fulvius Flaccus was sent probably with the normal two legions and allies to their aid. His route is not specified in the sources but it appears likely that he marched by way of the Alpine passes and through the territory of the Vocontii. He defeated the Saluvii and Vocontii in battle, but there is no indication as to where these battles took place.[2]

By the opening of the campaigning season of 124 a new consul, Gaius Sextius Calvinus, had arrived. He continued operations in Gaul until 122. The sources claim that he defeated the same tribes as Flaccus had, which seems to indicate that Flaccus's successes had not been decisive. The combined actions of both consuls seem finally to have solved the problem of the Saluvii. The next reference to them is a rebellion in 90.[3]

In addition to his military activity, Sextius established a garrison at Aquae Sextiae (Aix-en-Provence) in 123 where he seems to have won a battle against the Saluvii. Aix replaced the main town of the Saluvii Entremont, which was perhaps destroyed during this campaign. The garrison was located at an important road junction that served to protect the coastal route and as a further measure of security the tribes were forced to pull back from the coast. The foundation of Aix marks the next stage in Roman penetration of the area. For the first time there was a permanent Roman presence in Transalpine Gaul. It appears that Massalia was no longer capable of protecting the eastern part of this vital route for Roman campaigns in Spain.

The campaigns of Sextius did not mark the end of Roman intervention. The king and some of the leading men of the Saluvii fled to the Allobroges, a larger and more important tribe whose territory was situated along the Rhône north of the Saluvii, and which extended from the River Isère east to the Alps. They had also attacked the Aedui, whose land lay north of the Allobroges in

Burgundy and who now appealed to the Romans for aid. They were one of the most important of the Gallic tribes. At some point before the late 120s they had concluded an alliance with Rome and were recognized as related by blood to the Romans, perhaps on the basis of a myth of a common Trojan origin. Why the Romans did so is not clear. There is a parallel in the relationship with Saguntum, which also lay deep in Carthaginian territory and in a period when Rome had no manifest interest in Spain. It is possible that the Romans saw such an alliance as a way to deter powerful tribes from attacking the coastal route. They would be able to use the threat of the Aedui who lay to the enemy's rear as a buffer.[4]

The refusal of the Allobroges to return the Saluvian fugitives led to the sending of another expedition under a consul of 122, Gnaeus Domitius Ahenobarbus. War with the Allobroges led to a wider conflict. The Allobroges were subordinate to the Arverni whose territory lay in the Auvergne in south-central France. They were the most powerful tribe in southern France. Some later sources talk of an Arvernian empire extending from the Pyrenees to the Rhine.[5] But it is more likely that, as was the case with the Allobroges, they had a number of weaker tribes as clients. For unknown reasons Domitius did not begin the major phase of his campaign until the following year. The chief of the Arverni, Bituitus, sent an embassy to meet with Domitius, perhaps to persuade him to call off the campaign. Since Bituitus's envoys refused to hand over the Saluvian chiefs or to settle other Roman grievances the embassy ended in failure. Domitius defeated a combined army of Arverni and Allobroges under the command of Bituitus at a site called Vindalium. Its exact location is unknown but it appears that it lay about 6 miles (10km) north of Avignon.[6] Although we lack any details about the course of the battle the sources report heavy casualties among the Gauls.[7]

Once again, in 121 another consul, Quintus Fabius Maximus, was sent out who seems to have operated jointly with Domitius. Domitius' victory may have weakened the Gauls but it had not put an end to the conflict. Fabius moved north and somewhere near the confluence of the Rhône and the Isère decisively defeated a combined army of Allobroges, Arverni and Ruteni (another client of the Arverni who lived in the southern Massif-Central). The date was 8 August 121. Bituitus was captured and deported to Italy where he was detained at a villa south of Rome. Fabius and Domitius both celebrated triumphs in 121. The Allobroges as well as the Saluvii were now under Roman control of some sort, while the Arverni and the tribes to the north were left independent.[8]

Fabius followed a standard Roman practice and added the title *Allobrogicus* to his name in recognition of his victory. He further memorialized it by the erection of a triumphal arch. Domitius's celebration of his victory was more exotic. According to Suetonius, the biographer of his descendant the emperor Nero:

> During his consulate after defeating the Allobroges and Arverni he was carried through the province on an elephant accompanied by a crowd of soldiers as though he was celebrating a triumph.[9]

Other sources mention the fact that Domitius had elephants with his army and had used them to great effect against the Gauls who presumably had never before encountered them.

Domitius's procession through southern Gaul had less colourful aspects as well. He gave his name to a new road, the Via Domitia, which ran from the west bank of the Rhône at Tarascon to a major pass over the Pyrenees at Le Perthus. The road speeded the movement of men and supplies to Spain where the Romans were still engaged in pacifying the tribes of the centre and west of the peninsula. The road has yielded the earliest Roman milestone we possess, which bears the name of Domitius and records that it marks the 20th Roman mile from Narbo Martius (Narbonne).[10]

Narbo, founded probably in 118, was, unlike the garrison at Aix, a citizen colony; the first founded outside of Italy. In part it must have fulfilled the same function as Aix and Massilia in protecting, in this case, the portion of the route to Spain that lay to the west of the Rhône. It was also located at a site of great commercial importance, and even before the advent of the Romans the site had played an important role in trade. It sat astride an important trade route that ran through Toulouse and linked it to Aquitania and the Bay of Biscay. Although the major reason for this colony as for other Roman colonies was strategic, there is no doubt that the commercial benefits of the site were readily apparent and Italians were quick to take advantage of them. The foundation of the colony was followed by a growth in Italian imports and an increase in local coinage based on the standard Roman coin the *denarius*.[11]

Its foundation should be linked as well to political problems at Rome. Access to and ownership of land had become a pressing social and political issue. The devastation of southern Italy during the Second Punic War had driven many peasants off their land. Added to this pressure were the constant demands of prolonged military service outside of Italy. The peasant soldier had normally been the main source of labour on his farm and his absence, often for as much as six years, outside of Italy led to severe economic consequences for his family. Added to this was the effect of Rome's conquests, particularly in the eastern Mediterranean. Enormous wealth in the form of booty flowed to the Roman state, but especially into the hands of the aristocracy. The prestige and safety associated with land ownership led the aristocracy to expand their land holdings at the expense of peasant farmers. Adding to the pressure on small-holders was the importation of slaves acquired in Rome's wars and their use as agricultural labourers on the elite's estates. It has been estimated that between the beginning of the Second Punic War and the middle of the first century about 500,000 slaves were imported into Italy. Seasonal labour on estates, which had been used to supplement peasant income, was now no longer available. The pressure on this group is evident in the continued movement of population from the countryside into the cities of Italy.

All of these factors had an effect on Rome's armies. Military service in the legions was based on the possession of a certain minimum amount of property. Most of those who served were drawn from the rural population. As they lost their farms they no longer qualified for service and this created manpower problems for the levy. Added to this was a conflict in Spain where the Romans were involved in a prolonged guerrilla war that offered few prospects of booty for the average soldier.

By 133 this had become a major issue in Roman politics. After a difficult political struggle one of the tribunes of the plebs, Tiberius Gracchus, passed a law distributing plots of Roman public land to landless citizens. Despite his death in a brawl with his political enemies, a commission established by the law continued with the distributions but by about 120 the available public land in Italy seems to have been all but exhausted. It is in this context that we can place a proposal by Tiberius's younger brother Gaius, in 123 or 122, to found a colony on the site of Carthage. With the death of Gaius in 122, also as the result of political conflict, the plan for a citizen colony at Carthage was abandoned.[12]

These struggles over the issue of land and other benefits for the Roman lower classes had become deeply intertwined in elite politics. A division opened between those who pushed for such legislation and those who fought against it. A variety of economic and political interests were involved on both sides as members of the aristocracy struggled with each other for prestige and political office. Just as there had been in the case of the colony at Carthage, so there was a great deal of resistance to the founding of Narbo. The proposal was seen as a manoeuvre by those favouring popular legislation to enhance their political position. Despite opposition in the Senate to the measure it was carried. Some scholars have claimed that the basis for the opposition was the distance and isolated position of the colony.[13] This does not seem persuasive. Earlier colonies in Italy, such as Placentia, founded in 218, had often been located at exposed sites. Also, southern Gaul offered a fertile area for Italian settlement. Its climate and topography were similar to Italy's. By the first century Pliny the Elder could refer to southern Gaul as 'more Italy than a province'.

The campaigns of 125–121 had been fought exclusively to the east of the Rhône; apparently the Romans had little trouble with the tribes west of the river. The inability of Massalia to maintain control of a vital route had drawn the

Romans into southern Gaul. They had subjugated an area extending on the west from the Pyrenees to the Alps on the east, and bordered on the north by the Massif Central and the Cevennes. The lack of any further conquests for seventy years supports the idea that Roman goals in Transalpine Gaul were limited. The main aim seems to have been to safeguard the route to Spain by land and to maintain control of the coastal ports. The more difficult question is what mechanisms they used to achieve those objectives.

The major controversy has centred on the formation of a province which the Romans called *Transalpina*, or Transalpine Gaul to distinguish it from the Gallic area on the Italian side of the Alps, *Cisalpina*. The basic meaning of the Roman term *provincia* (province) is the sphere in which a magistrate or promagistrate (a magistrate whose powers are continued after his term in office has ended) is empowered to act. The province need not be a military command; it designates any sort of politically approved activity. For instance, it included the legal activities of praetors in Italy at Rome or the various duties of quaestors including financial supervision. In 59 Caesar and his fellow consul were given the administration of Italy's woods and public pasturelands as their province after they left office. For the consuls and praetors, as well as proconsuls and propraetors, the sphere of activity was usually military. The consul and proconsuls were the magistrates that waged Rome's wars. Rome's first overseas provinces of Sicily and Sardinia/Corsica were governed by additional praetors, and two more were added to govern the Spanish provinces after 197. The need in these areas for continued oversight led to *provincia* developing a geographical meaning as an established administrative area. The process developed haphazardly, especially in the west. In the eastern Mediterranean the previously established administrative apparatus of Hellenistic kingdoms and states offered the Romans a system they could use as a basis for their own administrative organization. The lack of such structures in western Europe, and the diffuse nature of tribal authority, made the process far more difficult.

A province in the fullest sense would be a geographical area that possessed a Roman administrative structure under the supervision of a Roman governor. The origin of provinces as military command often meant that administration and control developed slowly and haphazardly. For example, Sicily was conquered by the Romans in 241 but it was not until 227 that a governor was sent. In Spain the process unfolded in the opposite direction. From 197 Roman Spain was divided into two provinces but it was not until 180 that a formal administrative structure developed.

The problem is complicated in the case of Transalpine Gaul. For one thing we know very little about the settlements with the defeated tribes after the campaigns of the late 120s. Caesar informs us that neither the Arverni nor the Ruteni were reduced to provincial status or had yearly taxes imposed upon them.[14] This may imply that Rome concluded treaties with them in place of governing them directly. There is more ambiguity about the status of the other tribes that Rome had defeated. The Allobroges surrendered unconditionally, as presumably did the Saluvii, Ligurians, and the Vocontii who occupied the western foothills of the Alps south of the Allobroges. It has been suggested that Rome bound the tribes by a series of treaties but is more likely that the area became a lightly administered province.[15] There is support for this in the sources, who mention that the Saluvii rebelled in 90. The remark implies that they were directly subordinated to Rome.

One problem with accepting the establishment of a province at this time has been the absence of evidence for a regular succession of governors. It makes it more difficult that an individual can be specified as having Transalpine Gaul as his area of action without any explicit reference as to whether he was also administering it. For instance, Gaius Valerius Flaccus, who had been consul in 93, is mentioned in the sources as proconsul in Gaul from 84–81, but this may have been in connection with the war then raging in Spain and so is no certain indication that he was the governor of the province. The first definitely-identifiable governor was Marcus Fonteius, who probably served in Transalpine Gaul from 74 to 72. But even this is not totally certain. By Caesar's time he can refer to all of south Gaul simply as 'the province', which provides our first unambiguous evidence.[16]

Prior to Fonteius the whole of southern Gaul seems to have often been administered by the governors of contiguous provinces. The western portion often fell under the purview of the governor of Nearer Spain while the part east of the Rhône was assigned to the governor of Cisalpine Gaul. This again implies nothing about the status of Transalpine Gaul. Caesar was assigned Transalpine Gaul as a supplementary command when he had been given Cisalpine Gaul.[17]

There is no definitive evidence for the status of southern Gaul until Caesar's time. In part this is the result of the absence of sources for this period. It is also a result of the relative absence of conflict in Gaul for most of the period before Caesar, except for a major crisis caused by the migration of two German tribes towards the end of the second century.[18]

In 113 a wandering tribe of Germans, the Cimbri, had been laying waste the Celtic kingdom of Noreia, which was allied to the Romans and located in the eastern Alps south of the River Danube. The consul Gnaeus Papirius Carbo, fearing a possible invasion of Italy, confronted them. After entering into negotiations with them he launched a surprise attack and was disastrously defeated. The Cimbri and their fellow Germans the Teutones seem to have begun a migration from their homeland in Jutland in modern Denmark around 120. The reasons for the migration were as disputed in antiquity as they are today. One possibility is that they were driven out by the slow encroachment of the sea on their homeland or some sort of climatic change. But there may have been other factors at work. The last two centuries BC are marked by the migrations of other northern European tribes and the Cimbri and Teutones may simply be part of this larger movement. Their actions and negotiations with the Romans suggest they were looking both for plunder and for new lands to settle in. Their initial movement was towards eastern Europe and the Danube. However, they were defeated by the tribes already established there and turned west, where they encountered Carbo. After his defeat the Germans could have crossed the Alps into Italy but for unknown reasons turned west again. They seem to have remained in the area of the Rhine for a year, where they were joined by Celtic tribes including the Tigurini, a sub-tribe of the Helvetii. Finally in 110, or a little earlier, they crossed the Rhine into Gaul.

In 109 the Cimbri defeated the consul Marcus Junius Silanus, probably near Lake Geneva. The Cimbri followed up their victory with a request to the Roman Senate for land to settle in, probably in Gaul, in return for performing military service. The Senate refused and it is not clear what land could have been given to them. Two years later a Roman army once again met the wandering tribes. The consul Lucius Cassius Longinus and his legate Lucius Calpurnius Piso had been operating near the colony at Narbo in an attempt to pacify the area, which had been thrown into turmoil by the arrival of the Germans. The Tigurini encountered Cassius in the territory of the Nitiobriges, which lay in south-west Aquitaine. Cassius fought the Tigurini under their war leader Divico near the town of Aginnum, probably modern Agen; and suffered a crushing defeat. Both the consul and his legate were killed and the survivors surrendered unconditionally. These two defeats shook Roman prestige in Gaul to its core. Soon after the campaigns of the 120s a garrison had been established at Tolosa (Toulouse) to guard the road to Spain where it ran west of the Rhône. It lay, as did Narbo, in the territory of the Volcae Tectosages, who may have had a treaty with the Romans. The loss of land to Narbo and the presence of the garrison at Toulouse were clearly irritants for the Volcae and with the defeat of Cassius they rose in revolt and imprisoned the garrison.

Given the unstable situation in Gaul a consul of 106, Quintus Servilius Caepio, was sent against the Volcae and suppressed the rebellion. He did not have to immediately face the Cimbri who were far to the north in the Seine basin. Perhaps Caepio's victory set them in motion once again, looking for an easier point of entry into the Roman controlled lands of the south. They moved east to the Rhône and then down its eastern bank as far as Arausio (Orange) in 105. One of the consuls, Gnaeus Mallius, was posted there awaiting the Germans. Caepio had been retained in command as proconsul and he seems to have been assigned the area to the west of the Rhône while Mallius was to keep watch to the east of the river. The appearance of the Cimbri and the defeat and death of his legate Scaurus led Mallius to summon Caepio to his aid, but relations between the two men were strained. The question at issue was seniority in command. As consul, Mallius would normally have been senior to Caepio who was now in 105 serving as a proconsul. But Caepio claimed his command was independent and not subordinated to Mallius. Caepio moved up to the Rhône's west bank but at first did not cross it. The dispute between the two continued until Caepio, in fear that Mallius would win the glory of a victory without him, crossed to the east bank and encamped between Mallius and the enemy in hope of defeating the Cimbri before Mallius could come up. Together the two must have had an army of about 50,000 to 60,000 men including four legions and allies. There seem to have been two separate engagements in which the Romans were outflanked and totally defeated. Both camps were then taken and sacked. The sources claim that the defeat, with a loss of 80,000 men, was the most devastating since Cannae in the Second Punic War. The date of the battle is given as 6 October 105, which was added to the religious calendar as a *dies nefastus*, an ill-omened day on which no public business could be conducted. The figure of 80,000 is clearly not credible, but it is clear that Roman losses were very heavy and southern Gaul was now open to invasion.

The tribes of northern Europe were certainly the most formidable foes that Rome faced in this period, but the series of Roman defeats against the tribes are surprising. During the campaigns of 125–120 the Romans had faced large Gallic armies and had consistently beaten them. There is no indication in the sources that the Germans had superior equipment. The weapons finds in German areas point to the dominance of infantry and the relative lightness of their equipment. Little body armour has been found but it may have been made of perishable materials. The finds do show the importance of missile weapons, which indicate a reliance on speed and agility among Germanic warriors. Unfortunately little is known about German tactics or strategy although it is clear that they were able to plan large-scale tactical movements. Their string of victories is all the more surprising in that for most of the next three centuries the Romans were normally able to win set-piece battles against them. The Roman disaster at the Teutoburger Wood in AD 9, where three legions were destroyed, was the result of an ambush not a formal battle. The difference in numbers is not a sufficient explanation. In general Greek and Roman sources give impossible figures. At a later battle the sources claim that the Germans had 300,000 warriors, but this seems impossible. The best that can be said is that in some of these encounters the German forces were larger. But as these later battles show they were hardly unbeatable. In the encounters of 113, 109 and 107 BC it may well be that superior numbers told. At Arausio it seems not to have been a question of numbers but rather of lack of coordination and incompetence on the Roman side.[19]

Luckily for the Romans the Germans did not immediately move south. They moved into Celtic territories which were closer and less strongly defended. The Germans tribes now separated, with the Teutones and Ambrones along with the Tigurini plundering the lands of the Arverni in south-central Gaul after failing to defeat the Belgae in north-eastern France. The Cimbri pillaged Languedoc and then moved south to the lands of Celts and Iberians in north-western Spain. Their plundering there was not successful. They were defeated by the Celtiberi of north-central Spain and turned north, re-entering Gaul by the spring of 103.

The fear of the northern barbarians and the string of Roman defeats created panic at Rome. A successful but difficult war had just ended against the Numidian prince Jugurtha in 105, after a series of campaigns that stretched over six years and were at times marked by incompetence and corruption. The war had damaged relations between the Senate and the broader mass of citizens. The victorious commander Gaius Marius celebrated a triumph for his victory on 1 January 104. Marius came from a locally-important family at Arpinum, a town 60 miles (96km) southeast of Rome. His rise to the consulship had resulted from patronage extended by certain leading aristocratic families, his ties to various financial interests and his military ability. The last had led to his appointment to command in the war against Jugurtha despite strong senatorial opposition. In the aftermath of Arausio he was the obvious choice and was elected as consul for 104 and given the command against the Germans. Many military reforms have been ascribed to Marius in preparation for the northern campaign, but many of them are dubious. Some seem authentic and seem to have been due to Marius's efforts, including the encouragement of a greater level of professionalism and the introduction of more intensive weapons-training and steps taken to increase the mobility of the legions.[20]

After their return from Spain the Cimbri reunited with the Teutones and the other wandering tribes near Rouen. It was here that a decision was taken to invade Italy. What prompted this decision is far from clear. Italy was to continue to attract northerners throughout antiquity and in this period, and later its wealth and climate were continuous attractions for those living north of the Alps. The Alps could be a formidable barrier at certain times of the year but the Cimbri had already crossed and re-crossed the Pyrenees, and the Alpine passes were easier to negotiate for those coming from the north than they were for movement in the opposite direction. In addition, the Romans must have seemed a less than formidable foe. Every time the tribes had encountered them they had beaten them and the Romans were the only power that had sufficient strength to successfully oppose them.

Whatever the actual numbers involved, it is probable that for logistic reasons, and perhaps to create additional problems for the defence, the tribes decided to descend into Italy separately. The Tigurini were to proceed by way of Noricum (part of Austria) and the Julian Alps into Cisalpine Gaul, the Cimbri, some way to the east by the Brenner Pass and the Adige River while the Teutones and Ambrones were to pass into Italy through the Roman province and then cross the Maritime Alps. The likeliest time for this decision would have been towards the end of 103.

The consul and his army, probably consisting of five legions totalling about 30,000 men and perhaps 40,000 allies, arrived in Gaul in the late spring or early summer of 104. He did not pursue the Germans but set about defending the east bank of the Rhône. The exact site of his camp is not known, but it was either at Arles, the lowest ford on the Rhône, or more probably near the confluence of the Isère and the Rhône at Valence where the valley of the Isère leads to the Alpine pass of the Little St Bernard. It may be at this point that Marius expected the German invasion would come down the Rhône and through the Maritime Alps. We do not know where his colleague Gaius Flavius Fimbria was, but it is not unlikely that he was posted in Cisalpine Gaul as was the case in 102. Perhaps because he did not trust the Allobroges or because they were unable to supply the number of troops involved, Marius had his men construct a canal linking Fos-sur Mer to the Rhône and its confluence with the Isère. It simplified the problem of moving supplies upstream in a river known for its strong downstream currents. It was probably built over the winter of 103/2.

Certainly the Romans had learned of the Germans' plans by the beginning of 102. While Marius was posted in southern Gaul the other consul of 102, Quintus Lutatius Catulus, was probably based at the road nexus of Cremona north of the Po to meet the invasion of the Cimbri, probably with a normal consular army of two legions and an equal number of allies.

The Teutones and Ambrones had been moving down the east bank of the Rhône when they encountered Marius's camp. The consul refused to engage them. The sources report that he remained in camp for three days without responding to attacks by the Germans. The reason they give for the refusal to fight does not carry conviction and it may be that Marius was looking for a more favourable location before engaging the enemy. The Teutones and Ambrones decided to bypass Marius and proceeded on towards the Alpine passes. The Germans moved along the valley of the Durance until they descended towards the plain of Aquae Sextiae. Marius must have skirted their main body and also arrived in the plain, while only the Ambrones who formed the vanguard of the German force had reached Aix.

Marius encamped on a hill overlooking the River Torse, which supplied the Romans with their drinking water. The Ambrones were camped on the opposite side of the river. It was from a skirmish at the river that the first battle developed. Roman support troops had gone down to the river for water when they were attacked by a party of Ambrones. The sounds of the struggle alerted the rest of the Ambrones, who then attacked en masse. The Ambrones lost cohesion as they crossed the river and before they could reform they were attacked by Celtic and Ligurian troops fighting alongside the Romans. While the engagement was taking place the legions came up in support and the Ambrones were routed and a number were cut down. After the destruction of the Ambrones Marius now had to face the more numerous Teutones.

Less is known about the origins of the second battle. Even the month is uncertain, although September has been suggested, and its exact location remains a mystery. It seems to have been deliberately sought by the Romans. It appears that Marius had decided to hold the Teutones in front while he launched an attack on their rear and flanks. Apparently, before the battle he sent a force of 3,000 infantry under his legate Marcus Claudius Marcellus to set up an ambush on some wooded hills to the rear of the enemy. He opened the battle by sending his cavalry down into the plain of Aix. The Teutones attacked the cavalry, which then retreated to the legions arrayed on the slopes of the hill where Marius had camped. The Teutones charged uphill, which was always a difficult manoeuvre, and while this was going on Marcellus's troops attacked their rear. The tribesmen lost cohesion and fled. There is no doubt that they suffered heavy casualties, but the ancient figures, which number up to 200,000 dead, seem greatly exaggerated.[21]

The defeat of the Teutones and Ambrones did not end the threat to Italy. The next year saw another great battle against the Cimbri who had crossed the Alps by the way of the Brenner Pass – which today connects Innsbruck, Austria to Bolzano, Italy – probably in the winter of 102/101, although an earlier crossing cannot be ruled out. Catulus, based at Cremona to the west, learned of the Cimbri's descent into the Veneto and marched to confront them. He reached the Adige and then moved for a considerable distance up the river valley. The terrain was mountainous and Catulus may have selected it purposely to minimize the enemy's numerical superiority. It has also been suggested that he hoped to catch the Cimbri before they had recovered from the rigours of their passage of the Alps.[22] It is also possible that, given the terrain, he may have wanted to try to defeat them in detail. If this was his plan it did not meet with success. Catulus was twice defeated and forced to retire behind the Po. In doing so he abandoned the plains north of the Po, which the Cimbri proceeded to pillage.[23]

At the end of spring 101 Marius with 30,000 troops joined Catulus, bringing the Roman forces up to about 50,000 men. With Marius in command the Romans now crossed the Po to seek a battle with the Cimbri. Surprisingly the battle took place in the western part of the plain of the Po near Vercellae (modern Vercelli), about 60 miles (100km) west of Milan. The site of the battle, the Campi Raudi, is unknown. It is difficult to explain why the Cimbri had moved so far west and the sources provide us with no explanation. It is not easy to accept that they moved west to link up with the Teutones as they must have known of their defeat as almost a year had passed, although one of the sources, Plutarch, claims this was the case.[24] One possibility is that, having pillaged their way across the Po valley, they were now seeking to return to Gaul where they could expect to meet less resistance.

The Cimbri entered into negotiations with the Romans before the battle, again asking for land to settle in as they had seven years before. This is further confirmation that the Germans were not simply raiders but migrating tribes. The Cimbri, through their king Boiorix, challenged Marius to battle and a day was set, 30 July. This is not impossible as most large-scale battles in antiquity required a decision of both sides to fight. The course of the battle is far from clear. The Roman accounts of the battle have been distorted by the memoirs of both Catulus and later Sulla, who were both opponents of Marius. Apparently the Romans drew up in their normal battle formation in three lines with the cavalry on the wings, though the implication of the sources is that the majority of the Roman cavalry was arrayed on the right. It may be as well that the centre of the infantry line was deployed somewhat to the rear of the wings. This may have been an attempt to draw the Cimbri in and then attack them on the flanks. But none of this is certain. Marius commanded the Roman right while Catulus took the centre. The commander of the left is unspecified but it might have been Catulus's legate Sulla.

The battle formation of the Cimbri seems rather unusual. Apparently, all of their cavalry, which numbered 15,000 men, was drawn up on their left. The biographer Plutarch in his *Life of Marius* provides a vivid description:

> (The cavalry) rode out in magnificent fashion with helmets made to resemble the jaws of wild animals or the heads of strange beasts. Their helmets had crests of feathers, which made the riders seem larger than they were and they wore iron breastplates and held glittering white shields. Each trooper carried a pair of javelins and a large heavy sword for hand-to-hand fighting.[25]

According to Plutarch the infantry of the Cimbri were drawn up in a square formation with their depth equal to their frontage and each side was approximately 3 miles (5km) long. There are serious problems with the extant descriptions of the battle. This formation seems impossible as most of the German infantry could not have engaged.

Plutarch mentions an opening manoeuvre by the Cimbric cavalry to draw off the Roman cavalry by swerving to the right to try to outflank them and pin them between themselves and their own infantry. The cavalry then disappear from Plutarch's account. The fifth-century Christian writer Orosius has the German cavalry being driven back by the Romans on their own infantry and throwing them into disorder.[26] The course of the rest of the battle is lost in the polemic between the commanders, with each trying to take credit for the victory. Certainly, Marius's election to an unprecedented sixth consulship indicates that at least in the eyes of the Roman populace he deserved the major share of the credit for the victory. A further indication of the Cimbric migration as an attempt to find new land for the tribe rather than as a raiding expedition is the final stage of the battle, which our sources have dramatically elaborated. After their victory in the field the Roman attacked the camp of the Cimbri, which as was normal in German migrations consisted of their encircled wagons. They had placed their women and children there for safekeeping. The women fought back as long as they could and then killed themselves and their children.

Unlike Aquae Sextiae this seems to have been a soldier's battle. No stratagems are mentioned on the Roman side. The accounts make much of the sun shining in the face of the Germans, as well as the effect of dust and heat on men from cooler climates. This implies a long, drawn out struggle rather than a quick decisive battle. One source mentions that there were few casualties on the Roman side but that 40,000 of the enemy were slain and a further 60,000 captured. The numbers are not impossible and are certainly more credible than the ones given for Aquae Sextiae.

With the defeat of the Cimbri the threat of invasion ended. The third group of invaders, the Tigurini, who were to enter Italy by way of the Julian Alps, retreated to Switzerland. The German threat to Rome was only to reappear centuries later. Although it has been claimed that the invasions made the Romans aware of the importance of Transalpine Gaul, there is little support for it.[27] There is no evidence for an extension of provincial boundaries or exceptional activity in the period after the invasions. One striking aspect of the turmoil in Gaul was the passivity of the southern Gauls. It is true that they suffered from the depredations of the invaders, which might have made an uprising against the Romans more difficult. Nevertheless there is no evidence of any major unrest in the Roman area of control during this period. Other Gauls had joined the Germans; those of the south did not. There were to be isolated rebellions of various tribes until the time of Caesar but there does not seem to have been any general movement to oust the Romans from the area. Even during the strains of the Gallic War it remained remarkably quiet.

There are only fragmentary references to Transalpine Gaul until the late 70s. Understanding the situation is made more difficult by the fact that the references to Gaul can refer either to Cisalpine or Transalpine Gaul, although the occasional reference to the 'Two Gauls' helps remove the ambiguity. The first possible governor of Transalpine Gaul is Lucius Licinius Crassus, who was consul in 95. As consul he was active in Cisalpine Gaul where he repressed raiders and brigands. He was then assigned to Gaul as proconsul. What is not clear is which Gaul is meant. He had a long history of association with Transalpine Gaul. As a young man he had been instrumental in passing the law that authorized the founding of Narbo and so had existing connections with the province. It is possible that he governed both provinces at the same time, but there is no firm evidence that he did so or operated as a military commander there.

The next reference to a Roman official operating in Gaul is to Marcus Porcius Cato, who had been a praetor. He set out for Transalpine Gaul in 91 and died there. There is, however, no evidence as to why he was in the province. It could have been for private reasons and have had no connection to the government of the province. However, it is just possible that Cato was acting in an official capacity. In 90 the Saluvii revolted and were put down by Gaius Coelius Caldus, who had been consul in 94 and was presumably acting as proconsul in Transalpine Gaul. Cato may have been operating against the Saluvii when he died since we do not know when the revolt began.

The situation in Gaul remains obscure over the next few years. Gaius Valerius Flaccus, consul in 93, suppressed a revolt of the Celtiberian tribes in north-central Spain, probably in 92. He was in Transalpine Gaul probably in the years 84–82 and held a triumph over Gauls and the Celtiberians in 81. It may be that he governed both Nearer Spain and Transalpine Gaul together. This would suggest that the Gauls he conquered were probably located west of the Rhône.

Flaccus's activity falls in a period when Roman control in Transalpine Gaul became much more crucial. A serious and difficult war had broken out in Spain in 83 and once again Gaul assumed its role as a vital supply route for Roman armies operating in the Iberian Peninsula. The war, which was to greatly affect both Spain and southern Gaul, had its origin in a fierce internal struggle in Rome that threatened its political structure and its hold on its empire.

The growth of Rome's empire had led to severe internal strains. The influx of wealth and the greater rewards for the elite that came with imperial expansion had intensified competition among aristocrats as mentioned earlier. It had also opened up opportunities for Roman knights (*equites*, members of the equestrian order) who were no longer defined by their cavalry service but by their wealth and were both landowners and businessmen. The empire offered important opportunities for them in performing public functions such as the collection of taxes, which could be extraordinarily lucrative, and presented them with new commercial opportunities in the provinces. One consequence of these developments was that their interests often tended to diverge from, and put them at odds with, those senators who commanded Rome's armies and governed her provinces.[28] In the same manner the pressures of war and economic dislocation had created difficulties for the peasant farmers who filled the legions. Forced off their lands and into the cities and towns of Italy they were eager to acquire new land and to share in the profits of empire.

The difficulties brought about by the loss of land and a bloody and un-rewarding series of wars in Spain had led to problems in levying troops. The minimum property necessary for service in the legions had been lowered several times and finally in 107 the practice began of admitting men into the legions without any minimum at all. Long and continuous service abroad and the absence of personal property requirement produced men who saw military service as a profession and not simply part of their obligations as citizens. Since these men could no longer return to their farms on the completion of their service, and the state provided nothing for them on retirement, they began to look to their generals to provide for them through special legislation. This financial tie to their commanders was strengthened by the development of personal ties to their generals due to the increased length of military commands. Caesar and his army in Gaul offer the best example of what these ties could mean. These close bonds offered opportunities for commanders or governors to use this military support for their own ends.[29]

The expansion of the empire had created other problems as well. Perhaps the most pressing as the first century began was the relation of Rome to her Italian allies. The burden of Rome's wars had fallen disproportionately on her Italian allies. In the course of these wars allied communities had often pro-vided twice as many troops as the Romans. In addition, they received a smaller share of booty and were subject to harsher penalties for violations of military discipline. Although Italian businessmen and merchants had benefitted hand-somely from the business opportunities that Roman expansion had opened up, they had little control over the direction of Roman policy. The land law of Tiberius Gracchus exacerbated the situation. Its distribution of Roman public land to Roman citizens threatened the interests of the Italian elite, which had used large amounts of this land for their own benefit. Without citizenship the Italian elites were unable to hold office and use the votes of their fellow citizens to influence Roman policy. In response to the increasing pressure, Rome had taken a number of steps that made the inferior position of the Italians even more galling.

Finally in 90 the storm broke. Frustrated in their attempt to gain citizen-ship, many but not all of the allies rebelled and joined together to wrest their independence from Rome. The bloody and large-scale conflict lasted for two years and ended in the military collapse of the Italian forces. Despite this the Romans granted a series of concessions that gave citizenship to most Italian communities south of the Po.[30] In the course of the war one of the Roman commanders, Lucius Cornelius Sulla, had been extremely effective and his success led to him being elected consul for 88.[31]

Despite the end of the war and the grant of citizenship, Italian demands had not been totally met. Citizenship had been granted but with certain restrictions that hindered its exercise. An attempt was made to remedy this situation by Sulla's opponents. Further complicating the situation was a new war in the east against the Mithridates, king of Pontus in north-central Asia Minor. The command was attractive both for the wealth that would accrue and the prestige that it would bring. Fighting erupted between Sulla and his allies with their opponents that led to the first march of the legions on Rome. Sulla attempted through a set of reforms to bring stability and assert the control of the Senate. He soon left to wage war on Mithridates and in his absence his opponents gained control. Sulla returned to Italy in the spring of 83 after his victory over Mithridates. His arrival resulted in a hard-fought civil war that lasted until November of 82, with mopping-up operations continuing for at least another year.

One of Sulla's adversaries was Quintus Sertorius.[32] He had fled Italy for his province of Nearer Spain after Sulla's victories in 83. Driven out of it in 81 by supporters of Sulla he returned to Spain in 80 and garnered widespread support among the natives because of his integrity, just dealings and charismatic personality. These qualities, as well as dissatisfaction with Roman rule, enabled him to raise a substantial army and an allied navy. He quickly gained control of much of Spain and defeated a number of commanders sent against him. Among them was Lucius Manlius, proconsul of Transalpine Gaul, who was twice defeated by Lucius Hirtuleius, a lieutenant of Sertorius, first in Nearer Spain and then in Gaul in 78. Despite the arrival the year before of a consular army in Spain, Sertorius was more than able to hold his own and by 77 retained control of much of Spain. The situation had become so serious that one of the consuls of 78, Marcus Aemilius Lepidus, was assigned both Cisalpine and Transalpine Gaul for 77, but staged a rebellion against the Senate and was killed before he could take up his command.

The sudden appearance of Roman commanders in Gaul is evidence of the renewed importance that Transalpine Gaul had now assumed. The intensi-fication of the conflict with Sertorius in Spain had a parallel with the Second Punic War, when Rome had first become interested in southern Gaul. It was once again a major conduit for men and supplies as it had been in the earlier conflict. The difficulties that the central government was having in Spain led to the dispatch of the young Pompey in 77, although he did not reach Spain until the next year. During his march to Spain he had to force a passage by defeating a number of Gallic tribes during the winter of 77/76 and was forced to winter in Narbo. He returned to Gaul over the winter of 75/74. There is no doubt that Pompey was involved in some serious fighting, although the trophy he is said to have erected in the Pyrenees recording the capture of 876 towns between the Alps and the Pyrenees as well as having pacified the whole province seems to have greatly exaggerated his real accomplishments. He apparently did make some modifications in the provincial structure of Transalpine Gaul. In addition, lands were taken from the Helvii, whose territory lay on the right bank of the Rhône, and their neighbours the Volcae Arecomici and was given to Massalia, which may have led to conflict.[33]

However, it seems most likely that the fighting was precipitated by Roman demands for money and supplies for the war in Spain. The situation was further exacerbated by a poor harvest in 74. The demands and the resistance to them are attested by a speech of Cicero defending Marcus Fonteius's conduct as governor of Transalpine Gaul on a charge of extortion brought by a number of Gallic tribes. Fonteius had been praetor in 75 and was probably serving in Gaul from 74 to 72. Cicero's speech in his defence was probably given in 70 or 69. Only part of the speech has survived but enough has survived to provide some revealing details about Fonteius's tenure.[34]

Fonteius's main task as governor was supplying the Roman armies in Spain. Cicero mentions that he had requisitioned substantial quantities of grain as well as levying considerable numbers of Gallic infantry and cavalry for service in Spain. Excessive demands seem to have led to violent local reactions. Fonteius fought against the Vocontii near Narbo and probably against the Volcae, who also directly menaced the Roman colony at Narbo. Cicero also mentions his eviction of Gauls on the orders of Pompey from their farms as punishment for their rebellion. We also learn that he carried out repairs on the Via Domitia, especially necessary with the war raging in Spain.

Fonteius instituted new administrative measures, including a transit duty on wine, which points to the importance of Roman trade with the south in this period. Cicero has a striking passage describing the economic penetration of the economy of Gaul by Roman and Italian traders and merchants in this period:

> Gaul is filled with traders and Roman citizens. No Gaul does business without a Roman citizen. No money changes hands without being noted in Roman account books.[35]

The Romans had not conquered southern Gaul for economic reasons, but the advance of Roman control was accompanied by an influx of Roman and Italian businessmen who could enjoy the protection of Roman governors and their subordinates. This development was not limited to Gaul but occurred in most of the territory into which Rome expanded.

There is a striking increase in the number of Italian amphorae (wine jars) found in Gaul in this period. They indicate that the consumption of wine increased tenfold after 125. By 100 Italian wines had totally replaced those of Massalia. The founding of Narbo placed the Romans astride important north-south and east-west trade routes. Although Narbo produced a wide range of goods locally, its role as a middleman in this trade was probably of more importance. Fonteius's decree instituting transit taxes for wine carried inland from Narbo is evidence for its importance of it as a port of entry.[36]

One major east-west route linked Narbo to Tolosa and a tremendous number of amphorae have been found along it and at Tolosa. The garrisoning of the site gave the Romans control of the Carcassonne Gap, a passage between the Pyrenees to the south and the Massif-Central to the north. A major route from Tolosa led north to the Atlantic coast and another turned south towards Spain. It seems likely that Tolosa became the major Italian trading centre west of the Rhône. This would suggest that the trade was in the hands of Italian merchants resident in Gaul. A major Gallic export appears to have been metals. Gaul produced silver, copper, lead and gold. Major concentrations of *amphorae* have been found in mining areas from this period. Another crucial export was slaves. A reasonable estimate has put the number of slaves imported into Italy during years when there were no wars with Rome at about 25,000 per year. Although of lesser importance, wool and hams were also imported.[37]

The trade and probably the increased Italian presence had important effects on Gallic society far beyond the borders of the Roman province. From the middle- or late-second century large centralized settlements appear in central Gaul. They are located at sites that were close to mining areas or along navigable rivers, which bears witness to the increased importance of trade in Gallic life. Luxury goods imported from the Mediterranean begin to appear in this area at about the same time that these settlements appear. Associated with them is a change in Gallic tribal coinage. Previously, issues had been small and irregular and limited to large denominations, mostly in silver or occasionally in gold. Their main function seems to have been to serve in gift exchanges. Coinage now issued in restricted areas implies centralized control over its issue, and smaller denominations appear first in silver and then in bronze. The smaller denominations point to the development of a local market economy. Political institutions in some Gallic states began to approximate the Roman and Mediterranean models. Certainly trade with Italy played an important role in these developments: what is less certain is the presence of Roman businessmen and merchants who might have influenced and accelerated this process.[38]

Trade was not the only economic opportunity created by Roman domination of southern Gaul. The political conflicts fuelled by the hunger for land of dispossessed peasants and veterans had continued unabated since the 130s. The Gallic province contained rich land suitable for agriculture or herding and had the further advantage that its climate was very similar to that of Italy. The founding of Narbo was a prelude to further Roman settlement. In 100, soon after Marius' victories in Gaul and Italy over the Germans, the tribune Lucius Appuleius Saturninus proposed a law to distribute to Romans and their Italian allies the land that the Cimbri had seized while in Gaul. Despite a great deal of violence the law was finally passed. The controversy about this and other legislation of the tribune has left it uncertain as to whether the law was actually implemented, but it is clear that the Romans saw Gaul as a place for settlement. There is evidence for Roman land surveys among the Vocontii, Volcae and Saluvii, though no clear evidence for settlement.[39]

The first clear evidence we have for Roman ownership of land outside the colony at Narbo comes from a speech for the defence given by Cicero in 81. Probably in the early 80s, the brother of Cicero's client Publius Quinctius, in partnership with a Sextus Naevius, bought land in southern Gaul perhaps near Narbo for ranching and agriculture. The suit between the partners over their mutual debts reveals as well that that Publius individually owned additional land in the vicinity of Narbo in his own name. What is striking is the assumption that land ownership in Gaul was nothing unusual. This seems to imply that many Romans and Italians owned land there. It is part of a wider pattern in which Romans acquired properties in many of the areas they had conquered. The scope for exploitation increased with the confiscations of native land in accordance with a senatorial decree made by Fonteius as governor in the late 70s.[40]

A later speech of Cicero's points to a different aspect of Rome's involvement in Gaul. In 63 Cicero spoke on behalf of Lucius Licinius Murena who had just been elected consul for the following year. Murena was accused of using illegal methods to gain the consulship. In the course of his defence of Murena's character Cicero brought forward Murena's actions as governor of Gaul the year before. He mentions that Gaul is full of Roman businessmen and Cicero singles out for praise Murena's diligence in helping Romans to recover debts owed to them by Gauls. It is clear as well from other evidence that debt was a heavy burden for the Gallic tribes in this period and was the cause of several revolts against Roman rule. The origin of the debts is less clear. Presumably, taxes and exactions such as those of Fonteius helped to exacerbate debt problems. The influx of Roman businessmen and merchants, often lending money at exorbitant rates, also contributed to it. They may also have taken over trading operations on which various tribes depended. It was helpful to have a friendly governor such as Murena on their side.[41]

The history of Roman Gaul until the arrival of Caesar as governor in 58 is poorly known, as the sources only contain sporadic references to the province. In 66 and 65 one of the consuls of 67, Gaius Calpurnius Piso, was assigned both Cisalpine and Transalpine Gaul, a not infrequent combination. He is mentioned as subduing a revolt of the Allobroges, which was probably caused by an unbearable burden of debt.

He was replaced in 64 and 63 by Murena, whom Cicero later defended. The difficult situation that faced the Allobroges had not improved. During the conspiracy of Cataline in the autumn of 63 in Rome, Allobrogan envoys who were in Rome to try to gain some measure of relief from the weight of both private and public debts were approached by the conspirators who hoped to coordinate their rising in Rome with a rebellion in Gaul. In light of Cicero's defence of Murena it is revealing that the Allobroges complained of the greed of Roman magistrates. The situation had still not improved in the next year when Gaius Pomptinus governed Transalpine Gaul. Once again the Allobroges found their situation intolerable and rebelled. The Roman campaign against them was a difficult undertaking. It appears that the rebellion began at Valentia (Valence) on the east bank of the Rhône about 65 miles (105km) south of Lyon. One of Pomptinus's legates, Manlius Lentulus, launched an attack on the city that was initially successful, as most of the inhabitants had fled and those remaining sent an embassy to seek peace. They were temporarily rescued by an attack on the Romans by the rural population near the town. In response the Roman commander Lentulus ravaged the countryside. The Allobroges assembled a much more formidable force under their leader Catugnatus and almost captured the legate. It was only when that force withdrew, probably due to lack of supplies (a perennial problem for Gallic armies), that Lentulus returned and finally captured the town. The climactic battle was fought at the town of Solonium, whose exact location is uncertain but which lay west of the Rhône, by the governor himself and all of his troops. The town was taken and this seems to have ended the phase of large-scale warfare. The Romans then proceeded to subjugate the remaining districts still in open rebellion.[42]

Pomptinus continued as governor into 61. Despite his success against the Allobroges the situation in Gaul looked potentially dangerous. Rome's close allies the Aedui had suffered a defeat at the hands of their eastern neighbours the Sequani in early 60 at the Battle of Admagetobriga, somewhere in Alsace.[43] In their war with the Aedui, the Sequani and their allies the Arverni had called upon the aid of the German Ariovistus, a Suebian chief. The Suebi were a confederation of various German tribes whose huge territory stretched from the Rhine to the Elbe and south to the Danube. The section of the Suebi under the control of Ariovistus had been invited in to help the Sequani in their war against the Aedui and their help had come at a high price. The Sequani had to surrender a third of their lands to Ariovistus and his Germans, who settled in lower Alsace.[44] They were now not only neighbours of the Aedui, but also bordered on the Allobroges, who with their frequent revolts had been a source of trouble for the Romans. Ariovistus' lands were also adjacent to and constrained the Celtic Helvetii, who lived in the area of modern Switzerland. The pressure of the Germans and other factors had persuaded the Helvetii to migrate and this posed a further threat to the Romans. The weakening of the buffer provided by the Aedui, the possible expansion of the Germans and the uncertain course of a Helvetian migration gave cause for worry.

The anxiety at Rome can be glimpsed in a letter of 15 March 60 by Cicero to his most intimate friend Atticus:

> For the present there is a great deal of fear that a war will break out in Gaul. For our brothers the Aedui have recently been defeated and the Helvetii without a doubt have taken up arms and make raids on the Province. The Senate has decreed that the two consuls are to be allocated the two Gauls as their provinces, that a levy should be held, all leaves cancelled and that a delegation with full powers should be sent to the Gallic communities to keep them from joining the Helvetii.[45]

The problems in Gaul died down of their own accord. Cicero could write that the war scare in Gaul was over and that his friend Metellus Celer, one of the consuls of 60, who had been awarded Transalpine Gaul, was now disappointed since the return of peace dimmed his prospects for a triumph.[46] As it was, Celer was deprived of his province in political infighting and died suddenly in April 59 before he could leave the city. Pomptinus most likely remained in command until Caesar's arrival in 58.

Chapter Two

Caesar and Gaul: The Prelude

By the beginning of 60 a political impasse had developed at Rome. Pompey had returned from his wars in the east with a string of victories against the Pontic king Mithridates, having added a number of new provinces and client kings in Asia Minor, Syria and Palestine to the empire. There was some anxiety at Rome that the victorious general might return from the east as Sulla had almost twenty years before and that a new civil war would break out. Pompey landed at Brundisium (Brindisi), the main Italian port for those sailing from the east, in December 62. He disbanded his army and peacefully returned to civilian life. He was less impressive as a politician than he had been as a general. He had two demands: the first was for his arrangements in the east to be ratified by the Senate and the second that land be assigned to his veterans. Both proposals were vital to maintaining his political position. His victories in the east had created a vast network of clients there and to maintain his standing with them he needed the Senate's agreement to ratify the measures that had benefitted them. The demand for land for his veterans was equally crucial. Other generals had provided such a benefit to their veterans and Pompey could do no less if he wished to retain them as clients who could be used in future campaigns for office or to offer him support in the increasingly-violent confrontations that marked Roman politics in these years.

His very success threatened the political balance and a faction of senators, whose moving spirit was the young Marcus Porcius Cato, fiercely opposed him. Despite the fact that Cato had only held the quaestorship, the lowest rung in the senatorial ladder of offices, his connections and the force of his personality made him Pompey's most effective opponent. Cato's faction had strong support from a number of senators who resented the wealth and glory Pompey had gained and were afraid that passing these measures would only solidify his position.

However others were also dissatisfied with the obstructionism of the senators allied with Cato. Marcus Licinius Crassus was one of them. He had enriched himself during the civil war under Sulla. His unsavoury reputation forced him to manoeuvre between those politicians who took up the popular cause and the conservatives who would later be found allied with Cato. His greatest weakness was his lack of military glory. He had defeated the slave rebellion under the Thracian Spartacus in 71, but a victory in a slave war never carried the same prestige as those over foreign states. What he had succeeded in doing was to become the wealthiest senator until the return of Pompey who, with the wealth acquired in the eastern wars, probably surpassed him. Crassus's money had been earned through the confiscations in the civil war and through adroit manipulation of the housing market in Rome, creating a slave fire brigade who would only agree to put out fires if the owners sold the property to Crassus at rock bottom prices.[1] He would then erect cheap tenements on the vacant land, which he let out at exorbitant rates. During the 60s he had developed his friendship with Julius Caesar and strengthened his ties to the equestrians, many of whom were engaged in fulfilling public contracts such as supplying Rome's armies or undertaking public works. Many of the wealthiest of these *publicani* had formed companies to collect taxes in several provinces. The most lucrative public contract was for the collection of taxes in the province of Asia. The company that bought the Asian taxes in 61 seems to have entered an unusually high bid. It is difficult to know why they did so, but their hopes for a significant profit were soon disappointed and by 60, if not earlier, they were pressing for a reduction in the amount they owed the government. Crassus took up their cause as a way of strengthening his already close ties to the equestrians but met with little more success than Pompey had on his return.

In 60 Crassus's friend Gaius Julius Caesar had returned from his tenure as propraetor in Further Spain during 61. Caesar stood for election to a consul-ship for 59 and was fiercely opposed by the senators who feared politicians with popular programs. Despite the opposition, and probably with the help of Pompey whom he had supported at crucial points over the previous decade and also from Crassus, he was elected, although his colleague for 59, Marcus Calpurnius Bibulus, was a close associate of Cato's and would bitterly oppose him during that year.

In 59 Caesar was in his forty-second year, the earliest date at which he could legally hold office. He had been born in 100 into an old patrician family that had been only moderately successful in the competition for office and honours. His father, who had died when Caesar was fifteen, had never reached the consulship. Of more importance was his father's sister Julia, who had married Marius, the conqueror of the Cimbri and Teutones. Caesar's first marriage at the age of sixteen to Cornelia, a daughter of one of Sulla's fiercest opponents, even more firmly linked him to politicians who favoured popular legislation. In his twenties he gained military experience through various minor offices and through serving on the staffs of various commanders. Even at this early stage he gave proof of his personal courage, winning the award of the civic crown for saving a fellow citizen's life. In 69 he began his senatorial career by holding the quaestorship and then the higher senatorial magistracies in regular progression. During this period he openly supported popular legislation, including commands for Pompey, and became an even greater object of suspicion to the traditionalists. In 63 he came into direct conflict with Cato on the question of the fate of Cataline's fellow conspirators, with both men making speeches supporting differing points of view.

After his praetorship in 62 he was sent out as proconsul to Further Spain in 61.[2] He owed such extravagant sums to his creditors that he only left the city with difficultly after Crassus had satisfied his most demanding creditors.[3] Many of the characteristics he would later display during his governorship in Gaul were already in evidence during his time in western Spain and Portugal. He sought military glory that would ease his path to the consulship and money to help stave off his creditors. Immediately on arrival he raised ten cohorts (equivalent to a legion) in addition to the twenty already there. Brigandage had become endemic in the western part of the province and Caesar quickly launched a campaign to end it. He moved north to the Herminian Mountains (the modern Serra da Estrela) north-east of Lisbon in central Portugal where the tribes responsible for the province's troubles lived. He ordered these tribes to resettle in the Douro valley below the mountains where the Romans could more easily control them. Their refusal to do so, which Caesar probably expected, led to what must have been a difficult campaign given the harsh topography of the area. Despite this, Caesar successfully drove them out of their mountains. They fled west to the coast and made a stand on an unknown island. After an abortive attempt to ferry his men across on rafts, Caesar brought up a fleet and defeated the tribes who had sought refuge there.

Caesar showed the same energy in administration that he had shown on the battlefield. He lifted some of the impositions that had been placed on communities dating back to the Sertorian War a decade and a-half earlier. Caesar also resolved pressing debt problems in the province. As Roman activity in Gaul makes clear, wherever the Romans imposed themselves debt became a serious problem. Caesar had also made himself wealthy and had been hailed by his soldiers as *imperator*, which qualified him to request a triumph. At the end of his year he returned to Rome to stand for the consulship.

Despite his victory in the elections Caesar faced serious problems. His legislation would face strong opposition in the Senate and his colleague belonged to the faction that hated him. Also, before the election the Senate had, as legally required, designated the provinces that would be given to the successful candidates after their year in office. Caesar and Bibulus were assigned the supervision of the byways and woodlands of Italy. What exactly this meant is a matter of some dispute. It is probable that, given the unsettled situation in Gaul, it was a way of keeping the ex-consuls in readiness should an emergency arise. But for an ambitious man like Caesar this offered little scope to win further military glory.

Pompey and Crassus had no doubt supported Caesar's candidacy and had helped him get elected. However, each of the three faced the prospect of frustration and diminished prestige because of senatorial opposition. To obtain their political objectives the three men banded together. In office Caesar, with the support of the other two, was to propose and pass legislation that would give them what they wanted. This alliance between the three has been given the name of the First Triumvirate. Unlike the Second a decade and a-half later it had no legal standing. It was simply a private alliance, which their enemies called the 'three-headed monster', between these men for their own political advantage.

Caesar first turned his attention to obtaining land for Pompey's veterans.[4] He tried to make the law as conciliatory as possible, but such a measured approach proved useless. His colleague Bibulus did everything he could to obstruct Caesar. On the day the measure was brought before the assembly things became so heated that someone dumped a pot of manure on Bibulus's head and his friends had to remove him for his own safety. Through unrelenting pressure and adroit management, and with the help of Pompey's veterans and Crassus's supporters, Caesar brought the measure to a vote and it passed. A little later Pompey's arrangements in the east were ratified. Within a few months Crassus was satisfied when the Asian tax gatherers were given a remission of one-third of what they owed the government.

There remained one problem: Caesar's province after his consulship. Two provinces had particular appeal; Cisalpine Gaul and Illyricum. Cisalpine Gaul was a major recruiting centre and was well-placed for watching events in Italy and protecting the interests of the three allies in Rome, where the unpopularity of the Triumvirate was increasing. It would also serve as a base for reinforcing Transalpine Gaul should the already troubled situation there deteriorate further. For a man eager for military glory and the wealth that successful war could bring, Illyricum was full of possibility. The province bordered north-eastern Italy and guarded the approaches to the Julian Alps, the easiest approach to Italy from the other side of the Alps. To its north-east lay the expanding kingdom of Burebista, who ruled the Dacians whose centre lay in Transylvania. Burebista had already expanded south of the Danube towards the Julian Alps and the eastern coast of the Adriatic. Although events dictated otherwise, the threat and opportunity presented by the Dacians persisted and it was while he was planning a campaign against the Dacians that Caesar was assassinated in 44.

One of the tribunes, Publius Vatinius, an ally of Caesar and later to serve as a legate under him in Gaul, brought a bill before the people assigning Cisalpine Gaul and Illyricum to Caesar for five years, along with the three legions that were then based at Aquileia on Rome's north-eastern border. Pompey strongly supported the bill, which was passed. In addition, Pompey proposed that Transalpine Gaul, now vacant, with its one legion should be added to Caesar's command. The bill passed. It may have been now or soon after that Caesar obtained for Ariovistus, the Suebian victor over the Aedui, recognition of his title of king by the Roman Senate as well as that of 'Friend of the Roman People'. The award of such a title appears a little surprising given the longstanding relationship with the Aedui. It is best explained as an attempt to stabilize the situation in central Gaul without the need for military intervention. The failure of the Senate to react to a request by the Aedui for help against the Germans in 61 indicates the same lack of interest in the part of Gaul that lay beyond the province.

Caesar's consulship ended in the same acrimony with which it began. His political enemies tried to launch an inquiry into his conduct as consul, but when the matter came before the Senate it refused its support. Caesar remained on the outskirts of Rome, waiting on developments within the city. Finally he set out in March 58 for his new province, when he received news of further possible trouble in Gaul. He was to remain there for almost nine years, and when he left – at the beginning of his invasion of Italy in January 49 – Rome controlled all of Gaul from the North Sea to the Mediterranean and from the Atlantic to the Rhine.

The most important source for Caesar's Gallic campaigns is Caesar's own *Commentaries on the Gallic War*.[5] It consist of seven books, written by Caesar and covering the years 58 to 52, with an eighth book added by Aulus Hirtius, who had been a legate of Caesar in Gaul and was to hold the consulship in 43, which took events down to 50. The Romans distinguished the commentary from a history. A historical work was composed within a moralistic framework and with conscious literary art. The commentary was developed from memoranda, official dispatches and administrative reports. It could supply the framework for the writing of a formal history. A clear example is provided by the request by Cicero to his friend Lucceius to write a history of Cicero's consulship. Cicero promises to supply his commentary on his consulship so that Lucceius can use it as a basis for his history.[6] By the generation before Caesar, publication of such factual accounts of their achievements by the elite had developed into a means of self-promotion and justification, and as a way to enhance the influence and standing of their families. Caesar shared these preoccupations, in addition to a more immediate purpose. As long as he remained as proconsul he could not be prosecuted in the courts by his political enemies. If he could pass directly from his command to a second consulship in 49 he would be safe from prosecution until the end of that consulship, and who knew how his political fortunes might improve in the meanwhile. Certainly one motive of Caesar's in writing the commentaries was to show himself as a triumphant military commander who had added vast areas to the empire of the Roman people. In Roman elections military success played a dominant role.

The core of *Gallic War* was provided by the dispatches that Caesar as a proconsul periodically sent to the Senate to keep it informed of his actions and to broadcast his successes. But *Gallic War* is clearly far more detailed than such reports would have been, and contains sections such as the discussions on the Gauls and Germans in Book VI or the section on Britain in Book V that would have had no place in official dispatches. There has been some controversy about how the work was composed. Was each book written at the end of the year's campaign or was the work composed all at once? The first possibility seems preferable.[7] No earlier book makes a reference to a later one and there are contradictions between books that would surely have been removed had Caesar composed the work as a whole. For instance, in Book II he claims that the military manpower of the Belgic tribe of the Nervii was almost totally destroyed in battle in 57, but within three years we find them along with other tribes besieging a legionary camp. More strikingly, at the end of the events of 57 Caesar makes a claim that all Gaul was pacified, which makes little sense in light of the campaigns that follow. Caesar was known to have written with amazing speed and it is likely that at the end of the campaigning season, during the winters he spent in Cisalpine Gaul administering justice, he composed each book which was then dispatched and circulated at Rome. It was perhaps only when Hirtius added his eighth book that the individual books were brought together as a single work.

That the work was written to enhance Caesar's reputation and influence his impending election is undisputed but the audience for whom it was written is not. It would be a natural assumption that it was directed to the elite but there are certain passages that makes this questionable. Before the battle against Ariovistus in 58, while the army was refitting and waiting for provisions at Vesontio (Besançon), Caesar reports that there was panic in his army at the prospect of facing the Germans. He states that it began among the military tribunes, prefects and others who had followed him from Rome. He then claims that this panic infected the rest of the army. To combat this problem Caesar made a rousing speech that finally turned the situation around. It is striking that it was the legionaries and centurions who were in the forefront of this change of heart.[8] Another marked feature of the work is the number of passages devoted to the exploits of centurions. The centurion Publius Sextius Baculus is mentioned a number of times, the most dramatic being in the battle against the Nervii when Baculus, although wounded many times, managed to help reform his cohort on the right wing and held the line until Caesar brought help.[9] Baculus is presented as a paradigm of military virtue and courage.

Other ranks are also mentioned, such as the bearer of the eagle of the Tenth Legion who, during the hasty invasion of Britain in 55 when his fellow soldiers were hesitant to advance to the shore from their boats, leapt over the side bearing his eagle towards the shore. The loss of the legion's eagle would have brought immense dishonour and so the men followed.[10] Ordinary soldiers too receive praise for their valour and endurance, especially Caesar's favoured Tenth Legion. A marked feature of the work is the frequent references to the Roman people, who are mentioned forty-one times. The first book presents a series of justifications for forays beyond the province's frontier that are presented in terms of defending the honour and dominion of the Roman people.

Caesar had spent his career as a popular politician and his family had connections with such politicians that dated from the beginning of the first century. In the course of his career he had made many political enemies, especially among the senators. His military triumphs would do nothing to change their minds in his favour. In fact, the prestige and potential power such successes brought Caesar made them even more implacable. The successes produced strains as well with Pompey and Crassus, who were unhappy and uneasy at his spectacular achievements. These might hearten his supporters but they could not change the balance of power among the elite. They could however raise his chance of success with Roman voters. Although many of these might have been incapable of reading his work; there was a tradition of oral performance of such works that would have allowed them to reach a wide audience. On balance it seems best to regard the audience as a combination of Caesar's political supporters and allies as well as the Romans who would be voting in the electoral assembly when Caesar stood for office.

Gallic War has no parallel in the literature that has survived from antiquity. It is a contemporary account of a war written by the commanding general. Added to this is the seeming objectivity of the account heightened by Caesar's use of the third person for himself. It is written in a spare, simple, and lucid style. The purity and elegance of Caesar's writing was recognized by Cicero who, although no friend, characterized it as a work 'of unaffected and lucid brevity'.[11]

However, even in antiquity *Gallic War* drew criticism. Suetonius, the biographer of the Caesars writing in the early-second century, records that Asinius Pollio, a man who had been consul and an author of an important history, criticized the work as carelessly written and with too little a regard for truth.[12] He accused Caesar of being too ready to listen to the accounts of others and of manipulating facts for his own benefit. In at least one instance this may be true. At the battle with the Tigurini at the River Arar in 58 Caesar claims credit for their defeat without mentioning his senior legate Titus Labienus. Labienus, who joined Caesar's enemies during the civil war, disputed Caesar's claim.[13] Certainly other ancient accounts give a very different picture of Caesar's actions in Gaul. Suetonius presents him as purposely seeking out conflict and using any pretext, whether just or not, as a reason for beginning a war. The overall portrait is negative. The third-century historian Dio Cassius is equally critical of Caesar.

Much of this criticism was due to the ambiguous image of Caesar during the Empire. He was the founder of Rome's first imperial dynasty but he had come to power through civil war and had overthrown the Republic for which the senatorial class of the imperial period nostalgically yearned. Even the first emperor Augustus, who owed his position to his adoption by Caesar, kept the figure of his adopted father discreetly in the background. In addition, Caesar was under constant political attack while in Gaul and attempts were made to terminate his command. Cato at one point argued that Caesar ought to be handed over to the Germans to erase the curse on Rome caused by what he claimed was a violation of a truce with them by Caesar. Both the condemnation by some of Caesar's contemporaries and the ambivalence of posterity explain much of the negative portrait that later sources present of Caesar's conquests in Gaul.[14]

The basis of any narrative of Caesar's governorship in Gaul must be *Gallic War*. There are other sources but none can compare with its wealth of detail and analysis of events. The work was written in a heated political atmosphere and to present Caesar in a favourable light. One might expect widespread distortion of the facts in Caesar's favour but this appears unlikely. Upper class Romans seem to have been well-informed about the Gallic campaigns. Letters from Caesar's officers about events in Gaul seem to have regularly reached Rome. Cicero's brother Quintus was Caesar's legate from 54 to 51. We know from his brother's correspondence that he kept Marcus informed of events there. For instance, in 54 Marcus mentions a letter from his brother sent from Britain containing an account of Caesar's expedition there. A speech of Cicero's delivered in the Senate in April 56 assumes widespread knowledge of events in Gaul on the part of the senators. The common knowledge of events in Gaul makes it extremely unlikely that there is widespread falsification of the basic facts in *Gallic War*. This is borne out by the fact that even where we can challenge Caesar's presentation of his role, it is Caesar himself who supplies the means to do so. For example, during the Gallic revolt of 52 Caesar attacked the main town and fortress of the Arverni, Gergovia near modern Clermont-Ferrand. Caesar underestimated the difficulties of taking the town. In the course of the siege he launched a surprise attack that failed. Caesar blames the failure on the over-eagerness of his troops but it is clear that Caesar had misread the strength of the Gallic force, which was larger than his own, as well as its resilience. It was a mistake in judgment on the part of Caesar, not the misplaced enthusiasm of his men that caused the attack to fail. In general the narrative is factual and clear. There are occasional points where events remain obscure, which must have been due either to the difficulty of obtaining information or to the confused nature of the events. In the end Caesar's narrative remains our essential source.

The other two sources that offer a narrative on any scale are Plutarch's *Life of Caesar* and portions of Dio's *Roman History*. Plutarch's aim was biography, not history, and his portrayal of the Gallic Wars focuses on events as a window into Caesar's character. He does supply some supplementary information which seems reliable, but nothing more. Dio offers the only connected narrative account that, despite its fragmentary nature, directly challenges Caesar. The picture presented of the governor is strongly negative. Caesar is portrayed as deliberately seeking war for his own profit and glory. His conduct is portrayed as duplicitous, provoking the German Ariovistus despite the fact that Caesar had obtained recognition for him as a 'Friend of Rome' during his own consulship. Dio alleges that Caesar's negotiations with him were merely a device to give Caesar a suitable pretext for war. He underplays Caesar's successes and presents a negative picture of Caesar's relations with his troops. These are matters of interpretation. There are some factual differences between Caesar and Dio and it is possible that Dio used some additional source. However, for the most part Caesar supplied the factual material and Dio added his own interpretation of it. Dio cannot serve as a corrective to *Gallic War*.

There are summaries of Caesar's campaigns in Gaul in later writers. They add nothing. The only secure basis for a reconstruction of those campaigns is Caesar himself.

Chapter Three

58: The Helvetii and Ariovistus

The Helvetii

It was the news of the migration of the Helvetii that hastened Caesar's departure from Rome in late March of 58. According to his account the migration had long been planned and was set to begin on 28 March, when the Helvetii had agreed to muster at the Rhône. He states that planning for the migration had started in 61 and that it formed part of a plot by a leading Helvetian named Orgetorix to seize the kingship over his people.

Caesar claims that Orgetorix easily persuaded the Helvetii to migrate from their homeland in the area of modern Switzerland. He made the argument that they were hemmed in by natural barriers on every side, which prevented movement and limited their opportunities for raiding neighbouring peoples, a normal Gallic practice.[1] Their goal would be the land of the Santoni in south-western Gaul (Départment of Charente-Maritime).[2] The plan was approved and two years were set aside to prepare for the move that was to take place in the third. Orgetorix was placed in charge of organizing the migration and began to visit neighbouring tribes to conclude agreements with them that would allow peaceful passage of the Helvetii through their lands.

During his visits Orgetorix concluded a political alliance with a prominent member of the Sequani, Casticus, and with Dumnorix, a leading member of Rome's allies the Aedui. These two like Orgetorix sought kingship over their own people. Orgetorix promised to aid them with the power of his tribe. The three swore an oath that once they had become kings they would between them seize all of Gaul.

Orgetorix's plot was revealed by informers and he was brought to trial by his own people. If he was proven guilty the penalty would be to be burnt alive. To intimidate his rivals he brought 10,000 of his dependents to the hearing. The figure gives some indication of the huge entourage of relations, clients and debtors that a Gallic noble of a powerful tribe could muster.[3] The number was sufficiently threatening and the trial was called off. His opponents summoned their own supporters, intending to meet Orgetorix's threats with violence but he died mysteriously. There was a rumour that he committed suicide but no certainty. Despite his death the plan to emigrate went ahead.[4]

It is difficult to know what to make of this story. Caesar does not tell us how this migration to the land of the Santoni would aid Orgetorix in his quest for the kingship, a form of government that was disappearing in Gaul during this period.[5] The same can be said of the new homeland the Helvetians had chosen among the Santoni. The territory is more accessible than the mountainous homeland of the tribe but no reason is given for that particular choice. Whether it would relieve the overcrowding that Caesar alleges played a role in the movement is uncertain. There was a more pressing reason for the Helvetii to leave. Their territory was now hemmed in between the Germans under Ariovistus to the north in Alsace and the Romans to the south. The year that the migration was approved, 61, was shortly before the victory of Ariovistus over the Aedui and the settlement of his Germans across the Rhine. An expanding German presence in the north and an inflexible border in the south may have set the migration in motion and would explain the fact that the death of Orgetorix made no difference to the plan. The Helvetian raids on the province mentioned by Cicero in a letter of 60 may have been a result of this German pressure.[6] Settling among the Santoni would have reduced Roman pressure as their lands were farther from the province and Roman presence had not been as oppressive in the west.

One further aspect of the plot reported by Caesar needs to be examined and that is the claim that the three Gauls had conspired to support each other (not unlike the triumvirate of Pompey, Caesar and Crassus at Rome) in their quest for the kingship and to join together to rule all of Gaul. There is no doubt that the Helvetii, given their military strength, could have been of use to Casticus and Dumnorix; what is less clear is how they would return the favour. More interesting is the intent for the three tribes to dominate all of Gaul. Caesar is using Gaul in a restricted sense here. In the opening chapter of *Gallic War*, Caesar describes Gaul as divided into three parts: a central area which is Gaul proper; a south-western portion where the Aquitani live; and the north-east, home to the Belgae. He differentiates the three peoples in terms of physical appearance and culture. In the early books of *Gallic War* he uses 'Gaul' to refer to the central area and this is the case here. Given the presence of Rome and the Germans, an alliance between the three tribes would create a coalition powerful enough to maintain itself against them and assert control over central Gaul. If this had been the case it seems that the death of Orgetorix and the disaffection of the Helvetii ended any chance of forming such a coalition.

The function of this narrative is to justify Caesar's response to the Helvetian migration. It is noticeable that here, as in the conflict with Ariovistus later in the year, Caesar goes to great lengths to justify his actions. In later conflicts he feels no need to do so. Since he was acting beyond the boundaries of his province these justifications were meant to shield him from accusations that he was undertaking unnecessary wars for his own benefit.[7]

Before they were to set out in 58 the determination of the Helvetii to migrate was made abundantly clear by the steps they took to render their home territory uninhabitable. Caesar mentions the burning of their twelve towns and 400 villages, as well as isolated farmsteads. In addition they set fire to their grain stocks with the exception of the grain they were to carry with them. Swiss archaeologists have linked a burnt layer on Mont Vully near Fribourg with the burning. In addition, they persuaded other tribes to join the migration, the Raurici, Tulingi, Latobrigi, and the Boii.[8]

Two routes lay open to them. The one that ran north of the Roman province through the lands of the Sequani from the Jura to the Rhône was difficult for wagons and could be blocked in the Jura at the Pas de l'Ecluse. The more southerly route ran through the Roman province starting at Lake Geneva and was far easier. Given these considerations the Helvetii chose the easier southern route.

It appears that Caesar was caught unawares. Problems in Gaul had subsided after 60 and it appears that with the death of Orgetorix the Romans thought that the Helvetii had abandoned their plans. Receiving the news Caesar hurried from Rome to Geneva in the territory of the Allobroges. He was ill-prepared militarily to face the Helvetii. The province had a garrison of only a single legion, probably the Tenth Legion, perhaps stationed at Narbo. His three other legions (Seventh, Eighth and Ninth) were stationed at Aquileia in extreme north-eastern Cisalpine Gaul, presumably in preparation for a campaign near the Danube. At first Caesar issued no orders for the legions at Aquileia to march but hurried to Geneva, 430 miles from Rome, which he reached in eight days, an astonishingly-quick progress. On his arrival he quickly saw that the situation was extremely serious and that his forces were inadequate. He immediately set about recruiting local forces and ordered the bridge over the Rhône destroyed.

The news of his arrival reached the Helvetii and they sent envoys to request permission to proceed through the province. They promised they would cause no harm, adding that they had no other suitable route. It is clear that Caesar had no intention of allowing the migration to proceed. He invokes the memory of the defeat and death of the consul Lucius Cassius in 107 by the Tigurini, a sub-tribe of the Helvetii, portraying them as innately hostile to Rome. He also argues that the passage of the Helvetii through the province would inevitably cause damage; in this he is certainly right.[9] Despite the supplies they carried the Helvetii would have had to live in part off the land they journeyed through. Caesar put the delegation off by saying that he would meet with them again on

13 April and deliver his answer. This was merely a ploy to give him time to strengthen his defences, to bring his legions from Aquileia and to levy additional troops.

As a stopgap he had his men construct a fortification line from Lake Leman (Geneva) to the Jura. It consisted of a ditch and a sixteen-foot rampart, seventeen miles in length, to the point that divided Helvetian territory from that of the Sequani. Traces of it were found in the nineteenth century.[10] Forts and outposts were also constructed and garrisoned. When the Helvetian delegation returned Caesar made it clear that he would stop any attempt by the Helvetii to move through the province. Some Helvetians ignored him and attempted to ford the Rhône but were forced back.[11]

The only other feasible route, by the Pas De L'Écluse, ran through the territory of the Sequani and could not be used without their permission. The Helvetii turned to the Aeduan Dumnorix, the brother of Diviciacus, who was pro-Roman and a close friend of Caesar's. Clearly still valuing his Helvetian connection, Dumnorix persuaded the Sequani to allow the Helvetii to pass as long as they refrained from doing any damage.[12]

The choice of this alternate route by the Helvetii meant that the only way the migration could be stopped was by force. Caesar simply did not have sufficient troops on hand to stop it. Leaving his most trusted legate, Labienus, in charge he set out at full speed for Cisalpine Gaul to raise additional legions while summoning the three at Aquileia. The two legions that Caesar levied were raised illegally. Normally a magistrate required senatorial authority to raise new legions. They became the Eleventh and Twelfth. Caesar disregarded this requirement now and would again in the future. Leading out the three legions from their winter quarters at Aquileia together with the new legions, he marched at full speed across the Alps to Transalpine Gaul. Caesar's march was contested by local tribes in the passes through the Cottian Alps. After his hard-fought crossing he reached the territory of the Segusiavi, which lay on the western bank of the Rhône across from the province immediately south of the Aedui.

By the time that Caesar arrived the Helvetii were already through the defiles of the Jura, had passed through the lands of the Sequani and were now among the Aedui. The Aedui sent an urgent message to Caesar that their territory was being ravaged and that they were unable to defend themselves. The Allobroges sent a message that they were suffering as well. If Caesar had wanted a pretext to conduct further operations against the Helvetii he now had it.

The Helvetii now had to cross the Saône. Caesar was informed by his scouts of this and decided to attack them while they were crossing and vulnerable. He set out from his camp at about midnight with three legions to launch a surprise attack; about three-quarters of the Helvetii had already reached the other bank of the river when Caesar came up. The Helvetii were surprised and unprepared for the attack. Most of the Helvetii on the eastern bank of the river were slaughtered and the rest sought shelter in the nearby woods. The tribal sub-group that he attacked was the Tigurini who had had killed Lucius Cassius. Harking back to the incident he had mentioned earlier in his justification for war with the Helvetii he adds a further rationalization for his actions, linking the honour of the Roman people with a personal injury he had suffered:

> So either by chance or by the will of the immortal gods that portion of the Helvetii that had inflicted a notable disaster on the Roman people was the first to pay the penalty. In this matter Caesar was avenging not only a public wrong but a personal wrong as well because they killed the legate Piso, the grandfather of his father-in-law Lucius Piso, in the same battle as Cassius.[13]

Then Caesar had a bridge constructed over the Saône to its western bank and set out in pursuit. Unsettled by the slaughter at the Saône and still hoping to negotiate a passage the Helvetii again sent an embassy to him. It is evidence of their state of mind that they offered to settle and remain in any area that Caesar wished. This might have ended the matter then and there. However, it is doubtful that the eventual solution forced upon them by Caesar – that is, a return to their devastated homeland – would have been accepted. Caesar made further demands for reparations for the tribes allied to Rome whose lands the Helvetii had pillaged, and for hostages. The Helvetii refused. They had a reputation for success in war and had not yet been defeated in battle, as their envoys pointed out. Caesar's demands were in accordance with normal Roman practice. But to accede to them would have been an open acknowledgement of Roman superiority, an acknowledgement the Helvetii were not yet ready to make.

The next day the Helvetii broke camp and continued their trek. Caesar followed them with his legions and 4,000 auxiliary cavalry drawn from Gauls living in the province, along with the Aedui and their allied tribes. At this point it appears that the Helvetii were moving north-west through Beaujolais and Charolais just east of the Massif Central (Départment of Saône et Loire). Caesar sent all of his cavalry forward to scout the Helvetian column. These were drawn from Gallic auxiliaries, as the Romans no longer fielded their own cavalry. They approached too closely to the Helvetian camp and the enemy cavalry rode out against them. Although they numbered only 500, the Helvetian cavalry were able to get the better of the engagement and inflicted casualties on Caesar's men. Given the lopsided nature of the engagement their success did much to restore their morale and they began to act more aggressively, trying to provoke the Romans to engage them, but the Romans refused. The Romans followed them closely with no more than four or five miles between them and the enemy.

A key problem for Caesar was the question of supplies. As it was probably early May the grain was not yet ripe in the fields. One of the strengths of the Roman army was its superb supply system and grain would normally have been carried up the Saône by ship, but the Helvetii had turned away from the river so that the Romans now depended on local supplies. The Aedui had promised to supply the Romans but their shipments had not been forthcoming. Rather than grain they offered excuses and the situation was becoming serious as the date for the distribution of grain for the army was drawing near. Finally, Caesar summoned representatives from the Aedui to find out the reasons for the delay. It became clear that there was an anti-Roman faction among their nobility. Caesar blames Dumnorix in particular, but it seems likely that he was not the only noble involved. He was also probably not the only member of the elite with personal connections to the Helvetii.[14] Further, it might appear that supporting the Helvetii would be a safer course. As they passed through Aeduan territory there was raiding and destruction but they were a passing problem. Past Roman behaviour indicated that the Romans were here to stay and so might in the end turn out to present a more serious problem. Interestingly, Caesar resolved the matter without punishing Dumnorix which may indicate that during this point in the campaign he thought it better not to alienate an important Aeduan nobleman.

After the meeting Caesar learned from his scouts that the Helvetii were camped seven miles away at the foot of a hill, probably Sanvignes six miles east of the River Arroux, a tributary of the Loire.[15] He sent out scouts again to see whether the other side of the hill offered an easy ascent and finding out that it did planned a pincer attack. He sent out Labienus at the third watch (around midnight) with two legions to scale the hill and take possession of the summit so that he could attack the Helvetii from the rear while Caesar mounted a frontal assault. By dawn Labienus had reached the summit and was in place for the attack. At the fourth watch (around 3am) Caesar set out with the remaining legions and all of his cavalry. He sent his cavalry and scouts, along with Publius Considius, a man who had extensive military experience, to assess the situation. By dawn Caesar was a little more than a mile from the Helvetii and Labienus was in position on the crest of the hill. Labienus had evaded detection by the Helvetii and was getting ready to attack when Considius reported that the enemy was in possession of the hill. That false report led to an immediate change of plan. Caesar withdrew to a nearby hill and deployed for battle. Labienus had been instructed not to attack until he saw Caesar, and so he remained inactive. It was only late in the day that Caesar learned that the report was false. He followed the Helvetii at a distance and then encamped about three miles from their position.

Encumbered with all the paraphernalia of a tribal migration and the presence of women and children, the Helvetian column was slow-moving and shadowing it presented no problem. The need to re-supply, especially as the date for the grain distribution was only two days away, diverted Caesar to the town of Bibracte about 15 miles away. It was located on a hilltop at modern Mont-Beuvray. The town was the capital of the Aedui and given the difficulties Caesar had experienced in receiving his supplies from the Aedui it was an obvious choice. It would give him access to substantial stocks of grain as well as a way to pressure the Aedui to fulfil their commitments.[16]

The Helvetii set out in pursuit. Why they did so is unclear. Caesar offers alternative explanations, all of which are possible but none of which are compelling. It may simply be that they now found the constant pressure of his pursuit intolerable, and although the narrative does not mention it they may have been in supply difficulties themselves. Caesar's close shadowing of their column must have hindered their foraging. They may have been encouraged as Caesar suggests by his earlier refusal to engage. Caesar, learning of the approach of the Helvetii, deployed his six legions on a nearby hill and sent his cavalry forward. He arrayed his four veteran legions (Seventh-Tenth) in the standard triple line, consisting of cohorts from each of the legions arranged in three lines, with the third line normally forming a reserve. The two untested legions, Eleven and Twelve, that Caesar had recently raised in Cisalpine Gaul, were posted on the crest of the hill with Gallic auxiliary troops to guard the baggage train. Caesar then sent away all of the horses, including his own, making it clear to his infantry that he would share their fate. This is the first instance of a significant aspect of Caesar's success as a general; he made it evident to his men that he would share their hardships and dangers. This style of leadership is praised by ancient writers who understood that in mass formations and in close combat morale was a crucial factor. Caesar had a strong sense of theatre and used it to bind his men to himself.

The Helvetians arrived and piled their baggage in a single place. They repulsed the Roman cavalry and then formed up in what Caesar calls a phalanx. Since the normal offensive weapon of the Gauls was the long slashing sword, their formation was more open than the traditional Greek phalanx and Caesar must use the term simply to indicate a close formation. The Helvetii then advanced on the Romans. It is difficult to understand why they launched their attack at this point. They were attacking uphill, which was bound to blunt the force of their charge and hinder their use of missile weapons. It may be a symptom of their desperation that they did so. As their adversaries were mounting the hill the legionaries discharged their *pila* to break the enemy formation before they drew the short swords that were their main offensive weapon. The Roman *pilum* was a mass-produced javelin about 7 feet long with a barbed or pyramidal head. The remains of a number of them have been found at second-century BC Roman military camps in Spain. Normally each legionary carried a heavy and a light pilum, with the heavy probably weighing about ten pounds and the lighter about half that weight. Its maximum range was probably about 30 yards. Even if they failed to kill or wound *pila* were designed to bend or break on impact so that they could not be pulled out of shields. Caesar remarks about the difficulties created for the Helvetii by *pila* embedded in their shields and the fact that in many cases the Gauls were so constricted in their movements that they preferred to discard their shields and so made themselves more vulnerable.

Exhausted by what was an unequal struggle the Helvetii retreated to a hilltop less than a mile away. As the Romans advanced against them, 15,000 Boii and Tulingi who had served as their rearguard at the end of their column attacked the Roman right flank, the unshielded side, while the Helvetii, heartened by this attack, renewed their frontal assault. The flexibility of the Roman formation allowed the third line to turn around and face the new threat from the right. At this point the battle became a prolonged slogging match that lasted from shortly after noon until darkness. The Helvetii, giving away under Roman pressure, retreated to the hill from which they had started their attack, while the Boii and Tulingi were forced back to the tribes' wagons and baggage. There a fierce struggle took place that finally ended with the Romans in possession of the Gauls' baggage and their camp.[17]

Caesar claims that 130,000 of the Helvetii survived the battle and moved off through the night, and with almost continual marching reached the lands of the Lingones, which lay to the north around modern Dijon. The Romans refrained from pursuit for three days. The hard fought battle had caused a number of casualties. Time was needed to aid the wounded and bury the dead. It is clear from the following narrative that a number of Tulingi, Boii and Latovici had also survived the encounter. Caesar was in no mind to let these fugitives escape. He sent a letter to the Lingones with the threat that if they provided food or other assistance to the fugitives he would consider them an enemy. If the Lingones had had any intention of aiding the Helvetii Caesar's threat was sufficient to deter them. The loss of their provisions when their camp and baggage had been captured as well as the refusal of the Lingones to help them reduced the Helvetii to desperate straits and they were finally compelled to send emissaries to Caesar to beg for peace. Caesar ordered that the Helvetii should remain in place until his arrival, which they did. Caesar demanded the surrender of their weapons, hostages and escaped slaves. While this was taking place 6,000 men belonging to a tribal subdivision made their escape and headed for the Rhine to seek refuge with the Germans. Instead of sending his own forces in pursuit Caesar ordered the peoples through which they would pass to capture them and return them to the Romans. Caesar's orders were obeyed and the fugitives were brought to him. The fact that these tribes, probably the Sequani among them, complied is evidence for the impact of Caesar's victory over a large and warlike tribe. Caesar reserved them for special treatment. He says that he treated them as enemies. What he means by this is not clear but it probably means that he either enslaved or executed them. The rest of the Helvetii made an unconditional surrender which the Romans called a *deditio*. He ordered the surviving Helvetii, Tulingi and Latovici to return home. He gives as the reasons for this command the fear that if their territories were left vacant it would invite German settlement in an area bordering the Roman province. At the request of the Aedui the Boii were allowed to settle in their territory. Given recent events the reinforcement of manpower would have been welcome to the Aedui and the Boii were eventually assimilated by them.

In the aftermath of the battle Caesar claims that tablets were found in the Helvetian camp written in Greek characters containing lists of men of military age, women, boys and the elderly who had joined the migration.[18] There were also counts of the other tribes who accompanied the Helvetii for a grand total of 368,000, of whom 92,000 were capable of bearing arms. Caesar then records a census taken when the Gauls returned home which totalled 110,000. It is difficult to assess the accuracy of these figures and this is the only case in *Gallic War* where Caesar refers to such lists. The Gauls did write Celtic in Greek letters. Numerous inscriptions in Celtic written in Greek characters have been preserved. The figure of 92,000 warriors is plausible if the total of 368,000 is accepted. In pre-modern populations about one-quarter of the population consisted of males of military age. The total number for all of those migrating is also in the realm of possibility. The 110,000 survivors representing a third of those who set out is more of a problem. The loss of more than two-thirds is possible but it must have had a number of causes. The migration from beginning to end probably consumed about three months with the final battle in late May or early June. Many, especially the sick and the infirm, may have perished along the way and others simply settled along the route of the migration. Once battle casualties are included, which Caesar does not give, the figure for losses stills seems too high but there is no other evidence and at least it is in the realm of possibility.[19]

The exact route of the migration and the precise location of the battle cannot be identified. It is likely that after the Helvetii turned off from the Saône near Mâcon they moved up the valley of the Petit Grosne.[20] The final battle was in the neighbourhood of Besançon, and locations can be found to correspond with Caesar's description but no certainty is possible. Ancient battle descriptions rarely allow the exact location to be identified. Caesar's victory had been impressive but the defeat did not end Helvetian opposition to Roman control. During the great revolt of 52 the Helvetii are once again found fighting the Romans.[21]

Ariovistus

Sensing which way the wind was blowing a delegation of Gallic chiefs, Caesar claims from almost all of Gaul, came to congratulate him on his victory.[22] They also requested a secret meeting, which he agreed to. According to Caesar's account they begged for his help against Ariovistus and his Germans. Caesar mentions Diviciacus as the main speaker.[23] The Aeduan was a close associate of the Roman general and so collusion is possible. Caesar promised help. He said he would restrain the German through his influence for it had been Caesar who had had him named a friend of the Roman people during his consulship. It is hard to know how seriously Caesar meant this or whether he really believed that the matter could be settled by any measure short of military force. Caesar once again felt the need to justify his conduct as he did in the case of the Helvetii.[24] This time on the basis of the wrong done to the Aedui and the threat of the Germans first to Gaul and then to Italy.

Perhaps to further justify his conduct Caesar sent messengers to Ariovistus requesting a conference at a place midway between the two that the German could choose. Ariovistus was less impressed by the victory over the Helvetii than the Gauls had been. His reply was meant to show his indifference to Roman power. If Caesar wanted anything from him Caesar should come to him. He did not enter those parts of Gaul under Caesar's control and found it surprising that the Romans were concerned about Gaul as it was his by right of conquest.

Caesar's reply to what could only have been seen as an insulting message was to dispatch a set of conditions that he must have known would be refused and would end in war: Ariovistus should stop bringing additional Germans over the Rhine, return hostages to the Aedui and Sequani and refrain from attacking the Aedui and their allies. The German refused to accept these conditions, as must have been expected. He explicitly asserted his military supremacy: 'Caesar could attack when he pleased and he would see what the undefeated Germans could do'.[25] Caesar now details a timely recitation of the wrongs that the Aedui and the Treveri, who lived in Gallia Belgica between the Meuse and the middle Rhine and who were neighbours of Ariovistus, suffered. Of particular significance was the complaint of the Treveri, who reported that 100 clans of the Suebi had settled on the east bank of the Rhine and were trying to cross the river. Caesar decided to forestall Suebi. He gathered supplies and set out by forced marches to prevent them from linking up with Ariovistus. From the first

Caesar had decided on war. He must have known in advance that Ariovistus would reject his conditions.

After having marched for three days Caesar was informed that Ariovistus was making for the main town of the Sequani, Vesontio (modern Besancon), and had already advanced three days beyond his own frontier. Vesontio was a vital base for both men. It contained an abundance of supplies and was well protected by the Doubs River, which almost surrounds it, and the part of its perimeter that was not sheltered by the river was closed off by a high hill (Colline de la Citadelle). In addition to these natural fortifications there was a wall around the base of the mountain that linked it to the town and made it into a natural fortress. Given the importance of Vesontio and knowing that Ariovistus was advancing against it Caesar marched day and night and was able to throw a garrison into it before the German chief arrived.

Caesar remained at Vesontio to gather grain and other necessary supplies. During the halt he reports that the prospect of fighting the Germans caused a panic in his army. He notes that the panic began among the military tribunes, prefects and the customary entourage of friends from Rome, primarily young men holding no office but on the make, who had accompanied him to the city and had no military experience.[26] The contagion had spread to the legionaries, who were terrified at the prospect of fighting the Germans. Caesar called a council of all of his centurions and severely upbraided them. He then rehearsed the victories of Marius over the Germans, pointing out that there was nothing to fear and that if they and their men refused to follow him he would march out with only the Tenth Legion, for he was confident in their loyalty. Caesar's speech had the desired effect, with the Tenth Legion thanking the general for the confidence he had expressed in it and the rest of the army affirming its loyalty and its willingness to fight. The same sense of theatre and its effects is visible here as in the gesture of sending away his horse before the battle with the Helvetii. Caesar was able to create and sustain these bonds with his men until his assassination in 44. There was trouble, such as the mutinies at Placentia (Piacenza) in 49 and again in Rome in 47, but these were only occasional problems. The allegiance of the Gallic legions, as well as of other units, during the campaigns in Gaul and during the civil war that followed is striking. Even after Caesar's death his heir Octavian owed much of his success in gaining military support to the fact that he was Caesar's adopted son.

With his grain supply now assured Caesar was ready to march. His trusted Aeduan advisor Diviciacus supplied him with a route through open country, which would involve a detour of 46 miles but would avoid wooded areas where ambushes could be set. The route probably went by way of Voray, through the valley of the Ognon, a tributary of the Saône in Franche Comté, and the Arcey, also in Franche Comté. After seven days of continuous marching his scouts brought him the news that Ariovistus' camp was only 22 miles distant. Learning of his arrival Ariovistus sent to Caesar asking for a meeting. A large open area almost equidistant between the two camps was selected. Ariovistus requested each party be accompanied only by cavalry, an arm in which the Germans excelled. Caesar agreed to this but revealed the level of trust he had in his Gallic cavalry. He mounted the Tenth Legion on horses taken from the Gauls to serve as his escort. Caesar reports the substance of his own and Ariovistus' arguments at the meeting. He brought up his claim that he was fighting in defence of the Aedui. Ariovistus asserted that Gaul belonged to him by right of conquest. If it came to a battle he would crush the Romans and Caesar's death would be welcome to many aristocrats and leading men at Rome. Caesar replied that the Romans had campaigned in Gaul long before Ariovistus's arrival. What is remarkable about this statement is the shift it represents from the claim that he was defending the province or protecting Roman allies and clients to a naked assertion of the Roman right to dominate Gaul.[27] The parlay ended in a scuffle between the Germans and Caesar's Tenth Legion. Interestingly, two days later Ariovistus made a request for another parlay. Caesar refused to go himself as he thought that there was nothing left to discuss but sent two envoys in his place, one of whom was a Romanized son of a man who had been granted Roman citizenship by Valerius Flaccus.[28] They were promptly proclaimed spies by Ariovistus and thrown into chains.

By doing this Ariovistus signalled that further talks could achieve nothing; battle would have to resolve the conflict. On the same day he moved his camp to the foot of a mountain 5.5 miles from Caesar's. The next day he moved his campsite 2 miles beyond Caesar's camp. Here he would be a threat to Caesar's supply lines to the Aedui and Sequani. For another five days Caesar led his men out of camp and deployed, trying to provoke a battle. Ariovistus remained in camp but daily sent out his 6,000 cavalry and their accompanying 6,000 light infantry to engage the Roman cavalry. Caesar describes the Germans' tactics. The infantry acted as a support force. If there was trouble their cavalry could fall back on the massed infantry. If one of their horseman was wounded and fell from his horse, the infantry would form a circle around him to protect him from enemy assault. These cavalry tactics persisted. Writing a century and a-half after Caesar the historian Tacitus describes German cavalry tactics that are identical to those mentioned by Caesar.[29] *Gallic War* indicates that the Gauls did not fight in this way but engaged in pure cavalry battles. Despite the successful record of German cavalry against the Gauls, defeating large forces with astonishingly small numbers, and the later record of German units in the imperial army, cavalry formed a small proportion of German tribal armies. They lacked horses suitable for cavalry service. Their own horses were smaller and slower than those of both the Gauls and the Romans. In 52, while on the march Caesar, recognizing his inferiority in cavalry in the face of Gallic attacks, sent for additional cavalry to German tribes across the Rhine. Upon their arrival he recognized the inferiority of their horses and substituted Roman ones. German armies were primarily infantry armies. Ariovistus's army probably numbered about 120,000 men if Caesar's estimate is correct, although this has been challenged. Thus only one-twentieth was cavalry. The usual proportion in Mediterranean armies was one-in-ten. They were drawn like other contemporary cavalry units from the nobility and the wealthy. Caesar was clearly impressed by them and perhaps as early as 57 he recruited them as mercenaries.[30]

Caesar realized the Germans would not leave their camp to fight. Interrogating prisoners taken he learned that Ariovistus would not join battle because the omens were not favourable. The old women who performed this divination had stated that the Germans would not be victorious if they fought before the new moon.[31] Given the necessity of re-establishing his supply lines Caesar moved his camp about a half-mile beyond the German camp. The march was conducted in the three-line formation that could quickly deploy for battle. Once he reached the campsite Caesar deployed his first two lines in defence while the third began constructing the camp. Ariovistus, realizing that his plan to cut off Caesar's supplies was in danger, sent out a large force of 16,000 lightly-equipped infantry and all of his cavalry to stop the construction of the camp. Caesar ordered his first two lines to repulse the enemy while the third continued building the camp. The German attack was unsuccessful. Caesar left a force of two legions and a section of auxiliaries in the camp and marched back to his first camp with his remaining four legions. In total he had about 25,000–30,000 infantry and perhaps 4,000 auxiliary cavalry.

With his supply lines now secure, the next day Caesar once again led out his forces from both camps and advanced a short distance from his main camp. Once again Ariovistus refused the challenge and remained in camp. Around noon Caesar led his forces back to their respective camps. After Caesar had returned, Ariovistus launched an attack with part of his army on the smaller camp. Fierce fighting ensued, which lasted until darkness fell but, despite many casualties on both sides, the assault failed.

Ariovistus seems to have hoped to defeat Caesar without a major battle by using only manoeuvre. The failure of the attack on the smaller camp marked the failure of that plan. In theory he could have moved his camp once again to cut Caesar off from his supply line, but the Germans could not sustain the same march discipline as the Roman army, which would have exposed his forces to attack. Even had he succeeded, Caesar could have countered him by also moving his camp. Ariovistus would have exposed his army to potential danger with no prospect of certain gain. By refusing to face Caesar in battle he risked damaging the morale of his own forces. He would have to fight Caesar sooner or later.

The next day Caesar once again tried to bring about a battle. He left garrisons in both of his camps and deployed his forces for battle. Before the smaller camp he placed all of his auxiliaries as a show of force, because he claims he had an insufficient number of legionaries. In personal command of the troops in the larger camp he drew them up in the usual triple battle line and advanced up to the enemy's camp. Ariovistus decided to lead his men out of camp to engage Caesar. The challenge was too direct to ignore; if he had refused, the loss of face might have led to the disintegration of his army, which was drawn from a number of tribal levies.

The Germans were arrayed by tribe at equal intervals from each other. They were: Harudes, Marcomanni, Triboci, Vangiones, Nemetes, Sedusii and finally Ariovistus' own Suebi, who probably formed the largest contingent. The other tribes seem to have had their homes in the Rhineland. The German formation was then partially surrounded, according to Caesar, by their wagons and carts, where their women were placed to spur on their men to battle. This was typical Germanic custom, which also occurred during the wars against the Cimbri and Teutones.

Caesar put five legates and his quaestor in charge of each of the legions, posting himself on the right. He decided to begin the attack there as he saw that that was where the enemy was weakest. Both sides rushed together so quickly that there was no time or room for the Romans to throw their *pila*, which were no doubt discarded before contact with the enemy. In response to the Roman attack the Germans formed a phalanx to meet it. There was fierce fighting with several Romans tearing the enemy's shields away with their bare hands and wounding them from above, which implies that the Romans must have been on higher ground. The enemy's left was at first forced back and then put to flight as Caesar had foreseen. On the other side of the battle-line the struggle developed differently. The German right, by sheer weight of numbers, forced back the Roman left. Quick action by Publius the son of Crassus, who was later to perish with his father at Carrhae and who was in command of the cavalry, corrected the situation. He sent in the third line of infantry to support the first two on the left. The added support was enough to transform the situation. The Germans broke and fled to the Rhine five miles away. A few swam across while others found boats. Among them was Ariovistus, who managed to escape. The rest were pursued by the cavalry and cut down. Caesar expresses great satisfaction at the recovery of his envoys from captivity, stressing his personal friendship with them. The incident, while not particularly important in itself, points to a crucial element in Caesar's success in Gaul. This was based not only on victory in battle but also on his ability to create and manipulate the personal relationships that he developed with various Gallic chieftains and nobles, such as Diviciacus and, later, Commius, who Caesar made king of the Atrebates, a Belgic tribe who lived around Artois.

The exact location of the battle, which was probably fought in September, cannot be determined, though many possibilities have been suggested.[32] It was fought in Lower Alsace on the edge of the Vosges Mountains somewhere in the region of the modern city of Mulhouse, although a case can be made for a location near Belfort. The inability to pinpoint the exact location of many of the battles that Caesar fought in Gaul is partly due to the often vague descriptions of such locations by Caesar and other ancient authors, as well as the fact that given Caesar's audience and motives in writing *Gallic War*, such details would have complicated the narrative without advancing his purposes. One strange omission in the account of the battle is the absence of the German cavalry. Crassus, who commanded the Roman cavalry, had time to organize an infantry response to the German attack on the Roman left, which implies that his own men were not engaged. Since the German cavalry were very active in the earlier phases of the campaign this remains a mystery. As opposed to the precise figures offered for the Helvetii, Caesar makes no attempt to assess German casualties. The best that can be said is that the battle completely destroyed Ariovistus's power in Gaul. This is evident from the actions of a group of Suebi who had reached the eastern bank of the Rhine, intending to cross into Gaul and join Ariovistus. Hearing of his defeat they set out for home. They were attacked by locals on the way emboldened by Ariovistus's defeat.[33]

After these two victories Caesar led his army into winter quarters in the land of the Sequani a little later than was usual, perhaps in October. From there they could keep watch on the Aedui, the Helvetii and meet any German advance over the Rhine through the Belfort Gap. He placed his most effective legate Labienus in charge and then set off for Cisalpine Gaul for the winter months. This was his normal practice, except during the winters of 54/53, 52/51 and 51/50, when troubles in Transalpine Gaul made it impossible for him to leave. Caesar's ties to Cisalpina were close. After serving as quaestor in Further Spain in 68, on his return to Rome he stopped in the area of the province north of the Po, which had yet to receive the Roman citizenship given to the rest of Italy. There was much agitation over the issue and demands were made that citizenship be granted. Although the unrest came to nothing, Caesar openly supported these demands, which must have won him the friendship of many influential men in the area.[34] Much of a governor's time was consumed in judicial duties and Caesar was very scrupulous about such matters, as well as fulfilling his other duties there. That province was of particular importance for him. Its closeness to Italy and Rome was a key advantage for him. Its garrison was the nearest of all provincial garrisons to Rome. Its position also allowed him to keep abreast of the political situation in the capital through his numerous agents and informers. Further, it was the prime recruiting ground for the legions in this period, as Caesar himself had amply demonstrated. It could also serve as a base for campaigning in Illyricum if the opportunity arose.

Caesar's campaigns against the Helvetii and Ariovistus had established Rome as the dominant power in central Gaul. These had been campaigns of opportunity. It is probable that when he had received the provinces of Cisalpine Gaul and Illyricum he had looked to the east and the Dacians as the theatre where he could display his military talents.[35] Transalpine Gaul had been added as an afterthought, because of the death of the man who had been assigned to govern it. After his victories in this first year Caesar seems to have determined on the conquest of all or most of Gaul. His wintering of his legions outside the province and the events of the next year showed his determination to carry out that conquest.

Chapter Four

57: Caesar and the Conquest of the North

While Caesar was in Cisalpine Gaul he received reports that the Belgae were mobilizing against the Romans. A letter from his legate Labienus in Trans-alpina confirmed these reports. Caesar gives a number of reasons for this action by the Belgic tribes but the most persuasive is that they feared that the Romans would now move against them. Now that central Gaul had been subdued their frontiers were exposed. They must have seen the quartering of the legions among the Sequani, which the Romans could use as a staging area for an invasion of Belgic territory, as proof of their danger.

In response Caesar raised a further two legions, the Thirteenth and Four-teenth, both of which were not authorized by the Senate. The scale of Caesar's profits in Gaul to this point is revealed by the fact that he maintained them out of his own funds. Once the campaigning season opened he sent them off under the command of his legate Quintus Pedius. When fodder for his cavalry became available Caesar followed after, instructing the Senones who lived between the Loire and the Seine and bordered the Belgae, as well as other friendly tribes, to send out scouts. They reported that the Belgic tribes were mustering and forming a united army.

The area that the Belgae inhabited lay to the north of the Seine and Marne, extending into modern Belgium and stretching as far as the Rhine and the North Sea.[1] The Belgae did not see themselves as Gauls. They emphasized their differences and claimed that they were mostly of German origin. This seems to simplify what was a complex situation. The Belgae were probably of mixed Celtic and German heritage. There is no evidence that their language was anything but a dialect of Celtic. Their territory can be divided into three general regions. The Bellovaci, the most powerful of the Belgic tribes, a section of which migrated to Britain, inhabited the south-west. In the east there were the Nervii and a number of other smaller tribes who were intermingled with Germanic groups. Finally, a third group to the south-east was formed by the Treveri, famous for their cavalry, and other tribes with links both to the Germans and to the other Belgae. Whatever their ethnic origins the archaeological evidence also indicates differences from the communities of central Gaul. This emerges most clearly when we compare the *oppida* of the Belgae to those of central Gaul. They are smaller and less cohesive, with a greater prevalence of hill forts in place of towns. This implies a society with far less centralization. The area towards the Rhine is in general less developed then the other sections of Belgica. The Belgic tribes also seem to have had a less elaborate political structure than those of central Gaul, with kings and war leaders in place of the magistrates found among tribes such as the Aedui.

The Roman army reached the borders of the Belgae in fifteen days, perhaps stopping at Chalons-en-Champagne (formerly Chalons-sur-Marne) in the territory of the Belgic tribe of the Remi. The Remi were settled in the valleys of the Aisne, Vesle and Suippe with a particular concentration in the middle Aisne. Their territory was situated at a vital crossroads for routes leading in all directions. They had contacts with the Mediterranean world that the other Belgic tribes lacked and this may help explain their attitude towards Caesar. When he arrived the Remi sent envoys to him. They stated that they were willing to commit themselves and all they possessed into the faith and power of the Roman people. In effect they were offering unconditional surrender. They claimed that they did not agree with the other Belgae in opposing the Romans and would obey all of Caesar's orders as well as admit him and his men to their towns. Crucially, they also undertook to supply Caesar with grain and other necessities. The Remi remained faithful to the Romans offering a crucial logistics hub for Caesar's operations in the north-east. Even during the great rising of 52 when most of the Gallic tribes went over to open rebellion they kept to their Roman alliance and even endured a siege of their chief town Bibrax during the Belgic campaign.[2] In return they were accorded a privileged status from which they were to reap great economic benefits. Their behaviour in 57 illustrates one of the prime problems the Gauls had in dealing with Caesar; their inability to forge a coalition that would reconcile their divergent interests and goals. Further, within the tribes Gallic nobles aligned themselves on the basis of personal benefit. Among the Aedui it was clear from the beginning of Caesar's tenure in Gaul that his presence magnified political conflict within the tribe. This could be the case even within families. The brother of Caesar's closest Gallic friend and advisor Diviciacus Dumnorix pursued a persistently anti-Roman policy and was finally killed by Caesar in 54. Even a large-scale coalition formed in 52 to oppose Caesar had problems over leadership, which hampered its efforts. It remains questionable as to whether the Gauls, even if they had formed an effective union, could have expelled the Romans. Nevertheless Gallic disunity greatly helped Caesar.

The Remi informed Caesar that all of the other Belgae were fiercely determined to resist and had been joined by Germans from the Gallic side of the Rhine. They then provided Caesar with invaluable intelligence on the size of the opposing forces. The most powerful of the tribes, the Bellovaci, who could muster 100,000 men, had agreed to send 60,000 to the coalition army. Their neighbours the Suessiones around modern Soissons under their king Galba would provide 50,000 and the Nervii, with a reputation for being particularly fierce, pledged to supply the same number. Other smaller tribes, including the Atrebates, the Morini and the Atuatuci, had supplied lesser contingents totalling 96,000 warriors. The so-called German Belgic tribes would send 40,000. These figures total 296,000, which seems high. Once again we have only Caesar's numbers to go on. It is important to remember that these numbers represent promised troops, not those who actually served. The whole force was placed under the command of Galba.

After encouraging the Remi, Caesar summoned Diviciacus and instructed him to have the Aedui launch a diversionary raid on the Bellovaci to prevent them from joining the rest of the Belgic force. Caesar discovered that the Belgae had now united and were marching against him. Their exact route is unknown. They may have assembled at Noyon then marched via Laon towards the south-east. Learning that they were now close to his position Caesar speedily moved to meet them. He crossed the River Aisne (ancient Axona), which lay at the extremity of the territory of the Remi, and there pitched camp. A camp has been identified that may well be that of Caesar on the high ground between the Aisne and the Miette rivers. It has an area of 104 acres. Ditches and ramparts have also been found linking both sides of the camp to water barriers.[3] One side of the camp was protected by a riverbank and so secured Caesar's rear. This provided a safe route by which the Remi and other allies could ferry supplies to him. There was a bridge over the Aisne and to guard it he assigned one of his legates, Quintus Titurius Sabinus, with six cohorts, about 2,500 men in all, instructing him to build a camp with a 12-foot ramp and an 18-foot ditch.

Eight miles from Caesar's camp lay Bibrax, belonging to the Remi, which the Belgae now attacked straight from their line of march. Taking it would send a strong warning to the Remi to abandon their allegiance to Caesar, as well as providing abundant supplies. The townspeople held out with great difficulty. At this point Caesar gives a description of the siege methods, which he claims are practised both by the Belgae and the Gauls. They first surround a town and bombard the walls with stones to drive the defenders from them. Once that is done they form a 'tortoise' in Roman terminology, that is they interlock their shields on all sides forming a moving wall of shields at the front, top and sides of their formation, and then approach the walls to undermine them. The Roman tortoise, or *testudo*, was basically the same formation in sieges, although slightly different formations with the same name could be used on the battlefield. What is striking is the absence of the machinery that always accompanied sieges by Roman armies.[4]

Initially the stone-throwing achieved its aim and the wall was denuded of its defenders. Iccius, the commander of the town, sent an urgent message to Caesar asking for help. He claimed that without it the town would be lost. Caesar sent forward light-armed troops around midnight, including Numidian and Cretan archers, as well as slingers from the Balearic Islands. Their arrival heartened the garrison and discouraged the Belgae, who now broke off the siege. One of the great advantages that the Romans enjoyed was their organizational and technological superiority in such warfare.

After breaking off the siege the Belgae advanced on Caesar and encamped about a mile-and-a-half from his camp. Caesar claims that the Belgic camp had a perimeter of 7 miles and this may well be true. But no deductions on the numbers of Belgae are possible from the size of their camp since we have no idea of its layout. Caesar states that at first he avoided battle because of the size of the enemy force and their reputation for bravery in battle. After daily cavalry skirmishes he realized that his own men were in no way inferior to the Belgae and so decided on battle. It is not clear how cavalry skirmishes could serve as an indicator for what would be essentially a struggle between infantry. It is more likely that he realized that supply difficulties would either eventually break up the Belgic army or force them to give battle on unfavourable terms.

He decided to pursue the second alternative first. He left his two newly-raised legions in camp as a reserve, as he had done in the battle with the Helvetii, and deployed the rest of his army in front of the hill on which it was encamped. The area was slightly elevated in front above the plain and was large enough to hold his six legions. On its flanks it sloped steeply while to its front it offered a gentle rise, which would give impetus to Roman missiles and aid in case of a charge. The steepness of the flanks would help protect his own from the superior numbers of the Belgae. To further protect his flanks he had a ditch constructed 3,000 feet long at right-angles to each side of the hill. In addition, there was a marsh created by the Miette to the front separating the Romans from the Belgae.

Both sides were now drawn up and neither was anxious to cross the marsh, which would have seriously disordered their ranks. The infantry of both sides kept their position while a cavalry skirmish raged, which went in the Romans' favour, and they then returned to camp. It is difficult to believe that Caesar thought the enemy would cross the marsh to engage him, although there was always the chance that they might be foolish enough to do so. It is more likely that the deployment was an attempt to keep up his men's morale while he hoped that logistical difficulties would disperse the Belgic army, and the tribes could be dealt with one by one.

After Caesar returned to camp the Belgae moved quickly to attack Sabinus's outpost and destroy the bridge over the Aisne, or failing that to ravage the territory of the Remi. This would cut off Caesar from his supplies and would either force him to retreat or bring about a battle on more favourable terms. The Belgic commanders must have been aware of their own supply difficulties and were trying to bring about a battle in which their numerical superiority could be used effectively. The sophistication of this end-run around Caesar's flank indicates a high level of tactical awareness by the Belgic leaders.[5]

The Belgae found fords across the river and launched their attack. Sabinus reported the impending assault to Caesar and then marched out to meet the enemy with a force composed of cavalry and light-armed troops. He crossed the bridge to attack the enemy while they were fording the river and disorganized. The attack appears to have resulted in a slaughter rather than a battle. Many of the Belgae were killed while still in the river and others, frantically trying to cross back over the river, were greeted with showers of missiles, while the few who had already crossed were cut down by the Roman cavalry.

The tribes were in a quandary. Their attempt to either cut off Caesar's supplies or to force a battle had failed and they were now running out of food. A conference was called and the decision was taken for each tribe to return home and for all of them to bring aid to whatever tribe the Romans attacked. This would alleviate the immediate supply problem as each tribe could supply itself from its own resources and in the initial encounter with the Romans would have the advantage of fighting in their home territory. The Bellovaci, who could have significantly affected the outcome of the struggle, were under pressure at home as the Aedui were advancing against them. This decision might alleviate the immediate supply problem but tribal mobilization was a slow business and it gave the Romans the opportunity to defeat the tribes individually.

After the decision had been taken, at the second watch somewhere between 9 and 10pm, the Belgae broke camp. The decision to return home meant that the Belgae no longer had an overall commander and this probably resulted in their lack of discipline in maintaining their column of march as they retreated. Scouts had informed Caesar of their departure but he was unsure of its significance and so kept his men in camp.

At first light, after he had confirmed their departure, Caesar sent all of his cavalry in pursuit under the command of Quintus Pedius and Lucius Aurunculeius Cotta, along with three legions under Labienus to support them. They pursued the enemy column for many miles, attacking its rearguard. In the absence of any attempt to coordinate the movements of the column as a whole the rearguard put up a determined resistance but suffered heavy casualties. At nightfall the Romans finally returned to camp.

The next day Caesar marched out of camp hoping to strike the enemy before they had recovered from their disastrous retreat. He entered the territory of the Suessiones, neighbours of the Remi who had joined the other Belgic tribes that were opposing Caesar. He launched an attack on their main city Noviodunum (probably Pommiers west of Soissons).[6] The attack failed, even in the absence of a garrison, because of its strong fortifications. Caesar constructed a camp and then ordered his men to begin building siege machines.

The following night the Suessiones, who had been with the main Belgic force, entered the town. In response Caesar brought up his siege machines to the fortifications, which terrified the Suessiones who had never seen such equipment and they immediately sent envoys to offer surrender. At the urging of the Remi Caesar accepted their submission. The Suessiones handed over their weapons and gave hostages to Caesar.

The Romans now moved against the Bellovaci who retreated to their main town Bratuspantium – whose location is uncertain – with all of their goods. When Caesar and his army were about 5 miles from the town the leading elders came out to meet him and pleaded with him to accept their unconditional surrender. He then moved closer to the town and camped outside its walls. The townspeople now joined in the elders' pleas for peace. At this point his close friend and advisor, the Aeduan Diviciacus, urged Caesar to grant them their appeal. The general acceded to his request. There were pressing reasons to do so. The aristocrats who had led the opposition to him had fled to Britain. This is the first mention of that island in Caesar's narrative and may have given him a reason and a pretext to later invade it. Caesar also pursued a policy of strengthening and supporting the Aedui. In part this was a continuation of earlier Roman policy that was over half a century old when Caesar arrived in Gaul. There were also more immediate considerations. The Aedui were a large and powerful tribe who could provide supplies and serve as a useful military adjunct, as their invasion of the territory of the Bellovaci had shown. Their size and prominence also sent a clear signal to other Gallic tribes that support for the Romans could bring considerable advantages. The grant would further strengthen the Aedui, since they relied upon support from the Belgic tribes in their military campaigns.

The grant of peace was accompanied by the surrender of 600 hostages as well as all of the weapons in the town. The taking of hostages occurs frequently in *Gallic War*, not only by the Romans but by the Gauls and the Germans. Of the approximate 100 Gallic and German tribes mentioned by Caesar, thirty-seven provided him with hostages. Most were given, as in the case of the Bellovaci, as part of a formal surrender. Usually the hostages were family members or dependents of the tribe's leading men. Occasionally, they were drawn from among the nobles themselves. In 54 on the eve of his second invasion of Britain, Caesar took with him leading men from most of the Gallic states. Presumably he thought his absence from Gaul might give his opponents an opportunity to cause trouble.[7] To avoid encumbering his baggage train Caesar deposited them at the Aeduan town of Noviodunum on the banks of the Loire. The hostage policy proved singularly ineffective. It is a striking fact that Caesar never mentions reprisals being taken against hostages as the result of a tribal revolt. The reception of hostages on his part may have been owed more to traditional Roman practice in cases of unconditional surrender and a desire to conform to local practice in this matter rather than any expectation that it would be an effective deterrent.

Probably in late summer Caesar moved north-east towards the coast against the Ambiani, whose home lay in the Somme basin in modern Picardy where their main town was Samarobriva (modern Amiens). They immediately surrendered unconditionally.

On the eastern border of the Ambiani were the Nervii, who alone among the Belgic tribes put up substantial resistance against Caesar and almost defeated him in battle. They occupied parts of modern Belgium and north-eastern France, with their centre at Bavay near Valentines, ancient Bagacum or Bavacum. His campaign against them is the centre-piece of his account of the events of 57. To heighten the effect of his victory over them Caesar prefaces his account with an ethnic description, stressing their freedom from the debilitating effects of wine and commerce in luxury goods. This is a commonplace in Greek and Roman ethnographic description and should only be accepted with caution. Other sources ascribe their ferocity in battle to their German origins. Caesar applauds the courage and determination to resist him.[8]

After a three-day march Caesar learned that the River Sabis was about 9 miles from his camp. The identity of the Sabis is a problem. Caesar does not tell us whether he was marching through the territory of the Nervii or the Ambiani. If the former then the Sabis is the Sambre or the Selle; if through the lands of the Ambiani it is the Escaut (in German and Dutch the Scheldt). However, the absence of good strategic reasons for a defence of the Sambre makes the Selle, where a hard battle was fought in the last month of World War I, a more likely candidate.[9] He also learned that the Nervii, under their supreme commander Boduognatus, were camped across the river along with their neighbours and allies the Atrebates and the Viromandui. Further, he discovered that they were awaiting the Atuatuci, whose lands lay to the east of the Nervii and who were marching to their aid. The Nervii had concealed all of their non-combatants in a marshy area that was inaccessible to a large force. Since he was close to the enemy Caesar decided to set up camp and sent forward scouts and centurions to select a suitable location for it.

Caesar learned later from prisoners that some of the Gauls and Belgae accompanying the Romans were daily observing the army's order of march and had suggested to the Nervii that they launch an attack on the Romans while they were still in marching formation. The normal marching order was that each legion had its baggage to its rear so that the legions were separated from each other. In addition, the men normally carried heavy packs, which would encumber their movements. The Gauls and Belgae suggested to the Nervi that they attack the first legion once it had entered camp, before the others came up, and plunder its baggage. They said that once this happened the other legions would put up no resistance and flee. One further circumstance favoured such a plan. Given their lack of cavalry the Nervii had used trees to construct barriers against raids by the cavalry of their neighbours. These consisted of trees whose branches were interwoven to create hedges that obstructed scouting and channelled the enemy force into paths known to the Nervii. Although cavalry is mentioned when Caesar first encounters the Nervii he does not specify whose cavalry they were. They may well have belonged to allies of the Nervii. If so this does not contradict his general statement that they did not have a strong cavalry force.

The Romans had chosen a hill for the campsite, with an even gradient that sloped down to the Sabis. Opposite it on the other bank of the river a hill with a similar gradient rose from the other river bank. It was bare for about 1,000 feet and above that it was heavily wooded. The Nervii had concealed themselves in these woods.

Caesar sent his cavalry out first and then followed with the legions. Knowing the close proximity of the enemy he had changed his marching order, as Roman generals did when danger threatened. Six lightly-equipped legions (Seventh–Twelfth) now marched together, not separated by their baggage. This order would allow them to deploy without having to deal with their baggage. Behind them came the army's entire baggage train, guarded by the two newly-recruited legions, who also served as a rearguard. Caesar's order of march seems designed to counter an enemy with weak or non-existent cavalry. In situations where enemy cavalry was strong, Roman and auxiliary cavalry rode on the flanks and rear of the infantry column.

The Roman cavalry and light-armed troops crossed the river, which Caesar mentions was only 3 feet deep, to screen Roman movements and to keep the enemy busy while the Romans constructed their camp. They engaged the enemy cavalry who, under attack, retreated to their comrades in the woods and then returned once more to engage the Romans. While this was happening the six legions at the head of the column were busy constructing the camp.

The main force of the Nervii in the woods formed up, waiting for the baggage train to come into view before launching their attack, according to Caesar. Nevertheless, the reasons for an attack at this point are not easy to understand. The main point of the plan had been to engage the legions separately; this was no longer possible. Only the two newly recruited legions were separated from the rest and they had not yet come up. It may well be that the Nervii decided to attack while the Roman line was weakened by the detachment of units for construction and as the two legions guarding the baggage had yet to arrive.

When the baggage train came into view the Nervii launched their attack. They easily drove off the Roman cavalry on their side of the river and then with amazing speed rushed down to the river, crossed it and ran up the hill to where the Romans were constructing their camp. Caesar stresses that the suddenness and speed of the enemy's attack created severe difficulties for him. He had little time to issue the call to arms and to form up his men for battle. He notes that it was the quality of his troops that saved the situation. It was their training and experience in prior battles that prepared them to respond effectively without orders. He also praises the conduct of the unit officers, who had been instructed to remain with their men and who were equally capable of action without orders from above.

Caesar issued what orders he could and came up to encourage the legions. He reached the Tenth Legion on the left of the line and gave them what must have been a very short speech of encouragement. Caesar then gave the signal for battle and moved to his right to continue to hearten other troops. The advance of the enemy had been so sudden that the troops had no time to deploy in a regular line. They formed up as chance dictated.

The fighting was equally haphazard. Clashes erupted at different locations with the men facing in all directions. The thick hedges of the Nervii hindered any overall view of the battle and made it extremely difficult to issue general orders and to render effective aid where it was needed. Given the fragmented nature of the combat the fortunes of the legions varied greatly. The Ninth and Tenth Legions on the left threw their *pila* and then charged the Atrebates who were facing them. The Atrebates were worn out from their dash across the river and weakened by wounds, probably from the volley of *pila*. The Romans, attacking from higher up the hill, drove them back into the river. The Atrebates had difficulty crossing it and the Romans caught up with them and a slaughter ensued. The two legions now crossed the river and attacked those who had reformed on the other bank; despite the disadvantage of attacking uphill they routed them. In the centre the Eleventh and Eighth faced the Viromandui and defeated them. They then advanced downhill to fight on the river bank. The Twelfth on the right, along with Seventh, were still in a position to cover the Roman camp, but the advance of the other legions had exposed the front and left side of the camp. Boduognatus saw the gap in the enemy's line and took the opportunity to exploit it. He formed his Nervii in a compact column and marched on the exposed sections of the camp. Part of the column made to encircle the legions on their exposed left flank while the rest advanced on the camp. The Nervii first encountered the Roman cavalry and light-armed troops who had fled the initial Belgic advance and had sought shelter in the camp. Once again these were forced to flee. The camp servants and the men stationed with the baggage also took flight. The situation considerably worsened when the Treveri, from the Eifel and the Ardennes, who provided the Romans with their best cavalry, thinking the battle lost rode off home.

On the right Caesar noticed that the men of the Twelfth had become so closely packed together that they could no longer use their weapons effectively. In addition, a number of their centurions had been killed. Among the surviving centurions was a certain Publius Sextius Baculus, who had received a number of wounds and could only stand upright with difficulty. He realized that the situation was deteriorating rapidly, that the legion was losing cohesion and that it was on the verge of defeat. Already some in the rear ranks were leaving the battle-line to avoid the enemy missiles. The enemy pressure on the Roman line was unremitting. He had come up without his shield and so he snatched up one from a soldier in the rear ranks and made his way to the front. There he ordered the men to advance and open ranks so that they could use their weapons effectively. These actions restored the men's morale and they checked the Nervii's progress to some degree. This is not the only reference that Caesar makes to Baculus. In the next year Baculus is found campaigning with Servius Galba against Alpine tribes and advised his commander to make a sortie that resulted in heavy enemy casualties and allowed the Romans to escape from an untenable position. In 53 he rose from his sickbed and helped defend Atuatuca, an action that almost cost him his life. In Caesar's account Baculus serves as a model of Roman courage and virtue. He is only the most conspicuous example of centurions who played such a role in *Gallic War*. The attention given to him and to other centurions helps to explain the unbending loyalty that Caesar commanded among his troops.

While this was happening Caesar saw that the Seventh Legion, which was close by the Twelfth, was being hard pressed. He ordered the military tribunes of the two legions to gradually close up their legions and for the rear ranks to wheel about so that they could fight off enemy attacks on their rear. The change in formation had the desired effect and the legions now began to fight with renewed vigour.

The new legions assigned to guard the baggage heard news of the battle and hurried to aid their comrades. As they crested the hill on which the camp was situated the Nervii saw them. At the same time Labienus, who was serving as the commander of the Tenth Legion, which had taken over the enemy's camp, saw the perilous situation and moved to assist.[10] The appearance of these units transformed the situation. The enemy was now exposed on his flanks and rear. Although the Nervii resisted courageously, with their men continuing to fight standing on the bodies of their comrades, they were in a hopeless situation and the battle ended in a complete Roman victory.

After the battle the women, children and old men who had taken refuge in the marshes, realizing the hopelessness of their situation, sent a deputation to Caesar. He allowed them to return home and gave them back their lands and towns. Despite this, it is not clear how they could manage to survive the coming winter given the losses the tribe had suffered. Caesar also ordered neighbouring peoples to refrain from injuring them now that they were utterly helpless. The treatment of the Nervii is characteristic of Caesar's displays of clemency. He was later to pardon many of his enemies during the civil war. On many occasions Caesar was prepared to do exactly the opposite. In 55 his harsh and deceptive treatment of two German tribes allowed his political enemies to attack him. In the Senate Cato advocated handing him over to the Germans he had attacked to atone for his show of bad faith. The pattern is clear in *Gallic War*. He granted clemency when circumstances permitted and it could bring him political benefits. In the case of the Nervii, since they were no longer a military threat, clemency might help reconcile them and the other Belgic tribes to the Roman conquest. The lack of it with respect to the German tribes served as a warning to deter further German ventures into Gaul. His conduct at Uxellodunum in 51 made clear the costs of continued rebellion against him. It was in the end a clemency tempered by political expediency.[11]

Caesar claims that the battle almost annihilated the Nervii; out of 60,000 men of military age only 500 survived. This is clearly an exaggeration, as Caesar himself later makes clear. Within three years they were capable of mounting an attack on a legionary camp along with their client tribes. During 52 we find them supplying 5,000 troops to the Gallic rebels. If they were hardly as devastated as Caesar claims, nonetheless the later references to them seem to indicate that if they were not annihilated they were at least substantially weakened.

The battle was a near-run thing. Much of the blame for it attaches to Caesar. Despite the scouting difficulties that Caesar stresses, he knew where the Nervii were and it is hard to believe that over 400,000 men could remain undiscovered even if they were hidden in the woods across the river. His change in march formation is evidence that he was conscious of the threat they posed. Granted that it would have slowed the construction of the camp if he had drawn up a battle line and detailed perhaps a third of his units to fortification work, not doing so in the face of the enemy was an extreme example of the readiness to take chances that he displayed on many occasions. Earlier Roman generals faced with the same situation had shown far more caution. Over a century before in 168 the proconsul Lucius Aemilius Paullus, faced with the prospect of building a camp at Pydna in Thessaly in the presence of the enemy, deployed his legions to screen and protect the soldiers detailed for construction duties.[12] Again, the difficulty of the terrain may have made it harder to control his battle line, but the advance of the Tenth over the river, even if the fault lay primarily with its commander Labienus, exposed Caesar's left to an outflanking manoeuvre by a vastly superior enemy. Caesar had vastly underestimated his opponent. In the end the victory was due more to luck and the fighting qualities of the Roman soldier than to Caesar's generalship.

One tribe, the Atuatuci, who were part of the Germans living on the Gallic bank of the Rhine and on the banks of the Maas near Liége, had arrived too late for the battle and on hearing the news of Caesar's victory returned home. Caesar mentions that they were descendants of the Cimbri and Teutones, which must have made a favourable impression on his Roman audience.[13] Whether it is true is a different question with no definitive answer. Expecting Caesar to attack them, they abandoned their towns and strong points and concentrated in one town with superb natural defences whose location is unknown. The town was surrounded by sheer and steep cliffs except at one point where there was a gently sloping approach to it, but this was only 200 feet wide. This weak spot was reinforced by a high double wall and fronted by rocks and stakes. The withdrawal into the town was a sensible decision on the part of the Atuatuci, who were familiar only with Gallic siege techniques. Their position seemed impregnable and a prolonged siege in an attempt to starve them out appeared to be the only option.

As soon as the Romans arrived the Atuatuci made frequent sorties and fought repeated skirmishes. The Romans responded by constructing a siege wall of about 4.5 miles in length, which surrounded the town, and furnished it with a number of towers. When the townspeople saw penthouses moving up, an earthwork being built and a tower being constructed in the distance, they ridiculed these preparations at the same time as they jeered at the Romans' small stature.

As the towers approached their walls, although Caesar does not tell us how this was done given the natural strength of the position, the Atuatuci sent a delegation to ask for peace. They agreed to surrender but asked to keep their weapons so that they could protect themselves against their neighbours. Caesar, stressing his clemency, agreed to accept their surrender if they made it before the battering ram touched their walls. But he insisted that they surrender their weapons. The delegation returned with Caesar's answer and the Atuatuci agreed to his conditions. They threw a huge number of weapons over their walls. Caesar states that so many were given up that the piles equalled the height of their walls. They then opened their gates to admit the Romans.

Under Caesar's orders the soldiers withdrew from the town at nightfall. The Atuatuci, who had according to Caesar's calculation kept back about a third of their weapons and were supplementing them with hastily constructed shields, made a sudden attack soon after midnight on the Roman fortifications in hopes that with the coming of peace the Romans had relaxed their guard. The surprise failed and the Atuatuci found themselves fighting on difficult ground with the Romans bombarding them with missiles from the towers and the siege wall. Courage was not enough and 4,000 were killed while the rest were forced back into the town. The next day the gates were broken down and the Romans entered. As an object lesson the whole population of 53,000 was sold into slavery. This is the only precise figure in Caesar that we have for such a sale, but the sale of slaves was a major source of profit during the Gallic campaigns.

With the defeat of the Atuatuci the campaign in Belgica came to a close. Caesar had dispatched one of his legates, Publius Licinius Crassus, the son of his fellow triumvir, with a single legion – probably the Sixth or Seventh – on a campaign against the tribes who lived along the north-western coast of Brittany and the Normandy coast. Caesar names them as the Veneti, the Venelli, the Coriosolitae, the Osismi, the Esubii, the Aulerci and the Redones. Of these the Veneti were the most important and influential. They had a large and fertile territory rich in resources. In addition, they were engaged in various crafts, especially the making of ceramics, but trade with Britain across the channel as well as with neighbouring peoples was their most important economic activity. The territory of the Veneti lay near an important trade route that ran from the Roman province via the Loire or the Aude and the Garonne. The Veneti possessed the largest fleet in Gaul, which the Romans would encounter in the following year.[14]

It is remarkable that Crassus was sent with only a single legion and accompanying auxiliaries to subdue this region. It seems likely that some sort of prior agreement had been reached with these tribes after Caesar's initial victories so that no opposition was expected. In effect, Crassus was showing the flag rather than expecting to fight a serious campaign. This also raises the question of what exactly the tribes expected their submission to consist of. The only model that they had was that of Gallic tribes that had become clients of other tribes, as the Bellovaci were of the Aedui, and expected that few demands would be made of them. In this they were soon to be disappointed.

Caesar claims that with the submission of these tribes all Gaul had now been pacified.[15] By this he must mean the properly-Celtic area of central Gaul and Belgica, as the Aquitani in the south-west had not yet submitted to the Romans. He notes that the fame of his achievements was such that German tribes from the other side of the Rhine sent embassies to him offering to obey him and surrender hostages as a guarantee of their good faith. He put them off asking them to return during the following summer as he was in a hurry to proceed to his other provinces of Cisalpine Gaul and Illyricum. He then ordered the legions into winter quarters. Crassus encamped with his single legion in the territory of the Andes near Angers south-west of Paris, two legions were stationed to the east in the lands of the Carnutes and Turones between the Seine and the Loire, and four remained in Belgic territory while the Twelfth, along with auxiliary cavalry, was sent under Galba to open the Alpine passes.

Galba's expedition in the spring of 57 proved unsuccessful. He was sent to the territories of the Nantuates, Veragri and Seduni, who bordered the Allobroges, to occupy the Great St Bernard Pass in the western Alps that ran from Italy into Gaul. After a series of successful battles and the taking of a number of enemy strong points the tribes gave hostages and concluded peace. Galba had been given permission by Caesar to go into winter quarters in the area. He detached two cohorts to camp among the Nantuates while he and the other eight cohorts established their quarters among the Veragri near the village of Octodurus (modern Martigny in Switzerland), which lay south-east of Lake Geneva. It was not an ideal location as the area had little level ground and was surrounded by high hills. The valley was divided in two by a river, with the Romans occupying one part and the Gauls assigned to the other. Despite the Gauls having concluded peace, a number remained unreconciled to the Roman presence. Caesar specifies a number of reasons for this, including the small size of Galba's forces, the fear of a permanent Roman presence and, in addition, although Caesar does not mention it, the Gauls must have been upset by the loss of half of their valley. For all of these reasons the peace proved unworkable and when the opportunity presented itself the Gauls decided to renew the conflict.

News of the impending attack reached Galba and he held a council, as Roman commanders normally did, to determine on a course of action. Despite the fact that the camp defences had not yet been completed and nor had sufficient food been stockpiled, the decision was taken to defend the camp and retreat only as a last resort. There was little time left for preparations before the Gauls attacked. They charged down from the heights throwing missiles at the camp. At first the Romans resisted fiercely, but given the disparity in numbers and the fact that the battle lasted for six hours, the difficulties of dealing with the wounded and the onset of exhaustion began to weaken their efforts. The situation became desperate enough that Galba took the advice of the senior centurion Baculus, as well as of a military tribune Gaius Volusenus, to make a sudden sortie to counter the enemy's attack.

The sortie was launched from all of the camp gates, which allowed the Romans to surround the enemy. Caesar claims that 30,000 attacked the camp and that of these a third were killed during the sortie. Whether accurate or not, the enemy losses were sufficient to force them to break off their assault. The Romans then returned to camp. By attacking the camp in a confined space the

Gauls had sacrificed their mobility, and in massed fighting on level areas they could not match the Romans. Although the Romans had the best of the fight, they were still short of supplies and Galba decided to retreat. He and his men returned to Gaul to winter among the Allobroges. Galba had been given an almost impossible task. The country was difficult and Caesar had under-estimated the size of the force needed to hold it.

Despite this minor reverse Caesar, confident that Gaul was now subdued, set out to inspect Illyricum in the autumn of 57 and remained there for part of the winter. His report to the Senate made clear the magnitude of his victories and accomplishments. In response the Senate decreed a thanksgiving of an un-precedented fifteen days. It could not have made his fellow triumvir Pompey happy that Caesar had been granted five more days than he had received for his victories in the east.

Chapter Five

56: Consolidation

Despite attempts to recall Caesar as early as 58, and even to hand him over to the Germans, his victories in Gaul had at least temporarily silenced direct opposition to him. But his political position in the capital soon sharply deteriorated. The coalition of Caesar, Crassus and Pompey had dominated Roman politics immediately after its formation. It had been powerful enough to make sure that the two consuls who succeeded Caesar in 58 would be its own men. That power grew in part from the violence and intimidation that had become an increasing part of Roman political life in this period. Cicero, in a letter to his friend Atticus written in July 59 when Caesar was still consul, reveals the increasing unpopularity of the three men. He describes an incident during a theatrical performance when a leading actor, Diphilus, openly attacked Pompey, who was not present, by declaiming the line; 'To our misfortune are you great'. It was a play on the honorific name of Magnus or 'Great' that had been accorded to Pompey for his victories. The audience enthusiastically applauded. The audience also showed its displeasure by withholding the customary applause when Caesar entered the theatre.[1]

This unpopularity made it all the more necessary to try to regain the people's support. To that end the three began courting Cicero, whose oratorical talents might help improve their position. But their quarry proved elusive. He viewed their actions as illegal and he made it known publically. In a speech for the defence of his co-consul in 63, Gaius Antonius, he made a series of remarks that deeply wounded Caesar. In response Caesar and Pompey took steps to allow Cicero's implacable enemy Publius Clodius to stand for the tribunate of 58. It was an attempt to frighten Cicero but it had unintended consequences. They attempted to dissuade Clodius from actually standing for the tribunate but failed. The efforts to block his candidacy alienated Clodius who announced that he would bring in a bill to rescind the legislation that Caesar had passed during his consulship. Despite the triumvirs' opposition he was elected. He then passed legislation, which greatly increased his popularity and turned to attack Cicero directly. The attack was successful and Cicero left Rome in March of 58 to spend his exile in Macedonia.[2]

Clodius, having gained sufficient popularity to act independently of the triumvirs, now began an assault on Pompey and Caesar. The assault was not merely verbally but also physically violent. The attack finally led Pompey to use his influence to bring about the return of Cicero from exile. The orator entered Rome on 4 September 57. Pompey's stunning success in bringing about Cicero's return clearly demonstrated his political pre-eminence. The award of a command in the same year to regulate Rome's grain supply was further proof of his standing. Crassus, the third member of the coalition, seems to have been inactive, although this might be due to the silence of the sources.

Pompey provided Caesar with perhaps his most difficult political problem. Unlike Caesar, he was in many ways a traditionalist.[3] The former's break with the conservative senatorial faction that had coalesced around Cato had resulted from their obstinate refusal of his demands on his return from the eastern wars. He wanted the respectability that they could provide and his political position was not fundamentally different than theirs. His goal had always been the maintenance of his position as the leading man in the state. The question for Caesar was how to maintain the coalition of the three and prevent Pompey from joining his opponents. His command in Gaul was set to expire in 55 and he needed to extend it. As long as he was proconsul he would be immune to whatever judicial attacks his enemies might mount against him. He had to have his command renewed until he could enter the safe harbour of a consulship after the statutory ten-year interval had elapsed.

As the year 56 opened, developments in the east threatened to further widen the breach among the triumvirs. In late 57 there was possibility of a new overseas command for Pompey. The king of Egypt had been driven from his throne by his own subjects and had asked for Roman assistance for his restoration. The king owed Pompey great sums of money so that a military command to restore him would be both prestigious and lucrative at the same time. It was just this prospect that caused great opposition to it in the Senate. Crassus favoured a different approach: a three man commission on which he would presumably serve, which would enhance his reputation and provide a chance for further wealth. The other senators liked neither alternative and voted to do nothing. The result of the struggle between Pompey and Crassus was to further widen the rift between them. Pompey now accused Crassus of plotting against his life. His own problems were intensified by his lack of success in remedying the city's grain supply difficulties. Caesar was once again attacked with the threat to repeal the legislation he had passed while consul. The triumvirate appeared to be breaking apart. With the end of his command in the following year the threat of political disaster loomed. Already one of the candidates for the consulship of 55, the aristocratic Lucius Domitius Ahenobarbus who was Cato's brother-in-law, announced that if elected he would have Caesar dismissed from a command that he considered illegal. Caesar experienced a further setback when two of his candidates were defeated in elections for minor senatorial offices. Clearly something had to be done before the triumvirate completely disintegrated.

In April Caesar met with both Pompey and Crassus.[4] It is unclear whether he met them separately, Pompey at Luca (modern Lucca) in Liguria but close to the border of Caesar's Cisalpine province, and Crassus at Ravenna in the Po delta within the province, or both together at Luca. The exact details of what was discussed and agreed upon are controversial but the results are not. It appears that Caesar offered that if the elections for the consulship were delayed until after the campaigning season was over he would release some of his soldiers so that they could get to Rome in time to vote and help secure the consulships of 55 for Pompey and Crassus. Despite this, when the elections finally took place in early 55, Pompey and Crassus had to resort to violence to secure office. Caesar agreed that they could use tribunician legislation, which he would not oppose, to obtain commands to follow their year in office. In return Caesar was to have his command in Gaul extended, as well as other benefits. Both Cicero and Clodius were to be checked and the former, despite his private feelings, began to speak on Caesar's behalf in the Senate. These meetings were crucial to the restoration of the compact between the three men. The year 55 saw them once again firmly in control at Rome. Domitius Ahenobarbus had to delay his election to the consulship, which he finally held in 54.[5]

Caesar reaped some immediate advantages in the form of senatorial decrees. The four legions (Eleventh to Fourteenth) that he had raised above the number he had been allocated when he entered his province were now to be funded by the state. In addition he was voted the right to appoint ten additional legates. The increase in numbers allowed Caesar to spread his patronage over a wider circle. The names of these subordinate commanders figure often in *Gallic War*. But, as opposed to the known legates of other commanders such as Pompey, these men were of relatively humble origin. This must be a reflection of the enmity that many aristocratic senatorial families felt for the governor of Gaul. The names of many of these men are known from *Gallic War* and from references in other sources. Only one, Titus Labienus, Caesar's most senior and effective legate, is known to have served with Caesar during his entire tenure there. Several had held political office before their service with Caesar, including Quintus Caesar, the orator's brother, who served from 54 to 52. The remaining men were young and had still not made their mark in politics when they arrived in Gaul. Eighteen of them went on to hold high political office, including six who held the consulship, but in almost every case as the result of Caesar's patronage. In the field some were given independent commands, such as Galba in his attempt to open the Alpine passes, or the

(*left*). Caesar: the Tusculum Bust. The 'Tusculum portrait' in the museum at Turin may be the only surviving likeness of Caesar made during his lifetime. It bears a strong resemblance to a bust recovered from the River Rhône near Arles in the autumn of 2007.

(*right*). The Vercingetorix Monument at Alise-Sainte Reine, the most likely site of the Gallic town of Alesia, the main city of the Mandubii. There is another monument dedicated to Vercingetorix nearby in the central square of Clermont-Ferrand.

. An aerial view of Bibracte on the hilltop of Mt. Beuvray the capital of the Aedui

4. A view of Alesia from the west from the Plain of Laumes. To the right is Mt Flavigny where Caesar's camp lay and to the left is Mt Penneville.

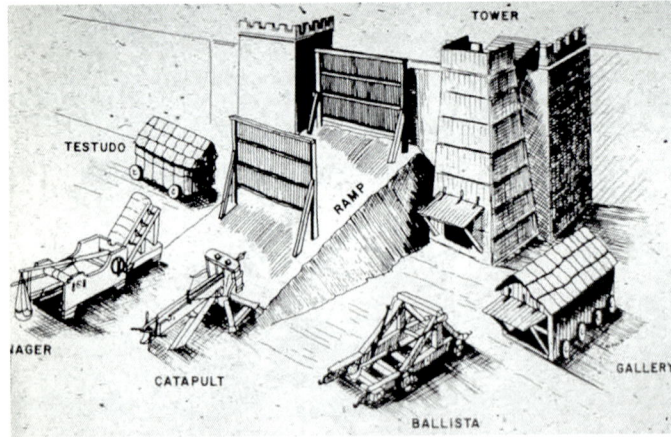

TOWER

TESTUDO

RAMP

IAGER

CATAPULT

GALLERY

BALLISTA

5. Drawings of Roman siege equipment. Many of them are based on Greek models.

6. The so-called Altar of Domitius Ahenobarbus which may have been dedicated by the consul of 122 BCE, who defeated the Arverni and the Allobroges. It depicts the five-yearly census. Note the equipment of the legionaries, including the oval shield which was later replaced by a rectangular one

. On several occasions Caesar had to fight in the front-line to encourage his men. During the battle of the Sambre river at a critical moment when the Roman lines were wavering he says he grabbed a fallen shield and rushed up to the front. Caesar also mentions the Gallic attack was so fast some of his men did not have time to put on crests or take the covers of their shields. Both of these points re included in the reconstruction as is the mixture of units seen by the various shield devices. Later t the battle of Munda Caesar once again had to fight at the front but there he adds he also fought bare headed so his men would recognise him. At Alesia he also says he stood out because of his distinctive cloak. Both these features have been added to this scene. (© *Graham Sumner*)

8. After believing they were guaranteed safe passage the besieged army of Sabinus and Cotta was wiped out in an ambush in a wooded ravine two miles from their camp. Amongst the casualties was Quintus Lucanius a Primus Pilus Centurion, who died trying to save his son who had been surrounded. He wears military decorations befitting his rank and sports an old fashioned Hellenistic style helmet. Many Roman troops chose to take their looted possessions with them in the baggage train rather than their winter equipment. (© *Graham Sumner*)

While his engineers begin the construction of the fortifications around the hillside, Caesars's
-erman auxiliary cavalry keep the Gallic cavalry scouts away. In the background Alesia looms.

10. The Gauls have only just reached the outer edge of the siege-works surrounding Alesia but are already being picked off by Caesar's missile troops mounted in the towers. Just beyond the arrow shafts visible in the ground can be seen the first of those defences, metal spikes protruding from the ground. Beyond them were eight rows of covered pits each with a sharpened stake, a booby-trap Caesar's troops ironically nicknamed 'lillies'! Then there were five rows of small ditches each filled with sharp tree branches creating a formidable hedge and two deeper ditches in front of an earth rampart topped with a palisade. (© *Graham Sumner*)

11. A reconstruction of the bridge built by Caesar in 55 for his first crossing of the Rhine.

12. A typical Ardennes landscape in the area where Caesar campaigned against the Eburones and other Belgic tribes. Somewhere in this region lay the camp of Cotta and Sabinus, which was destroyed in 54.

13. A view of the Jura Mountains. It was between these mountains and the Rhône that the Helvetii were forced by Caesar to move, instead of the easier route through the Roman province.

14. *Vercingetorix surrenders to Caesar*, a painting by
Lionel Noel Royer, 1899.

15. A gold stater, a coin first minted by the Macedonians and
adopted by the Gauls, weighing approximately one-half ounce
or fourteen grams. On its obverse is a stylized head of
Vercingetorix and a legend with his name. It is from Pisonat,
Puy-de-Dôme, France.

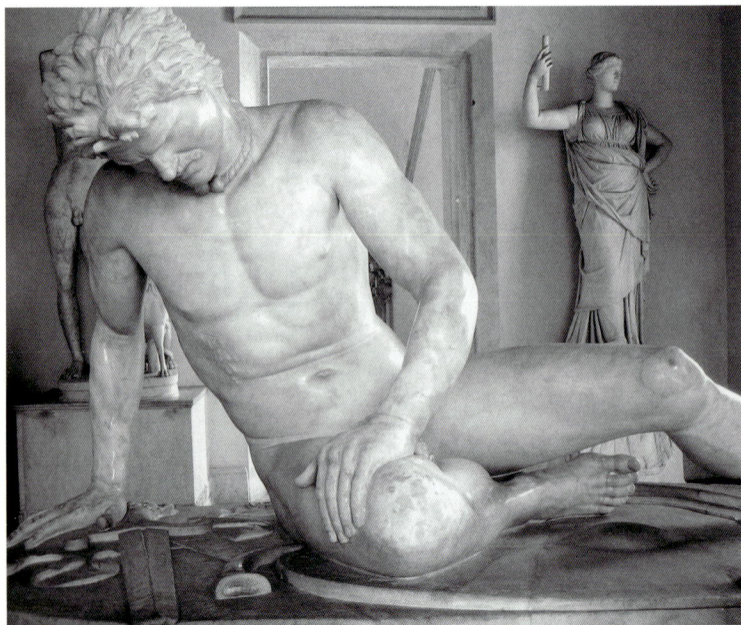

16. The Dying Gaul of
Pergamum. A Roman copy
of a Hellenistic sculpture of
the late-third century BCE.
It was commissioned to
celebrate the same victory
over the Gauls as the
Ammendola Sarcophagus.

promising young Crassus, active in Brittany and Normandy in 57 as well as the following year in the south-east. Occasionally, legates were given command of battle groups of several legions; the most conspicuous of them was Labienus, who was given command of four legions to operate against the Parisii and the Senones in the area between the Loire and the Seine in 52. In the major battles when Caesar was present they appear to have had little independent initiative. It is not clear whether this was in fact the case or whether Caesar has distorted his narrative for his own purposes.[6] The most important result for Caesar of his meetings with Pompey and Crassus came later in 55 when both men as consuls passed a bill that prohibited the discussion of a successor to Caesar before 1 March 50.

Events in north-western Gaul in the spring of 56, perhaps at the same time as Caesar was meeting with his fellow triumvirs, soon made his claim at the end of the campaigning season of 57 that all Gaul had been pacified ring hollow. Crassus, who had been wintering with his legions among the Andes near Anjou, needed to supplement his grain supply. He sent a group of officers to the maritime towns along the Atlantic coast to requisition additional grain. The presence of these men presented the Veneti with what they thought was an opportunity to retrieve the hostages they had given to the Romans. They retained two of them and persuaded the neighbouring tribes, the Osismi and the Coriosolitae, to do the same. Caesar stresses the influence of the Veneti on their neighbours because of the size of their navy and their control of the few accessible harbours along the coast. All of the coastal tribes in the area then formed a compact, sealed by oaths, to resist the Romans. An embassy was sent to Crassus to demand a return of the hostages if he wanted his own officers given back. Crassus sent a report of these events to Caesar, who was probably still in Cisalpine Gaul. He decided that the rebellion had to be suppressed and if he was still at Luca he could not have returned before the middle of May. On receipt of the news he issued orders to begin building warships on the Loire and for the recruitment of sailors from the Roman province.

In response the Veneti assembled as many ships as possible and sought additional allies. The result was a wide-ranging confederation that included the Osismi, Lexovii, Namnetes, Ambiliati, Diablintes and the Belgic Menapii and Morini. The number of tribes involved as well the extent of their territories, which stretched from Brittany to Flanders, indicates the seriousness of the rising as well as the general dissatisfaction with the Romans.

Caesar's account of the causes of the rebellion has been challenged. Some scholars have argued that the rebellion had an economic cause.[7] In 57 Caesar was already planning an invasion of Britain which, if successful, would have harmed the maritime trade of the Veneti and this was the spark that ignited their resistance. This is far from convincing. There is little evidence of Roman wars undertaken for economic motives beyond the immediate prospect of the booty that victory would bring. Nor is there conclusive evidence that Caesar contemplated an invasion of Britain this early. Although the geographer Strabo, writing towards the end of the first century BC, claims that the Veneti knew of Caesar's plans for an invasion of Britain and were afraid it would affect their trade, it is hard to believe that they could have been aware of his intentions.[8] Strabo's account once again raises the question of what these tribes thought their submission to Crassus implied. Perhaps, given the concentration of Roman forces in eastern Gaul far from their territory, they thought of it as nothing more than a way of avoiding conflict with the Romans and would in the end have no practical consequences. This seems especially true given the difficulty that Caesar experienced in trying to subdue the Veneti.

For any army whose main strength was in heavy infantry the campaign against the Veneti presented particular problems. Their territory in the modern departments of Morbihan and Finistère in Brittany was centred on the Gulf of Morbihan. The land routes were difficult because they were intersected by water courses. Their towns, which they now set about fortifying and supplying with grain stores, were mainly situated on headlands that were inaccessible by land at high tide and equally unapproachable by sea at low tide. Their formidable navy complicated matters even further. If they were too hard pressed they could bring their goods aboard ship and embark their people and sail away to another town.

Caesar provides our only description of these ships, which differed greatly in construction from those in use in the Mediterranean with which the Romans were familiar.

> Their ships were constructed and armed in the following fashion. Their bottoms are somewhat flatter than ours to deal more easily with shallows and ebb–tides. Their high prows and sterns were designed to deal with high waves and severe storms. They were entirely constructed of oak capable of enduring any force or buffeting. The cross timbers consisting of beams a foot wide were joined by nails as thick as a man's thumb. The anchors were attached by metal chains instead of rope. They used skins and leather stretched thin as sails either because they had no linen and so did not know how to use it or what is more likely because they thought that linen sails would be unequal to the force of such strong winds and severe storms.[9]

The Roman ships that faced them were of very different construction. The standard warship was the quinquereme or 'fiver', which became common in Mediterranean fleets during the third century. It could be constructed from a number of different woods including cypress, fir and oak. While at sea it relied on its sails for propulsion, in battle the sail was taken down and the ship depended on its oars for manoeuvre. The use of oars meant that it had to sit far lower in the water than the Gallic ships. The exact configuration of the rowers who gave the ship its name is uncertain and controversial. Naval tactics were of two types: they relied either on a bronze ram on the ship's prow below the water line to hole the opposing ship or the use of missiles followed by boarding the enemy vessel. Although at crucial periods such as the First Punic War (264–241) the Romans mounted massive and successful efforts at sea, they were primarily a land power. In the absence of any naval threat they allowed their fleets to atrophy. When need arose, as in Caesar's case, fleets were constructed but it is revealing of a lack of a naval tradition that rowers remained non-citizens even in the period when Rome manned standing fleets.[10]

The difference in ship construction created serious problems for the Romans. The traditional tactics of boarding and ramming were impractical. The oak construction of the Veneti's ships rendered the ram ineffective, while their height made the use of missiles futile. Equally, the flat bottoms of their boats allow them to seek sanctuary in water too shallow for Roman vessels.

Although Caesar had taken a number of towns it became clear that this could not bring an end to the war as long as their fleet remained in being. For the first and only time in the course of the Gallic War a naval victory was essential. He halted operations until his fleet arrived, possibly at Port-Navalo on the Gulf of Morbihan, under the command of Decimus Brutus, who was later to figure among Caesar's assassins. On sighting the Roman fleet, the Veneti and their allies put out into Quiberon Bay with 220 ships fully fitted out for battle. The Romans were at first at a loss as to what tactics to adopt. One innovation they made that was to be especially effective was to attach sharp hooks to long poles. These were hooked over the ropes that bound the enemy's yardarms to their masts. The Romans then rowed away, severing the ropes, and brought down the sails. In the absence of oars the Veneti's ships were helpless.

Despite Caesar's stress on the bravery of his men in this battle the hooks were decisive in disabling the enemy's ships and allowing the Romans to board them, although how they did so is not clear. The immobile ships were surrounded by two or three Roman ones and attacked from all directions. The loss of a number of ships convinced the Veneti and their allies that the battle was lost. As they turned in flight the wind suddenly dropped, allowing the Romans to capture most of the enemy ships before their crews could reach land. After ten hours, from about 8.30am to about 7.00pm, the Romans achieved a decisive victory. The historian Dio Cassius has a slightly different version in which the Romans did not leave port until the wind had dropped, but a source close in time to Caesar supports his version and this should be preferred.[11]

With the loss of their fleet the Veneti had no option but to surrender unconditionally. To make an example of them Caesar executed their senators and sold the rest of the population into slavery. Despite Caesar's claim, at least some of the Veneti remained free: during the great rebellion of 52 some of them were called up for service in the rebel army.[12] On more than one occasion Caesar used terror as a weapon to compel obedience, as other Roman commanders had done. He employed it again in 52 in mopping up operations after his great victory at Alesia. In 53, following the loss of a legion-and-a-half in an ambush by the Eburones, he decided to exterminate them. He first laid waste their territory, captured their town, and then invited the surrounding tribes to plunder and seize their land. In this case, added to the wish to make an example of them was the desire for revenge. After a long and difficult siege of Uxellodunum, the main town of the Cadurci in south-west Gaul, he had the hands of all those who had fought against him cut off. When he felt terror was a necessary instrument of policy Caesar showed no hesitation in employing it.

To isolate the Veneti from their northern allies Caesar sent his legate, Quintus Titurius Sabinus, with three legions and auxiliaries against the Venelli, Coriosolitae and the Lexovii whose territory lay on the northern coast of the Cherbourg Peninsula and the Cotentin.

The campaign opened with the Venelli in the Cotentin. There an allied army had assembled under the leadership of one of their chiefs Viridovix. He had been joined by the Aulerci, Eburovices and the Lexovii after they had executed their senators who had opposed the rebellion. Caesar portrays their army as composed of criminals and brigands, but there is no reason to follow him in this. There must have been a struggle between factions within these tribes that resulted in the victory of anti-Roman forces who were less motivated by plunder than by the desire to be rid of Roman control.

Sabinus arrived and encamped on a hill that gradually sloped upwards for about mile. Viridovix set up his camp a little less than 2 miles away and led his forces out of camp daily, trying to provoke a general engagement. Sabinus refused to be drawn. His refusal to engage convinced the Gauls that he was too weak to do so. Sabinus reinforced this conclusion by sending a Gaul from among his auxiliaries who pretended to be a deserter and bolstered their belief in his weakness. The feigned deserter claimed that Caesar's campaign against the Veneti was not going well and that Sabinus would as early as the following night break camp secretly to rejoin his commander. These false impressions, as well as the supply difficulties that beset all large Gallic forces in the field, persuaded the Gauls that the Roman threat could be ended by a mass attack on their camp.

The Gauls rushed the camp at full speed to surprise the Romans and to strike before they could respond. Their uphill rush exhausted them, as they were encumbered with the brushwood and other materials necessary for storming. A sortie by Sabinus's men from two of the camp gates quickly routed the disorganized and exhausted enemy. This victory took place at about the same time as the naval victory over the Veneti.

Before beginning his campaign against the Veneti Caesar, perhaps based at Nantes on the Loire about 30 miles from the Breton coast, had sent Labienus with the cavalry to the Treveri in eastern Belgica to secure the loyalty of the Remi and other Belgic tribes, as well as to prevent German forces who had been summoned from coming to their aid. The flight of the Treveri during the battle with the Nervii seems to have created a lasting question about the extent of their loyalty.[13]

Crassus was again dispatched to Aquitania, the area bounded by the Garonne, Pyrenees and the Bay of Biscay, with twelve cohorts (probably a reinforced Seventh Legion) and cavalry to prevent the Aquitani from aiding the Veneti and the other rebels. The Romans distinguished these peoples from Gauls on the basis of their different appearance, languages and customs, although Gauls had been settling there since the third century.[14] The Romans had been operating in Aquitania since the second century and had never thought it necessary to subjugate it. For the most part their tribal groupings were small and it is hard to see why Caesar felt that they were now a potential threat. It may be that he saw their submission both as rounding out his conquests in Gaul and as a means to secure the coastal road to Spain, in addition to the trade route that ran through the Carcassonne Gap to the Garonne and then to the Atlantic.

Before beginning his campaign Crassus saw to his grain supply and levied auxiliary cavalry and infantry, as well as calling up Roman veterans from Tolosa and Narbo. He then advanced into Aquitania against the Sotiates, whose territory lay in the area of the modern town of Nérac. Caesar notes that they were known for the excellence of their cavalry. They launched a cavalry attack on Crassus's force while it was still on the march, but they were beaten back. As the Roman cavalry pressed its pursuit it was ambushed by the enemy's infantry and scattered. After a long and difficult struggle the Sotiates, who had suffered many casualties, finally turned and fled. Crassus immediately proceeded against their main town, whose exact location is unknown. The Roman commander had siege towers and moveable shelters brought up to besiege the town. The Sotiates resisted, making sorties as well as mining in an attempt to destroy the Roman siege lines. Despite these countermeasures the Romans pressed the siege and the tribesmen finally surrendered. Peace was granted on the condition that they handed over their weapons.

While this was going on a sworn-brotherhood of 600 men under the command of a certain Adiatuanus attacked. Caesar simply names him as their commander, but later sources call him a king. Coinage issued in his name seems to confirm his title as king, but it may be that at this point he had not yet assumed it. The attempt was unsuccessful and he and his men were forced back into the town and likewise surrendered.

Crassus now moved against the Vocates and Tarusates, whose exact locations are unknown. These tribes formed a coalition and had sent for aid to peoples living in Nearer Spain who were probably related and whose leaders had had experience in fighting the Romans during the war with Sertorius. They constructed a camp and fortified it in the Roman manner while sending out patrols to prevent the Romans from gathering supplies. These attacks placed Crassus in a difficult position. He did not have sufficient manpower to garrison his camp as well as to protect his supply lines and, in addition, the enemy forces were growing in numbers. In such a situation there were only two sensible choices either to withdraw or to attack, and Crassus chose the latter.

At dawn on the following day Crassus drew up his army for battle. He deployed in a double rather than the traditional three lines, presumably because he needed to counter his numerical inferiority by extending his line. If the figure of 50,000 given by Caesar for the enemy's army is correct then he must have been outnumbered three to one. The Gauls, perhaps having heard of Roman success on the battlefield, refused to engage and decided to continue with their strategy of starving the Romans out. This left Crassus with no option if he was to continue the campaign but to move against the enemy's camp. The attack on the camp provoked violent resistance. The break came when some of the Roman cavalry reported that a gate at the rear of the camp was insufficiently fortified and could be forced. Crassus summoned the cohorts who had garrisoned the camp and were still fresh and sent them with cavalry to make an attempt on the gate. They successfully eluded detection and entered the rear of the camp while Crassus pressed the siege at its front. The enemy was now encircled and could no longer hold their position. They must have fled as Caesar notes that the cavalry pursued them over the open plains outside the camp and only returned at dark. He claims that only about a quarter survived. The news of this success, following the earlier one against the Sotiates, persuaded the rest of the Aquitani to submit and surrender hostages.

However, the whole of Gaul was not yet conquered. The Morini and Menapii were still under arms. The Morini were situated in the modern Pas de Calais, while the territory of the Menapii lay in present day Flanders near the mouth of the Scheldt River, which formed the frontier between the two tribes. Also of importance to Caesar was the fact that the territory of the Morini possessed a port, Portus Itius, from which Caesar would launch his expedition to Britain. Despite the lateness of the year – it was probably autumn – Caesar decided to mount a campaign against them as he thought it would be over quickly. He quickly saw that they presented a different tactical problem from his earlier encounters with Gallic armies. The tribes were well aware that Gallic forces had been consistently defeated in open battle. Instead they decided to wage what was essentially a guerrilla war.[15] The countryside, filled with woods and marshes, was well adapted to such a strategy. They withdrew into these areas taking all of their property with them and refused to face the Romans in battle.

Caesar began constructing his camp on the edge of a forest. While his men were dispersed collecting building materials the tribes launched an attack from the woods on the scattered legionaries and on the campsite. The Romans repelled it but their pursuit of the Gauls into the forest led to casualties. To prevent a repetition of this attack Caesar had the woods cut down and used the timber to construct a rampart facing the enemy with extensions on both of the sides. The Romans managed to capture many of the enemy's cattle and a portion of their baggage but severe storms arose that ended the campaign. Before departing Caesar devastated the enemy's fields and burned their villages. Caesar then brought his legions into winter quarters among the tribes of Brittany and Normandy, among them the Aulerci and Lexovii. These quarters were chosen with an eye to making certain that the recently pacified area remained calm, and it allowed him if necessary to intervene in central Gaul. Such a position avoided the error of the previous year when the Romans had accepted what turned out to be a premature surrender.

The Morini was the more important of the two tribes once Caesar had decided to mount an expedition to Britain. In the next year while he was engaged in preparations for it he was approached by envoys from them who claimed that they were willing to make peace. He demanded a considerable number of hostages from them but nothing more. The lateness of the season and the impending British expedition left him no other choice. The submission had not been universal and some Morini were not reconciled to the prospect of Roman control. After his return from the first British expedition of 55, 300 soldiers who had disembarked from the Roman fleet and were marching to camp were surrounded by a band of Morini demanding that they lay down their weapons and turn over their booty. The Romans refused to do so and a fight developed involving an attack by 6,000 Morini. An energetic defence and the appearance of Roman cavalry quickly dispersed the Gauls.[16] This led to the mounting of a major expedition against them under the command of Labienus with the two legions in 55. The marshes where they had sought refuge in the previous year were too dry to afford them the same protection and they quickly surrendered. The Menapii were to prove a more difficult problem.

It seems likely that Caesar had formed his plan to invade Britain in early 56 before his meeting at Luca. He had more or less publically proclaimed the submission of Gaul and so had no plausible pretext to remain there after March of 54. The revolt of the coastal tribes, whatever difficulties the Romans had in subduing them, was politically advantageous as it gave Caesar a reason to stay in Gaul by emphasizing the difficulties of the conquest. It may be at this time that he formed his plan to invade Britain once the revolt was put down as he would again need a reason to remain in his province. This might also explain what turned out to be a rather useless incursion over the Rhine in 55 with equally unimpressive results.

Chapter Six

55: Britain and Germany

In 58 two German tribes, the Usipetes and Tencteri, under attack by the Suebi and unable to withstand the pressure, began a westward migration. Probably in January 55, after three years of wandering, they crossed the lower Rhine and entered the territory of the Menapii who had settlements on both sides of the river. At the arrival of the Germans they evacuated their settlements on the eastern bank and garrisoned the right bank to guard against a German crossing. Lacking boats the Germans entered into negotiations with the Menapii but these ended in failure. Pretending to retreat from the river the Germans deceived the Menapii, who relaxed their guard. A night attack by German cavalry killed the guards on the right bank and the Germans seized the Gauls' boats. Once across they gained control of part of the lands of the Menapii, using their provisions and occupying their dwellings.

Caesar was in Cisalpine Gaul when he learned of the German crossing. He set out for Transalpina earlier than usual to prevent a more serious situation from developing. After he joined his army he learned that the arrival of the Germans had had further repercussions. As the Sequani had done earlier, several of the Gallic tribes invited the Germans to serve as mercenaries in intertribal wars. Encouraged by these invitations the Germans had moved into the territory of the Eburones and Condrusi who lived in the area between the Meuse (German Maas) and the Rhine and were Roman clients.

In response Caesar called a meeting of Gallic leaders. Here he probably means those of the central Gallic tribes, to rally support and to remind them of where their loyalties lay. He also levied cavalry from them both for military reasons and as hostages to assure good behaviour. After making arrangements to secure his grain supply he set out in the direction of Coblenz to confront the Germans. When he was only a few days march from them they sent envoys to him and requested lands to settle in – either those they already held or some other area designated by the Romans – and in addition offered themselves as allies. Caesar refused their request for their settlement as it would have upset his relations with the Gauls and the stability he had achieved, but offered them land on the other side of the Rhine in the territory of the German Ubii, which lay between the River Lahn and the Taunus Mountains.

The envoys asked for three days to consider Caesar's offer. They requested that during the three days Caesar would not move his camp closer to their position. Caesar refused. He claims that the reason for this refusal was the fact that he had received intelligence that they had sent a large force of cavalry across the Meuse to loot and forage in the lands of the Ambivareti and that the delay was merely an excuse to put off fighting until the return of this force.

Caesar now advanced against them and when he was about eleven miles from their camp their envoys reappeared once again asking him to proceed no farther. Failing in this request they asked that he order his cavalry not engage them and to allow them to send an embassy to the Ubii. They said that if the Ubii accepted they would agree to Caesar's terms. They asked for another three days to accomplish this. Caesar claims that in spite of his misgivings he agreed to go no farther than another four miles in search of water, and he ordered the Germans to assemble where he halted in full force and he would make a decision about their request. He then sent a message to his cavalry commander not to launch an assault and if he was attacked to wait until Caesar came up with the infantry.

The majority of the German cavalry was still absent when the 5,000 Roman auxiliary cavalry came into view. Despite the odds the 800 German horsemen charged and threw the auxiliary cavalry into disorder. When the Roman cavalry turned to resist, the Germans dismounted as was their custom, stabbing the horses and pulling their riders off until they finally routed the Romans, killing seventy-four of them. The rest turned in headlong flight until they came up with Caesar's column. The disparity in numbers makes this rout surprising and it does seem suspicious. Caesar had already mentioned the fact that certain unnamed Gallic tribes had offered invitations to the Germans and they may have deliberately fled so as not to alienate the Germans. On the other hand there was a later occasion when a small force of German cavalry in Caesar's service defeated a much larger body of Gallic cavalry.

The cavalry battle now persuaded Caesar that instant action was unavoidable. The rout of the cavalry would be seen as a defeat and persuade the Gauls who were unhappy with the Roman presence that Caesar's forces were vulnerable. The next day a delegation of leading Germans appeared to apologize for the action, which may well have been unplanned. Caesar, who this time was not worried about violating the sanctity of envoys, detained them. He now marched against the leaderless Germans with his entire force, placing the cavalry at the rear as he was uncertain of their morale and loyalty. He deployed his army in a classic triple column of march so as to be ready for a sudden attack. Marching at the double he quickly completed the seven miles to the German camp and surprised them. The sudden appearance of Caesar and his army threw the unprepared Germans into confusion. The Romans broke into the camp. Those Germans who had arms resisted for a little while, fighting among their baggage and wagons; but the others, including the women and children, fled. Caesar sent his cavalry in pursuit. During the flight German morale broke down completely. They abandoned their weapons and standards rushed out of camp in an attempt to cross the river to safety. Caesar says that they fled to the confluence of the Meuse and Rhine: that is, to the Rhine-Meuse Delta in the Netherlands. But depending on the geography of the campaign, some place the battle near the confluence of the Moselle and the Rhine near Coblenz.[1] The first alternative is preferable. It is supported by the text and by a not entirely accurate description of the course of the Meuse earlier in the text. The flight was a disaster; when the Germans reached the Rhine a great number had been killed and many more drowned in the river.

Caesar claims that he had few casualties and none of them fatal. He gives the number of the combined tribes as 430,000 and a later source, his biographer Plutarch, claims that 400,000 of them perished.[2] These figures give one pause, especially Plutarch's figure for those killed. This seems an impossibly large number given that the pursuit and the slaughter extended over a significant distance and that some of the dead drowned in the Rhine. No figure can be regarded as even remotely accurate. It is difficult to believe that both tribes were as devastated as Caesar implies. Certainly they were still capable of causing further trouble for the Romans in the last decades of the century.

Caesar's enemies fiercely criticized his conduct in this campaign for the bad faith he had shown with the German emissaries.[3] A commission of inquiry was voted by the Senate but it is doubtful that it was ever sent. Caesar had the year before made one of his reasons for going to war against the Veneti the detention of Roman officials who were in fact not envoys. Although he does make an attempt to exonerate himself by suggesting the cavalry attack was purposeful, he does not hide the basic facts of the situation. His political enemies may have seen this incident as a weapon to use against him, but it is doubtful, given the Roman attitude towards the northern barbarians, that this act was politically damaging.

Caesar now decided to cross the Rhine. He thought a demonstration on the right bank of the river might act as a deterrent to further German attempts to cross into Gaul. In addition, if he crossed the river he would be the first Roman general to do so and this might further mute any criticism of his actions against the Germans and add to his prestige. He also wanted to pursue the German cavalry, which had been absent at the time of his victory over the Usipetes and Tencteri. They had crossed the Meuse in search of food and plunder and then retreated back over the Rhine to the territory of the Sugambri, whose lands lay between the Lahn and Ruhr rivers, and made an alliance with them. Learning of this Caesar sent messengers to the Sugambri to demand the return of the fugitives. They refused his request, claiming that Roman power ended at the left bank of the Rhine and that what they did was no business of Caesar's. His victory had not impressed many of the German tribes: only the Ubii sent a delegation and concluded a treaty of friendship with Rome. They had good reasons to do so. They, like the Usipetes and Tencteri, were under pressure from the Suebi, and Caesar provided a possible solution to that problem. They offered boats to ferry his army across the Rhine. Caesar rejected this offer. He was worried about the safety of the crossing. The Ubii may have appeared anxious for his help but how could he be sure of them? He adds that such a crossing would not be consistent with his own or the Roman people's dignity. Certainly, dignity was an important Roman political and social concept signifying the respect that other individuals or communities accorded a person or a group. It is hard to understand what it means in this context. Perhaps of more importance was the use of Roman engineering skills to impress the Germans. In place of the boats Caesar now had a bridge constructed. By a remarkable effort it was completed in ten days. Caesar gives a long, technical description of its building which has generated prolonged controversy over its detailed construction. Its location is equally uncertain but most probably across the middle Rhine between Andernach and Neuwied just north of Coblenz. The bridge was an impressive feat of engineering. In this area the Rhine is on average 1,300 feet wide and about 20 feet deep.[4]

During the construction Caesar was approached by a number of German tribes seeking peace and alliance. He received their requests favourably, asking that they turn over hostages as a pledge of good faith. It is not clear that these hostages were ever handed over, but later on Caesar was able to recruit German mercenaries so his action must have had some effect. Leaving a guard at the bridge the Romans marched into the territory of the Sugambri, who had already fled once they learned of the construction of the bridge. As some of the Gauls had done, they sought refuge in the forests taking all of their property with them. Caesar remained for a few days in the territory of the Sugambri laying it waste and then moved on to the lands of the Ubii. There he made an explicit promise to the tribe that he would aid them against the Suebi. Meanwhile he learned from Ubian scouts that the Suebi had assembled all of their men capable of bearing arms in the middle of their territory and would fight a decisive battle there with the Romans. The spot was too remote for an expedition and so Caesar recrossed the Rhine, destroying the bridge behind him.

Although Caesar claims that he had achieved his goals of overawing the Germans, punishing the Sugambri and of aiding the Ubii, it is hard to see the German expedition as a success. The few days spent in destroying the property of the Sugambri and the uncertain German promises of peace and friendship counted for little. The Sugambri had evaded him during his eighteen-day stay across the Rhine. He did not confront the Suebi, who were the main Roman problem in western Germany, and it is difficult to know how serious his promise of support to the Ubii was. Also Caesar exaggerates the importance of the Rhine as a dividing line between Gaul and the Germans. The German tribes of the Eburones and Atuatuci were already settled to the east of the Nervii.[5] It was not this campaign east of the Rhine that was significant but Caesar's string of victories in Gaul that made the difference. It is likely that had Caesar not campaigned, the Germans would have increased their migration into Gaul and occupied much of it.

Despite the fact that it was late in the campaigning season, probably in late July, Caesar made preparations for his expedition to Britain. At this point in his narrative he claims that the reason for the expedition was that the Gauls had received help from their kinsmen across the Channel.[6] The biographer Suetonius mentions another reason: Caesar's lust for pearls.[7] This is hardly persuasive. Although Caesar mentions other natural resources he is silent about the pearls, and some later Roman writers considered British pearls to be small, discoloured and dark. Writing within a generation of Caesar's death the geographer Strabo mentions that the island produced slaves, hides, gold, silver and tin but in Caesar's generation far less was known about the products of British mining.[8] Cicero mentions that he had heard that there was no gold or silver in Britain.[9] Caesar indicates that there was tin and iron but says nothing of precious metals.[10] There was a substantial trade with the tribes on the north-western coast as far south as the Loire. But this was not a Roman concern. Caesar claims that the merchants who traded with the Britons knew only the part of Britain facing Gaul and were of little help. It may well be that they were afraid of the effects of an invasion on their established routes and customers, but that does not indicate that they feared they would be replaced by Romans and Italians. An invasion would upset their established relationships and make movement unsafe. These were reasons enough to be reluctant to provide the Romans with information. There is no doubt that the desire for wealth played a role in Caesar's decision, but it was made for booty, not trade opportunities.

Caesar's claim that the Britons provided support to the Gallic tribes in their struggle with the Romans may be true but exaggerated. He records that south-eastern Britain was inhabited by Belgae, who had invaded the area and then settled it. Coinage and other archaeological evidence point to successive migrations by Belgae beginning about a century before Caesar's arrival on the island. There were certainly ties between the Belgic tribes in Britain and those on the continent. In his discussion of the continental Belgae Caesar mentions that within living memory Diviciacus the king of the Suessiones had also ruled

Britain, presumably in the Belgic south-east. In 57, after the defeat of the Belgae, chiefs of the Bellovaci who had persuaded their people to fight fled to Britain. In 55 on the eve of his first landing in Britain Caesar sent out Commius, whom he had made king of the Atrebates, to Britain as an envoy because he possessed great influence there, presumably among the Atrebates settled in Britain. Despite these ties Caesar provides no evidence of substantial British support for his enemies in Gaul.[11]

The most important reason for the invasion is to be found in Caesar's political position at Rome. If he had originally planned the invasion for 56 his attempt to link it to the security of Gaul, which he now claimed was pacified, would provide a further reason to extend his command. His prestige would be bolstered by being the first Roman to bring an army across the channel. The British invasion has its counterpart in his crossing of the Rhine. Both were ways of justifying Caesar's command and enhancing his standing. These actions seem aimed less at Germans and Britons and more at his political enemies in Rome. The quest for wealth was certainly a motive but a subordinate one.

The first landing in Britain in 55 was little more than a reconnaissance in force. Caesar brought his legions to the Pas de Calais in the territory of the Morini who, now overawed by the concentration of force, surrendered. The army he assembled for this campaign was certainly too small to accomplish more than to prepare the way for a larger expedition. It consisted of the Seventh Legion and his favourite, the Tenth, lightly equipped to save space, and a force of cavalry sailing in a separate convoy from a different port. He must have expected that he would be met by British tribes with whom he had already been in diplomatic contact before he sailed and that they would make a formal submission. Caesar does not mention the port from which he sailed in 55 but in the next year he sailed from Portus Itius, whose location is uncertain but may be Boulogne, and it may well have been the port he used the year before.[12]

When Caesar left the cavalry had not yet embarked and a change in the weather prevented it from joining him. When he had sailed on 26 August Caesar had chosen the natural harbour at Dover for his landing, but the steep cliffs covered with defenders made a landing there impossible. He sailed north along the coast, probably landing between Walmer and Deal.[13] The British had kept pace with his ships as they sailed from Dover and were ready to oppose his landing. Despite having to disembark in the water because of the sloping beach the troops forced their way onshore and routed the British, but pursuit was impossible without the cavalry. In this initial encounter the Romans had their first experience of chariot fighting. The chariot was still used by the British Celts long after it had been abandoned in Gaul and Caesar was impressed enough to add a digression on it to *Gallic War*.[14]

A storm four days later severely damaged Caesar's ships. This led to renewed fighting with the British, who were once again defeated. These successes had some effect. A number of tribes submitted and as a penalty for their initial refusal to surrender Caesar doubled the number of hostages he demanded and ordered the tribes to transport them to Gaul. Given the lateness of the season – it was close to the autumnal equinox – Caesar returned to Gaul. The expedition had almost ended in disaster because of the weather. The force was too small to achieve anything significant, insufficient attention had been paid to the weather in the Channel, and too little time had been spent in preparing for the crossing. Despite its shortcomings the British expedition produced the political results that were all that Caesar could have wished for: he was voted a twenty-day thanksgiving by the Senate.[15]

Chapter Seven

54: Gallic Resistance Grows

The invasion of Britain the next year was on a much larger scale. When Caesar left for Cisalpine Gaul he instructed his legates to begin ship construction. After finishing his judicial duties he set out for Illyricum to deal with a raid by the tribe of the Pirustae. With few available troops he raised a local levy. The Pirustae sent envoys to excuse their raiding. They offered satisfaction for the damage they had done and the matter was soon settled. At the end of May Caesar set out for Transalpine Gaul. A substantial number of transports and warships had been built for the crossing from Portus Itius to the British coast. Before assembling his army for the crossing Caesar took steps to make sure that his rear in Gaul was secure. He marched to the territory of the Treveri with four legions and 800 cavalry. The recent behaviour of the Treveri had been disquieting. They had failed to attend the council Caesar had called before the campaign against the Tencteri and Usipetes the previous year, where he had asked for cavalry support, an arm in which the Treveri were particularly strong, and not received it. Further, there were rumours that they were soliciting help from the Germans across the Rhine. The arrival of the Romans in central and eastern Gaul and their string of victories posed problems for all the Gallic tribes and the Treveri were no exception. Whatever the tribe's general attitude to Roman authority, a pro-Roman position could bring substantial benefits in the form of a powerful patron in internal political struggles. It also meant that once a noble had secured Roman political support his opponents would have to look elsewhere. In the case of the Treveri that naturally would have been the Germans. This seems to be exactly what happened. Two nobles, Indutiomarus and his son-in-law Cingetorix, were engaged in a contest for power with each other. Cingetorix had publically supported the Romans. At Caesar's arrival he met with him promising to maintain his loyalty and that of his tribesmen. He reported that Indutiomarus was preparing to fight, levying cavalry and infantry and hiding the rest of his followers in the Ardennes. The presence of Caesar proved too much for the Treveran chief, whose supporters now began to abandon him, and he sent emissaries to Caesar in an attempt to excuse his conduct. His protestations did not convince Caesar, but the need to start the

British expedition while the weather was still good made a quick solution the most expedient course. Indutiomarus appeared with the 200 hostages, one of them the son that Caesar had demanded. Nevertheless, Caesar's doubts about Indutiomarus remained and so to bolster the tribe's loyalty he met privately with a number of the other nobles and persuaded them to throw their support to Cingetorix. It was a solution that only increased Indutiomarus's bitterness and resentment. It would bear bitter fruit for the Romans in the near future.

With his rear secured Caesar now returned to Portus Itius. The ships were ready and Caesar had received the 4,000 cavalry he had asked for, and the Gallic tribal leaders he had summoned had now arrived. To further guarantee stability in Gaul while he was absent he took almost all of these men along as hostages, leaving only a few of unquestioned loyalty behind. It is clear that Caesar remained uncertain about the stability of his conquests.

He was right to doubt it and the most disturbing incident occurred among the Aedui to whom he had shown special favour. Dumnorix, the brother of his trusted advisor Diviciacus, who had already caused trouble for Caesar in 58, was once again creating difficulties. Given his past record Caesar particularly wanted him to accompany the British expedition. His anti-Roman stance had not altered in the past four years. Further, his political position guaranteed that as long as Caesar was in control there was little hope that he could attain political predominance within his tribe. He spread rumours that Caesar had offered him the kingship of the Aedui as a way of alienating his people from Caesar. As an independent people and as Rome's oldest allies in Gaul they would not have taken kindly to such an offer, although given the history of Dumnorix's relations to Caesar it is hard to believe that such a proposal would have been credible. Caesar presents him as headstrong, ambitious and influential and therefore an especially dangerous enemy.[1] Dumnorix tried to put off Caesar's request that he accompany him to Britain by claiming that he should be left behind in Gaul, alleging seasickness and religious obligations that would prevent his sailing. After Caesar refused to leave him behind he began to incite trouble among the other Gallic leaders. He claimed that Caesar had determined to strip the Gauls of their aristocracy and that once they arrived in Britain Caesar would execute them all. Fears of Roman domination and their own loss of status led to a common understanding among many of them which they strengthened by an exchange of oaths.

Caesar was well informed about Dumnorix's activities, and since he was prevented from sailing by a contrary north-west wind for twenty-five days he decided that something must be done about them. The Aedui were too important and Dumnorix too effective an opponent to ignore. Finally, the wind changed and the army began to embark. Caesar seems to have thought that he had the situation in hand when he learned that Dumnorix and the Aedui were leaving camp and returning home. Such open insubordination was impossible to ignore. He halted the embarkation and sent a large number of cavalry in pursuit with orders to kill Dumnorix if he resisted. He did so and was killed. The Aeduan cavalry, perhaps in fear of an attack if they flouted Caesar, returned to camp.

This was a far more substantial expedition than that of the previous year. Caesar took five legions (about 20–25,000 men) and 2,000 cavalry on board ship. He left three legions and the same number of cavalry to protect the ports and to oversee the grain supply. Finally, probably in early July, he set sail with a fleet of 800 ships and, despite a navigation error, by dint of rowing finally made land at the spot that he had chosen the previous year. Its precise location is unknown but it was probably once again north of Dover, somewhere between Deal and Sandwich.[2] This time the landing was unopposed; the Britons, frightened by the size of the fleet, had withdrawn inland and taken up a defensive position behind a river, probably the Stour.[3] The Roman camp was quickly built and garrisoned with ten cohorts and 300 cavalry, whose main task was to guard the fleet. Caesar learned the location of the enemy from his scouts and decided on a risky night march to surprise them at dawn. Taking a force of forty cohorts and 1,700 cavalry Caesar arrived on time and launched an attack on the British position. The legionaries easily thrust the British aside and then proceeded to attack their hill fort, which formed the strong point of the enemy's position. Forming a tortoise the Romans constructed a simple ramp and stormed the fort. The next day Caesar, thinking the enemy would not reform, sent out three columns in pursuit while he remained behind. However, at this point nature intervened and a storm developed that destroyed forty ships. After ten days of intensive labour the surviving ships were repaired with materials salvaged from those vessels that the storm had destroyed beyond repair. Caesar issued orders to Labienus to have more ships built.

The interval allowed the British to regroup under a war leader: Cassivellaunus, who may have been king of the Catuvellauni, a tribe that lived north of the Thames. As Caesar advanced the British made harassing attacks and set ambushes, in both of which the Romans suffered severely. The success of these tactics encouraged Cassivellaunus to launch a more massive assault. The enemy attacked from the woods as the Romans were fortifying their marching camp. Despite being driven back the Romans inflicted a number of casualties. The British then withdrew and camped on a height at some distance from the Roman camp. The next day they attacked men from three legions that had been sent out to forage. The legionaries, with the support of the cavalry, routed them, inflicting heavy casualties. The loss had serious consequences for the British. The lack of success affected morale and a number of them dispersed after this failure.

Caesar now decided to strike at Cassivellaunus's home territory as a way of ending British resistance. He crossed the Thames against light opposition. The inability to stop Caesar led to a change in British tactics. Cassivellaunus decided to abandon any attempt to meet the Romans in the field and turned to using his chariot force to harass and ambush them. The change in tactics proved effective and the Romans began to suffer. Internal British dissensions provided an opportunity for Caesar to bring the war to a successful conclusion. A number of smaller tribes who had suffered at the hands of Cassivellaunus's tribe saw an opportunity to use the Romans against them. They concluded an alliance with Caesar and handed over hostages and, more importantly, supplied the Romans with food. They also revealed the location of Cassivellaunus's stronghold hidden deep in the woodlands and marshes. The Romans successfully stormed it, and that, combined with the failure of an attack by his allies on the Roman fleet's camp, convinced Cassivellaunus that further resistance was useless.

He sent envoys to Caesar through Commius and terms were agreed upon. Caesar demanded hostages and fixed an annual tribute. The failure of the British resistance points out an important aspect of campaigns by the Romans against Celtic peoples. The Celts were unable to face the Romans in pitched battle. Superior Roman equipment, discipline and cohesion always prevailed. It has been estimated that a force of only two legions was sufficient to subjugate most of the Gallic tribes. The Gauls also lacked the unified command structure of their Roman enemies, which made it difficult even when they were superior in numbers to prevail. They suffered an additional disadvantage in that they did not possess the highly-developed supply system of their enemy. This is most apparent in the melting away of the Belgic army during the campaign of 57. Their only effective tactic was to use harassment and ambush to cut the Romans off from their supplies and force a withdrawal. Given Roman tactics and reliance on heavy infantry this could create severe problems as Caesar himself realized. Describing the attack by Cassivellaunus's chariot forces on the Roman camp he notes that:

> In this type of fighting since it took place in front of sight of everyone and in front of the camp it was noted that our men were not well adapted to this style of fighting because of the heaviness of their equipment; they could not pursue the enemy when he gave way nor dare to leave their formation.[4]

But even irregular fighting had its difficulties for the Celts, as the second British campaign makes clear. It required a long-term commitment to a struggle that was at odds with existing tribal frictions. Both in Britain and Gaul existing animosities could be used to Roman advantage. Superior Roman siege craft also made it difficult for the Celts to maintain fortified supply centres where they could organize and from which they could provision their forces. Despite the numerical disparity the Romans enjoyed significant advantages.

The two British expeditions had almost ended in disaster. Both times the weather nearly wrecked Caesar's plans. Despite the risks Caesar took there were few practical benefits. Rather, personal and political motives had driven Caesar.[5] The twenty-day thanksgiving after the first expedition had significantly added to his prestige. It had strengthened his position with respect to his partners in the triumvirate and greatly enhanced his personal standing at Rome.

British trade with the mainland did increase and this may have been due to a mounting interest shown by Roman merchants. The tribute that Caesar had demanded was probably never paid and he never returned to the island. His successors showed no interest in the conquest of Britain. British chieftains did from time to time flee to Rome to seek help. They did so under Augustus (30 BC–14 AD) and again under Caligula (37–41 AD), but their appeals did not result in any concrete action. The attitude of these early emperors can best be seen in a passage in Strabo:

> The British submit to heavy duties both for the goods that come from Gaul and on those they export to it so that there is no need to garrison the island. For at least a legion and a cavalry unit would be necessary to collect the tribute from them and would equal the revenues from them. Also it would be necessary to lessen the duties they owe if tribute is imposed and to undergo risks if force is used.[6]

It was not until eighty years after Caesar's death that a serious attempt was made to conquer the island under the Emperor Claudius (43–54 AD), who invaded in AD 43. Like Caesar, Claudius was motivated less by any practical benefits that would accrue to Rome than by personal and political needs. For an emperor without any military triumphs Britain provided an easy victory, although it would take several decades of campaigning before Britain was subdued and the Roman arms never conquered the Scottish highlands.

It was now September and the onset of stormy weather in the Channel. In addition, Caesar had learned of unrest in Gaul and was anxious to return. Despite further problems with his fleet Caesar and his troops safely returned. Once he had arrived he summoned a council of Gallic leaders to Samarobriva (Amiens), the capital of the Ambiani, which he used as a major supply base and a temporary headquarters. The main purpose of the assembly was to inform the Gauls about the locations of his legions' winter quarters. The quartering of the legions for the winter of 54/3 presented more difficulties than usual because of a poor harvest due to a prolonged drought. The legions would have to be dispersed over a greater area so as not to overburden local supplies. One legion under the legate C Fabius was stationed among the Morini, probably to secure control of Portus Itius and the route to Britain. A second under Quintus Cicero was dispatched to the Nervii. A third under Lucius Roscius was sent either to the Lexovii or Esuvii between the lower Seine and the Loire – the text of Caesar is uncertain at this point. A fourth was posted under Labienus on the borders of Treveri. Three more were concentrated in Belgica under Lucius Munatius Plancus, Marcus Crassus and Gaius Trebonius. Another legion Caesar had recently raised (the Fourteenth), as well as five additional cohorts, was stationed among the Eburones who lived in the area between the Meuse and the Rhine and placed under the joint command of Q Titurius Sabinus and L Aurunculeius Cotta. The use of two legates was probably the result of the larger number of troops. The legions' quarters stretched in an arc across northern France from the Channel coast to the Rhine in potential trouble spots, except for Roscius's force, which was located in a peaceful area. They were separated from each other by less than 100 miles or about six days march. In quartering the eight legions Caesar faced a very difficult problem. Separating them was necessary given the local supply situation: on the other hand, given the unrest that Caesar knew existed there was the possibility that the individual encampments could be attacked and taken before help could arrive. The uneasy situation prompted Caesar to remain in Gaul until all the legions had safely reached their winter quarters and had finished fortifying them.

Some hint of the problems to come surfaced as the legions were entering their winter quarters. Tasgetius, a leading man of the Carnutes and appointed as king by Caesar, probably in the winter of 57/56, was assassinated by his enemies. His appointment and death highlight an important aspect of the means that Caesar used to manage the tribes under his control. In the Mediterranean Romans had conquered organized states with existing systems of administration that commanded general obedience. Once the central government had submitted, the population and, more importantly, the leading men usually acquiesced in Roman control. Moreover, given the small number of Roman administrators, often fewer than one hundred, the Romans depended heavily on the local elite to carry out most of the day-to-day tasks of administration, such as collecting taxes. One of the most important functions of a governor was to establish good personal relationships with these local elites.[7] The situation was compounded in areas where tribal government prevailed and provided a far more difficult challenge for the Roman administration, as the 200-year struggle it took to subdue Spain made clear. The absence of a generally recognized central authority meant that even when the governor had chosen a man as the representative with whom he would deal, he could never be sure that his choice would be able to control his own people. This was a particularly acute problem in Gaul. Although there were certain tribes such as the Aedui with more formal governmental institutions, most tribes were ruled by coalitions of nobles whose supremacy depended on mutual agreement with each other and therefore were inherently unstable. Roman appointees had not only to deal with hostility towards their masters but also with rivalries with their peers. In Tasgetius's case Caesar does not provide us with enough information to determine what led to his murder, but the later behaviour of the Carnutes makes it likely that it was anti-Roman feeling that was the major factor in his assassination. Caesar's response was to shift Plancus's legion from Belgica to the territory of the Carnutes and to arrest Tasgetius's assassins.

Fifteen days after the legions entered winter quarters the first uprising broke out under the leadership of Ambiorix and Catuvolcus, the rulers of the Eburones. Caesar claims that the instigator of the revolt was Indutiomarus, who had good reasons to hate Caesar who had favoured his rival earlier in the year. It seems likely that the he saw the uprising as a prelude to a general rebellion against the Romans. Although Caesar presents it as the product of an individual noble's resentment, the response of the Eburones and then of other tribes indicates that hatred for Rome was widespread. At first the Eburones had welcomed Caesar's legates Cotta and Sabinus and supplied their camp at Atuatuca (the location is unknown, but perhaps in the neighbourhood of Liège or Tongres) with grain, but Indutiomarus changed all that. An attack was made on soldiers gathering wood and then the Eburones began a siege of the Roman camp. The attack was driven off by a strong defence of the camp and a victorious sortie by Spanish cavalry. The Eburones then asked for a parlay to settle matters.

Cotta and Sabinus sent as their representative Gaius Arpineius, a Roman knight who was a close friend of Sabinus, and Junius, who had had frequent contacts with Ambiorix. Ambiorix spoke of the earlier benefits that Caesar had conferred on the Eburones and his family and claimed that the attack on the camp was not of his doing but that he had been compelled to act by his tribe. He said that the tribe had been induced to do so by a general conspiracy of the Gauls. They had planned to attack all of the Roman camps on a single day so that they could not come to each other's aid. He had acted as duty demanded but felt that he owed a great deal to the Romans and he now wanted to repay their previous favours. He said that the situation would only grow worse. A great number of German mercenaries had been hired and had already crossed the Rhine. They would be here in two days. He asked that Cotta and Sabinus consider whether they should evacuate the camp and lead their men either to the camp of Labienus or Cicero, who was only about 45 miles away. If they did so he swore that he would give them safe passage.[8]

The envoys reported back to Sabinus and Cotta, who were greatly disturbed by the news. The unimportance of the Eburones gave credence to the notion that the rebellion was in fact general, so they called a meeting of the military tribunes and the leading centurions to discuss the matter.[9] It soon became apparent that the two legates held radically opposing views on what should be done. Cotta, with the support of many of the military tribunes and centurions, urged caution, saying that they should remain in camp unless Caesar ordered them to leave. He stressed that they had a sufficient supply of grain and that they would be able to hold off the Germans, as their defence against the Eburones had already shown. Help would come from the other camps and from Caesar. Finally, he pointed out that it was disgraceful to trust an enemy when lives were at stake.

Sabinus objected strongly. He argued that by the time their enemies had united with the Germans it would be too late, time would have run out. Caesar must have already left for Italy for neither the murder of Tasgetius nor the attack by the Eburones would have taken place if he had been present. He argued that, given the hatred of the Gauls and Germans for Rome, the only safety lay in flight. He argued that departure would be best: if the threat were not serious then they would reach the nearest legion in safety; if the danger was real escape was their only hope. If they endured a long siege where they were they were bound to suffer from hunger.

The argument between the two men and their supporters was long and vehement but in the end Cotta finally gave way and preparations for departure were begun. After packing all night the Romans finally left their camp at dawn (about 6.30am). Given the number of men and their heavy baggage the column stretched for quite a distance. The Gauls, aware of the departure because of the noise the column made, set up two ambushes in the woods through which the Romans had to pass and then awaited their arrival. When the column entered a deep ravine the Gauls appeared at both ends of it and began attacks on both its head and on the rearguard. The divided command complicated the Roman response. Sabinus tried to deploy the cohorts to meet the attack but seems to have been too unhinged to do so effectively. Cotta seems to have been more successful. Finally the commanders made a concerted response. Orders were given to abandon the baggage and to form a circle so as to be able to meet an attack from any quarter.[10] This was a standard defensive formation when a battle line could not be deployed or when it had been broken. Caesar criticizes this manoeuvre because being on the defensive would weaken the legionaries' morale and encourage the enemy's, but it is hard to see what else the legates could have done in such a situation. The more serious problem was that in forming up the soldiers lost contact with their units and many of them tried to rescue those items most precious to them from the baggage, which disordered their lines. In essence the legates lost control of their troops. While the Romans had at least temporarily lost formation the Gallic leaders made every effort to preserve theirs. They exhorted their men to ignore the booty for the present, promising that they would distribute it after victory.

Caesar claims that their courage and fighting ability were equal to the Romans, who were handicapped by Sabinus's incompetence. As always, in close fighting the Romans were superior and whenever a cohort advanced to the attack it inflicted heavy casualties. Ambiorix noting this ordered his men to keep their distance and to use missile weapons. When the Romans charged they should give ground and attack them as they returned to their positions. The same tactic would be used in the next year by the Parthians against Crassus at Carrhae in northern Mesopotamia.[11] In addition, the charges by individual cohorts created gaps in the Roman line that exposed the Romans' unshielded right side to attack. There was little advantage for the legionaries in maintaining their circular defensive formation. The dense mass meant that enemy missiles often found their targets and its immobility left the initiative to the enemy.

Sabinus finally asked for a parlay with Ambiorix and this was granted. He tried to persuade the wounded Cotta to accompany him but Cotta refused. He then ordered the military tribunes who were with him, as well as the senior centurions, to follow. As he approached Ambiorix he was ordered to drop his weapons, he did so and instructed his men to do the same. While discussions were being prolonged on purpose Sabinus and his men were surrounded and cut down.

Excited by this success the Gauls raised their battle cry and made an attack on the Roman lines, throwing them into disorder. Cotta died fighting along with most of his men. The survivors fled back to camp. With difficulty they held out until nightfall when they decided the situation was hopeless and they committed suicide. Only a few survived. Wandering along unknown trails they finally made their way to Labienus and told him what had happened. Some of these men must have been officers given Caesar's account of the council of officers at which the decision was made to leave camp.

Atuatuca was one of the two serious defeats that Caesar suffered in Gaul; the other being Gergovia in 52. His narrative makes every effort to place the blame for it on the dead Sabinus. Given the deaths of perhaps 6,000 men this is understandable. However, the portrayal of Sabinus's actions at Atuatuca is at variance with his previous record. He had played an important role in the battle at the Sabis, in command of a bridge over the river, and then had led Caesar's favourite legion, the Tenth, in the final battle against the Nervii. In 56 during the war with the Veneti he was sent with three legions to the Venelli and waged a skilful and successful campaign against them. In the following year in conjunction with Cotta he fought the Menapii without achieving a decisive result. However, Caesar ascribes the lack of success not to any fault in generalship but to the nature of the terrain in which he campaigned. We know less about the prior career of Cotta. Besides his campaign with Sabinus he is mentioned in the preliminaries to the battle against the Nervii as co-commander of the cavalry. These facts create a suspicion that Sabinus was used as a scapegoat by Caesar to divert attention from his own responsibility for what happened. The newly raised legion and the additional five cohorts were posted in an area that Caesar knew to be a centre of unrest. Its lack of experience and the need to integrate the additional cohorts would require time and training. Given the possible dangers, such time might not be available. The attack by the Eburones soon after the Romans entered winter quarters makes it likely that there had been little opportunity to create a cohesive force. In addition, the Eburones had not been conquered by Caesar and must have felt resentful at the demand for grain and other supplies. The situation was further complicated by the divided command. It had led to disaster earlier in Roman history. As the account of the council shows, at the very least it led to a rivalry that could not have helped the troops' morale. The argument between Cotta and Sabinus is not as clear-cut as Caesar presents it. The Romans were isolated in hostile territory with no certainty that if they held out in camp help would come. Caesar's own reference to general unrest made Ambiorix's claim of general rebellion plausible. His previous relations with Caesar gave some credibility to the claim that he had been forced into attacking the camp and would help the legionaries leave. Given these considerations Sabinus's arguments were sensible. After the Romans had marched out of their camp the one obvious failing of both commanders was the lack of adequate scouting. Once the men were trapped in the ravine their position was hopeless and the attempt by Sabinus to negotiate was more sensible than Caesar makes it appear, as there was no obvious alternative. In addition, the panic ascribed to him during the battle had little effect on its course. Once the army was trapped nothing beyond the enemy's agreement to let it through would have made a difference. By placing the blame squarely on Sabinus Caesar minimizes his own role in the debacle. To position a relatively-untried legion in an area that was restive was a mistake. Clearly Caesar was aware of the unrest. He remained in Transalpine Gaul far longer than he usually did. Despite his references to Gallic unrest he seems to have under-estimated the immediate threat. It would have made more sense to assign the unit to a peaceful area, as he had done with the legion under Roscius's command. It is significant that the second attack that year against a Roman camp took place in the same area.

The annihilation of Sabinus and Cotta's forces dealt a sharp blow to Roman prestige and Caesar's aura of invincibility. Encouraged by his victory, Ambiorix set out for the lands of the Atuatuci, which lay on both sides of the Meuse and so they were neighbours of his own tribe. They were easily persuaded to join the revolt. He went on to the Nervii, claiming that now was the chance to reclaim their liberty and to exact vengeance for their defeat. He urged them to launch an attack on Quintus Cicero's camp and destroy it, as the Eburones had done to Cotta and Sabinus. The exact location of Cicero's camp is unknown.

The Nervii readily agreed and sent out messengers to their client tribes to assemble as quickly as possible for an attack on Cicero's camp before the news of the annihilation of Sabinus and Cotta's forces reached him. Also, a sudden and unexpected attack was the best hope for capturing the camp. The Romans with their skills in fortification and siege craft normally had little trouble in taking fortified Gallic towns. The Gauls, without either the knowledge or the necessary skills, generally failed against prepared defences. Caesar claims that they had 60,000 men but it is hard to credit the figure. Certainly, the force was large as it included not only the Nervii and their allies but also the Eburones and Atuatuci.

The attack began in the same manner as had the one on Cotta and Sabinus. Roman soldiers who had been sent out to gather timber for work on the fortifications (which implies that they were not yet finished) were surprised by Gallic cavalry, cut off and then surrounded. The Gauls then began their attack on the camp. The Romans quickly armed themselves and mounted the camp's palisade. It was only with difficulty that they held out because of the suddenness of the enemy's assault.

Cicero failed in his attempt to send a message through to Caesar as the roads were blocked and the messengers were intercepted. During the night the Romans constructed about 120 timber towers with incredible speed. The perimeter of the camp would have been about 2.5 miles (about 4km). The towers would then have been spaced approximately 110 feet (about 33m) apart, which would have allowed an effective missile defence from any part of the wall. The next day, having collected even larger forces, the Gauls, after filling in the defensive ditch, renewed their assault. The Roman defence followed the same pattern day after day. There were constant attacks and then preparations at night to meet them the next day. The strain on the defenders was unrelenting. Caesar has high praise for Cicero's unstinting attention to these preparations, despite his poor health, although it is possible that Caesar exaggerated his efforts to curry favour with his brother.

The Gauls tried the same ruse that had proved successful in their assault on the camp of Sabinus and Cotta. They asked for a meeting with Cicero and this was granted. They put forward the same arguments that they had used earlier about the hopelessness of the situation. They claimed that their major objection to the Roman presence was the quartering of the legions on them and promised a safe conduct if the Romans agreed to leave. Quintus replied that Romans never accept any terms from an armed enemy.

After the negotiations had collapsed the Nervii began building siege works. They surrounded the camp with a rampart 10 feet (3m) high and a ditch 15 feet (4.5m) wide, with a circumference of 3 miles (about 4.8km). Caesar notes that these techniques had been learned from watching the Romans and from Roman prisoners. The absence of suitable tools compelled the Gauls to cut turfs for the rampart with their swords, a further indication of their lack of skills and equipment. Under the prisoners' instruction they readied siege towers, hooks to pull down the fortifications, and shelters to allow a protected approach to the camp rampart.

On the seventh day of the siege a strong wind blew up. The Nervii hurled fire-heated balls of clay and flaming missiles onto the huts inside the camp, which had thatched roofs. These quickly caught fire which, because of the wind, quickly spread to the rest of the camp. At this the Gauls raised a great shout and brought up their towers, shelters and ladders to mount the walls. Despite the fire and their losses the Romans remained on the ramparts and fought off the attack. The fighting took its toll but the Gauls suffered severely. A great number were killed and wounded as they had crowded together under the rampart and those behind them prevented any withdrawal of those in front. There was a short break in the fire and at a point where one of the Gauls' towers had reached the wall the centurions of the third cohort withdrew their men and challenged the Gauls to enter. None dared to. A volley of stones dislodged them from the tower, which was then set on fire.

The continuing siege began to take a heavy toll on the legionaries. Further attempts were made to send a message through to Caesar but they also failed. Some of the messengers who had been caught by the Gauls were tortured in sight of the camp and then executed. Finally Vertico, one of the Nervii who had fled to Cicero's camp, persuaded one of his slaves with promises of freedom and money to carry a message through enemy lines to Caesar. By pretending to be one of the Gallic warriors the slave slipped through enemy lines and reached Caesar at his headquarters at Samarobriva at about 4pm. At once Caesar sent a message to his quaestor Marcus Crassus who was camped about 23 miles (37km) away to set out at midnight and to join him as quickly as possible. On receipt of the message Crassus marched immediately. Caesar dispatched a second message to Gaius Fabius among the Morini to move his legion to the territory of the Atrebates, through which Caesar's route to Cicero's camp would run. He also sent a dispatch to Labienus to move into Nervian territory if he could do so safely. Mustering 400 cavalry from nearby camps and a legion from Samarobriva, Caesar decided to move immediately without waiting for the rest of his troops. Crassus speedily covered 18 miles (29km) and arrived before Caesar left. Caesar placed him in command of Samarobriva, where the Romans had stored their grain and other supplies as well the army's baggage, hostages and archive. Fabius met Caesar on the march, increasing his force to two legions (7,000–8,000 men), but Labienus informed Caesar that he could not move. The Treveri had taken up a position only 3 miles from his camp and if he left it would look as if the Romans had withdrawn in fear.

By forced marches Caesar reached Nervian territory. He bribed a member of the auxiliary cavalry to carry a message to Cicero informing him that Caesar was approaching and would soon arrive. Meanwhile, he encouraged Cicero to hold his position. The message was written in Greek to make certain that if it was intercepted the enemy would be unable to read it. This measure implies that he expected some of the Nervii to be familiar with Latin. Although certain Gallic tribes such as the Helvetii wrote their own language in Greek letters, it is unlikely that they understood the language. The Belgae were the least urbanized group in Gaul and Caesar mentions that the Nervii had little contact with merchants who might have introduced the language among them. Caesar told the messenger that if he could not reach the camp he was to fasten the message to a javelin and throw it inside the camp.

The Gaul, afraid of being captured, did as Caesar had instructed him and flung the spear into the camp. It happened to lodge in one of the defensive towers. It remained there for two days until it was noticed by one of the soldiers and taken to Cicero. He had the soldiers assemble and read the message to them. The boost to morale was electric and all doubt was removed when smoke was sighted in the distance, a sure sign that relief was near. The enemy's scouts also reported the approach of Caesar to their leaders and the Gauls abandoned their siege and turned to face Caesar. Once again Vertico found a messenger for Cicero who was sent to warn Caesar of the enemy's approach. He reached the general about midnight and Caesar informed his men of the situation and encouraged them with hopes of victory. This must have been necessary as, even if the figure of 60,000 for the Nervii and their allies is a gross exaggeration, the enemy must have substantially outnumbered the small force that accompanied Caesar.

The next day Caesar marched about 4 miles (7km) before he sighted the Gauls across a valley though which a stream flowed. His force was small and the ground unfavourable so he halted and camped. Given the disparity in the size of the opposing forces Caesar needed to draw the enemy on to ground where he could exploit the Roman superiority in discipline and cohesion. He had the camp constructed to give the impression that his force was even smaller than it actually was, hoping to convince the enemy to attack. There were minor cavalry skirmishes but both sides held their positions. The Gauls had delayed battle because they were waiting for further reinforcements. At dawn the next day there was a cavalry encounter close to the Roman camp. Caesar ordered his cavalry to give ground and then to retreat into camp as further evidence of the weakness of his force. To enhance the deception he had the camp's rampart raised and its gates barred.

His subterfuge worked and the Gauls drew up their army on unfavourable ground, as the camp was on a rise. To entice the Gauls closer to the fortifications soldiers had been withdrawn from the ramparts. The enemy started to hurl their missiles within the fortifications from all sides. When there was no response they advanced up to the ramparts, began to tear them down and started to fill in the defensive ditch. Having lured on the Gauls Caesar launched a combined infantry and cavalry assault from all of the gates that took them from behind. The victory was swift and many of the enemy were killed. He halted pursuit as the area was wooded and marshy, which would have made pursuit difficult and dangerous. He then made his way to Cicero's camp and held a review at which he heaped praise on the legion for its performance during a long and gruelling siege. It was then that Caesar learned of the fate of Sabinus and Cotta and called an assembly of his troops to inform them about it and to claim that their success had compensated for it.

The news of Caesar's victory spread, as he himself mentions, at incredible speed. He had arrived at Cicero's camp about 3pm and before midnight the news of it had reached Labienus, whose camp was some 55 miles (35km) away. There are other instances of equally rapid transmission. In 52 the news of a massacre of Roman merchants at Cenabum, a town of the Carnutes, at dawn reached the Arverni 100 miles (160km) away by about 8pm. When the news reached the Treveri, Indutiomarus, who had begun the uprising by persuading the Eburones to attack Sabinus and Cotta's camp, abandoned his attempt on Labienus' camp and led his army back to the land of the Treveri. Given the severity of the rebellion and the still uncertain state of Gaul, Caesar decided not to follow his usual practice of wintering in Cisalpine Gaul but to spend the entire winter at Samarobriva with three legions. The news of the reverse among the Eburones had stirred up talk of war against the Romans among almost all of the remaining Gallic states, an important index of the resentment and dissatisfaction that the conquest had created. It must have been especially worrisome that the Gallic tribes were conferring in secret about a revolt. In the almost-constant tension of the winter of 54/53 Caesar received a message from his quaestor Lucius Roscius, who was commanding the Thirteenth Legion, that the Armorican tribes had assembled a large army to attack his camp and were less than 8 miles (13km) away. The news of Caesar's victory dispersed the attackers and at least for the moment the rebellion subsided.

War was now replaced by diplomacy. Caesar summoned the leaders of each of the Gallic states for a meeting. Through intimidation and encouragement he managed to maintain the loyalty of most of them. But there were still holdouts, such as the Treveri. The major tribe of the Senones attempted to assassinate

Cavarinus, the man Caesar had made king. He barely escaped with his life. They then sent a delegation to offer excuses, but when Caesar summoned their council it refused to come. This was a significant development. If the Senones revolted they would threaten Roman supply lines to Italy. The behaviour of the Senones was a symptom of wider disaffection. Roman demands for food and other supplies must also have weighed heavily on the local communities.

The embers of rebellion had not yet been completely extinguished. Indutiomarus began marshalling forces to oppose the Romans with the support of his fellow Treveri. Initially he tried to obtain support from German tribes across the Rhine but the attempt failed. Despite this setback Indutiomarus began to muster and train his own men. Significantly he attracted widespread support despite the failures of the recent uprisings. Recruits flowed in from the Senones, Carnutes, Nervii and Atuatuci who together formed a ring around the pro-Roman Remi. Indutiomarus and his allies summoned an assembly of Treveran leaders to gather support and laid out their plans for the coming conflict. The first issue raised was the status of his pro-Roman rival Cingetorix, whom Caesar had recently restored at Indutiomarus's expense. Indutiomarus took his revenge: Cingetorix's property was confiscated and he was declared a public enemy. Indutiomarus informed the assembly that he had been summoned by the Senones and other tribes, presumably to form a coalition army to oppose Caesar. Once that was done he would then march into the territory of the Remi and ravage it. If he forced the Remi to oppose the Romans, their one secure base in Belgica would be gone. Before doing so it was critical to eliminate Labienus, whose camp was a bar to linking up with the other tribal armies and to launching an attack on the Remi.

Labienus's camp was well positioned to defend against an attack. It was protected both by the natural strength of its site and strongly fortified. Informed by Cingetorix of Indutiomarus's plans, he summoned cavalry from the neighbouring peoples. This was especially important as the Treveri were unusually strong in that arm. The Gauls were already creating problems for the Romans as they approached the walls and hurled missiles into the camp. As Caesar had done against the Nervii, Labienus kept his men in camp to give the impression that he was afraid to face the enemy.

Labienus managed to bring all of the cavalry he had called for within the camp walls without the Gauls being aware of their presence. In ignorance of this, Indutiomarus and his cavalry continued to ride up to the ramparts and hurl their missiles into the camp. At the approach of dusk they dispersed as usual. At this moment Labienus's cavalry sortied from two of the camp gates and attacked the dispersed enemy. They had been given instructions by their commander to concentrate their pursuit on Indutiomarus and ignore everyone else. Labienus also sent infantry cohorts in support. Indutiomarus was cornered and killed and his head brought back to camp. The death of the Treveran rebel leader led to the rebellion's collapse. Despite this the situation remained threatening among the Treveri. At Indutiomarus's death the tribe's leadership was transferred to his relatives, who kept on trying to obtain German help through offers of money.

Chapter Eight

53: Troubles at Rome and Growing Threats in Gaul

Despite the comparative calm the situation remained threatening. To meet that threat Caesar held a levy in Cisalpine Gaul through his legates. In addition he asked Pompey to send him the troops that the latter had levied as consul, since Pompey had remained in Italy as he was entitled to do rather than proceeded to Spain. Caesar's legates completed their levy of two additional legions and Pompey sent him one more. The three new legions, the Fourteenth, Fifteenth and First more than replaced Caesar's losses. The last legion was numbered 'one' since it had been raised by Pompey for service in Spain. The new legions allowed Caesar to reconstitute the Fourteenth and he now had thirty more cohorts in place of the fifteen he had lost. His army now totalled ten legions.

However, the situation at Rome was deteriorating.[1] The central problem was his relationship with Pompey and Crassus. In 54 strains had once again surfaced. The growing anarchy in the city had further complicated Caesar's political calculations. At least one of the candidates for the consulship of 53 was Caesar's man, and the other was not closely affiliated with Pompey or Caesar's enemies. But the prevalence of large scale bribery had raised such a political storm that all of the candidates were indicted and 53 began without Rome's chief magistrates in office. It was not until late in the year that an election was held with Pompey presiding. More disquieting for Caesar were the rumours that Pompey might be offered a dictatorship to re-establish order at Rome. Neither of the two consuls elected was allied with Caesar. In September of 54 Caesar's relationship with Pompey had sustained a serious blow. Julia, Caesar's daughter who had been married to Pompey to seal the alliance between the two men, died. Her death not only weakened the ties between them but also opened up the possibility of a new marriage for Pompey. There was always the chance that Pompey's desire for respectability and his jealousy of Caesar would cause him to throw in his lot with Caesar's enemies.[2] A further blow was to come in the spring of 53 when Crassus, in his quest for military glory to match his rivals, was defeated and killed by the Parthians at Carrhae in northern Mesopotamia.

Without the presence of Crassus there was a greater risk of a rupture between the two rivals. This may explain Caesar's kind words on Pompey's dispatch of one of his legions to him.

Despite earlier claims of calm in Gaul during the winter the situation was serious enough to keep Caesar there in Gaul. The Treveri had not given up their struggle against the Romans and had concluded a pact with Ambiorix of the Eburones. The Nervii, Atuatuci and the Menapii, along with Germans from the Gallic side of the Rhine, were also up in arms. The Senones had entered into talks with the Carnutes and other neighbouring peoples to form an alliance against Caesar. Given these developments Caesar decided to not wait until spring as usual to open his campaign but to march immediately.

He moved first against the Nervii. Taking four legions he was upon them before they had time to organize resistance. The Romans, experts in devastation, ravaged their fields and burned their houses while capturing many of them before they had time to flee. The devastation was so thorough that the Nervii surrendered and provided hostages. In such campaigns the Romans had a decisive advantage. Their excellent supply system enabled them to operate in winter conditions before there was grain in the fields, while their Gallic opponents without it suffered accordingly. To make matters worse for the Gauls, even if they dispersed and fled the lack of supplies made it impossible for them to hold out for any length of time.

Caesar returned to winter quarters after this brief campaign. At the beginning of spring he called another council of Gallic notables. Once again the Senones, Carnutes and Treveri did not attend. He decided to open his campaign against the dissident tribes immediately. His first target was the Senones, whose territory he reached by a series of forced marches. Acco, the leader of the anti-Roman faction in the tribe, tried to bring his people into the towns from the countryside but the same speed with which Caesar had moved against the Nervii proved equally effective against the Senones and Acco's plan could not be implemented. Resistance was hopeless and a delegation was sent to Caesar to sue for peace. The intervention of the Aedui in their favour persuaded Caesar to grant their request. By granting the appeal of the Aedui and restoring the Senones to their former status as clients of the Aedui Caesar both earned the latter's gratitude and gave them an interest in restraining their clients. A similar plea for peace came from the Remi in favour of their clients the Carnutes. Once again Caesar granted it. He had thus done favours for his major allies in central and north-eastern Gaul and given them an additional interest in maintaining the Roman presence.

Central Gaul was now pacified but Ambiorix and the Treveri in Belgica had yet to be subdued. Before he set out for the campaign against the Treveri Caesar called up cavalry of the Senones under Cavarinus. They would be hostages for the good behaviour of their tribe and Cavarinus, who was heartily detested by the tribe, would at least temporally be removed to safety.

Caesar was now faced with deciding on a battle plan. He realized, correctly as it turned out, that Ambiorix would not meet him in battle. More likely he would conduct a guerrilla campaign of small skirmishes, ambushes and constant harassment aimed at wearing the Romans down and cutting them off from their sources of supply. The first phase of Caesar's plan was to detach neighbouring peoples who were friendly to Ambiorix and from whom he could draw supplies and to whom he could flee if defeated. In this way Caesar would limit Ambiorix's area of operations and increase his supply difficulties.

The first attack was launched against the Menapii on the Belgian North Sea coast who had close ties to Ambiorix and also had alliances with the Germans. They had never acknowledged Roman suzerainty by sending representatives to any of the meetings of Gallic chiefs that Caesar had called. The lack of success of earlier Roman attempts to subdue them was not encouraging. They had fought against the Romans as part of the Belgic confederacy that had faced Caesar in 57 and two earlier expeditions by Caesar's legates against them had proved fruitless. Their territory was heavily wooded and marshes covered much of the rest. Rather than face the Romans they had retreated into these refuges. Guerrilla warfare presented many of the same challenges in antiquity that it does today. Roman armies basically consisted of heavily-armed infantry operating in conjunction with cavalry and auxiliary troops. They were designed to meet the enemy in a decisive encounter. Their heavy equipment and supply and baggage trains limited their mobility. They were vulnerable to small scale attacks, as Caesar's experience on his second British expedition or during the great rebellion of 52 make clear. Guerrilla forces also enjoyed the advantage of an intimate knowledge of the local terrain in confronting foreign invaders. Nonetheless, given the limitations of ancient weapons and the lack of organization and support available to the Gauls and Germans, such operations could never be decisive. Although they could create difficulties for the Romans, as they had done in Spain since the early second century, they could not win a war. Caesar's solution to his inability to come to grips with the enemy was to inflict a maximum amount of devastation on the enemy population, especially attacking their food supplies and dwellings. Deprived of supplies the enemy could neither fight nor survive. In all of his campaigns in wars of this type he used these methods, which were generally successful.

Before beginning his attack on the Menapii Caesar took steps to increase the mobility of his troops by detaching his baggage train and sending it to Labienus. He also dispatched two legions to him to protect it. Caesar's usual practice was to use newly raised and relatively inexperienced troops in this way and the two legions were probably the Fourteenth and Fifteenth he had raised during the winter. Caesar set out with five legions, now lightly equipped, for the territory of the Menapii. He divided his army into three columns, one under his own command, which consisted of three legions, while one legion each was assigned to his legate Gaius Fabius and the other to his young quaestor Marcus Crassus, who had already demonstrated his skill in earlier campaigns. The separation into three columns was an excellent tactical move. There was no reason to expect his army to be met by a large enemy force. The division's purpose was to spread devastation as widely as possible and to block the Menapii's likely escape routes. To deal with the problem of operating in such difficult country he had causeways constructed over the marshes. The campaign was a complete success and the Menapii quickly surrendered and provided hostages.

While Caesar was fighting the Menapii the Treveri had assembled a large force and were preparing to attack Labienus and his original sole legion. When they were only two days away from his camp (perhaps 20 miles or 30km) they learned of the arrival of the two legions that Caesar had dispatched with the baggage. Instead of continuing to the Roman camp they pitched camp about 14 miles away and awaited German reinforcements. Labienus decided to meet them in the field. Leaving a garrison of five cohorts to guard the camp he marched out with twenty-five cohorts (two and one-half legions) and a large cavalry force. The cavalry were particularly important as the Treveri could field as many as 5,000. He camped about a mile from the enemy. Between the two armies there was a river which was difficult to cross and had steep banks that precluded launching an attack across it by either side. The Treveri had a reason to hold off their attack as German reinforcements were arriving. The topography was similar to that which Caesar had confronted one year earlier in his campaign against the Belgae.[3] Since an offensive was impossible Labienus decided on a ruse analogous to the one Caesar had used. He stated in public that he would not risk battle but would at dawn strike camp and retreat. Given the number of Gallic cavalry that served with the Romans Labienus knew that news of his decision would quickly reach the enemy. That night he summoned his officers and explained that his retreat was a trick to draw out the enemy by pretending that his men were in a state of panic. He ordered them to strike camp with as much noise and commotion as possible to give the impression that his army was in flight. As he expected, the news swiftly reached the Treveri.

The Treveri fell for the deception and almost as soon as the rear of the Roman column was clear of their camp they crossed the river and attacked on unfavourable ground. Labienus did not immediately respond to the attack but waited until all of the enemy's forces were across the river. In addition to fighting on disadvantageous ground the Treveri must have lost cohesion as they crossed the river. Labienus finally gave the order to reverse the standards and move to the attack. The Treveri, totally unprepared, broke and ran. They sought shelter in the nearby woods but many were overtaken by Roman cavalry and either killed or captured. Caesar provides no information on the location of the battle except that it took place near Labienus's winter camp. It has been reasonably suggested that this was in the vicinity of Sedan.[4] One surprising aspect of the battle is the absence of Treveran cavalry. The narrative suggests that it was mainly an infantry battle, as does the pursuit of the routed Gauls. Hearing of the defeat, the Germans who had been en route to the Treveri returned home. The relatives of Indutiomarus, who had led the revolt, knowing that sure punishment awaited them fled with the Germans. Caesar rewarded Cingetorix once again by awarding him the leadership of his tribe. Given the fact that Cingetorix had failed to keep them loyal this appears an odd decision but it may well be that at this point Caesar had no one else to appoint.

Once Caesar had advanced into Treveran territory he decided to once again cross the Rhine. The second crossing had the same aim as the first. It was designed to inflict enough damage to deter the Germans from sending further aid to the Gallic tribes, and in this particular case to dissuade them from providing a refuge for Ambiorix. A bridge was built, as it had been in 55, and a strong guard was stationed to hold it and to deter the Treveri from creating trouble in Caesar's rear. Once on the eastern bank Caesar was approached by envoys from the Ubii. They claimed that they had not provided reinforcements for Treveri and had done nothing contrary to the terms of the agreement they had made with Caesar. Caesar says that he learned that the reinforcements for the Treveri had come from the Suebi, so he accepted their explanation and asked them about the best route to the land of Suebi. It is a curious episode. It is unlikely that Caesar was unaware of the tribal affiliations of the German mercenaries hired by the Treveri. Perhaps the best explanation is that some of the Ubii did participate as private individuals and that what took place was a public disavowal of their actions on the part of the tribe's leaders.

The Suebi had been informed of Caesar's crossing and were making preparations to meet him. They were assembling all of their forces and issuing orders to client tribes to send infantry and cavalry. Caesar, thinking that an invasion of Ubian territory by them was possible, selected a site for a camp and then secured his grain supply and other necessities and instructed the Ubii to bring all of their animals and other property into their towns before the arrival of the Suebi. He hoped that denying supplies to the Suebi would force them to fight in unfavourable conditions. He then received reports that the Suebi had now pulled back into the most distant corner of their territory to a forest that the Romans called the Bacenis, which served as a dividing line between the Suebi and their eastern neighbours the Cherusci. The Bacenis is either the heavily forested Harz Mountain chain or the Thüringer Wald.

The remoteness of the Suebi and possible supply problems persuaded Caesar to abandon his attack on them and withdraw. He had the section of the bridge that touched Ubian territory broken down and on the Gallic side he had a four-story tower 200 feet (60m) high erected, which he garrisoned with twelve auxiliary cohorts under the command of Gaius Volcatius Tullus. The second crossing of the Rhine was a demonstration of power, as the first had been. It is difficult to see what Caesar accomplished beyond making it clear to the Ubii that it was in their best interests to remain allied to Rome. Caesar's behaviour indicates that he saw the Rhine as the limit of Roman conquest in northern Europe and that his crossing was an attempt to make it apparent to the German tribes of the eastern bank of the Rhine that Gaul was now Roman. There is no proof but it is not unlikely that the demonstration was aimed at shoring up his reputation at Rome as well.

Probably at the beginning of August when the grain had ripened in the fields Caesar began his campaign against Ambiorix by marching through the Ardennes. Caesar sent all of his cavalry ahead under his cavalry commander Lucius Minucius Basilus to look for Ambiorix. By pure chance Basilus came upon Ambiorix's band, catching them unawares while engaged in foraging. Extracting information from his prisoners he made straight for Ambiorix, who he had been told had only a small cavalry guard with him. Ambiorix and his men were in a building surrounded by trees. In this confined space his men were able to hold off the Romans long enough for him to secure a horse and make his escape. The Romans captured all of his equipment, which forced him to disband his forces. His men made their way to the safety of the forests, marshes and the lagoons along the seashore. Ambiorix's partner in the rising of the Eburones in 54, Catuvolcus, was unable to flee and anticipated execution by suicide.

Two of the German tribes living on the Gallic side of the Rhine, the Segni and the Condrusi who lived between the Eburones and Treveri, sent a delegation to Caesar asking that he not consider them to be enemies, claiming that they had never aided Ambiorix. After investigating the matter Caesar accepted their claim and instructed them to hand over any fugitive Eburones in their territory.

Caesar now divided his force into three columns and sent the heavy baggage to Atuatuca. The site was chosen because of the existing fortifications, despite its unpleasant associations. In accordance with his normal policy Caesar left one of his newly enrolled legions, the Fourteenth, as a guard with 200 cavalry under the command of Cicero. Labienus was sent with three legions to the area that bordered the territory of the Menapii and the ocean, while Gaius Trebonius with three legions was dispatched to devastate the lands bordering those of the Atuatuci to Labienus's south-east. Caesar took the remaining three legions and made for the River Scaldis (the Scheldt) to where he had heard that Ambiorix was heading, accompanied by a small force of cavalry. Caesar claims that the Scaldis flowed into the Meuse, but it does not and perhaps never did. This seems to imply that he had not personally visited the area and is reporting misinformation supplied to him by his informants. Caesar stated that he would return in seven days, on the day that the grain ration for the Fourteenth Legion was due, and instructed both Labienus and Trebonius to return on that day as well if the situation allowed.

Caesar's campaign against the Eburones faced many of the same difficulties he had experienced among the Menapii and Morini. The Eburones did not mount a concerted defence but scattered, seeking safety where they could. The legions could not fight in formation and if they dispersed they became vulnerable to ambush, especially as the area was thickly wooded. Caesar was able to use the lure of booty to persuade the neighbouring tribes to do the Romans' work for them. He sent messengers to the neighbouring states to invite them to pillage and burn the territory of the Eburones. This heaven-sent opportunity lured many who assembled to take advantage of the Eburones plight. The news travelled across the Rhine and persuaded the Sugambri to assemble 2,000 cavalry and probably an equal number of infantry to join in the plunder.

Given the hopeless situation of the Eburones Caesar decided to return to Atuatuca as he had originally intended. However, the Sugambri, encouraged by their success, ranged more widely than expected. Informed that the Romans had stored their baggage and supplies at Atuatuca and that it was close by they decided to attack it and seize a far richer prize.

After the attack by the Nervii on his camp in 54 Cicero acted with extreme caution, keeping the garrison at Atuatuca within the fortifications. But on the seventh day Caesar had not yet arrived and Cicero had no information as to his location. In addition, the men were chafing at the lack of activity and pressuring him to be allowed outside the walls. Given the size of the Roman force and knowing that the enemy was scattered and presented little danger to his men he finally allowed them to leave camp. A force of five cohorts (about 2,000 men) was sent out to forage for grain. A further 300 men who had been on the sick roll were sent out separately to gather grain along with a train of pack horses and a company of camp servants who were probably unarmed. The area between the camp and the grain fields was only broken by a single hill. As Cicero's men were foraging the Germans arrived and made a dash for the camp's main gate. As their approach was partially screened by trees the Romans were caught by surprise and the cohort on guard at the gate barely withstood their first attack. The Germans scattered, looking for another way into the camp but the Romans put up a successful resistance. The fortifications and the natural strength of the site prevented the Germans from finding another point of entry.

The attack created panic in the camp, in part because the garrison consisted of newly raised levies with little experience of fighting. Meanwhile, the men out foraging had just completed their work when they heard shouting. The cavalry accompanying them rushed ahead to reconnoitre and saw the looming danger at the camp. When they saw the legionary standards the Germans at first thought that legions were returning, but then realized it was only a small body of troops and turned to attack them from all sides. The servants accompanying the Romans, pursued by the Germans, rushed in among the Roman ranks, disordering them. The veterans, who constituted a separate unit and were normally used for garrison duty, formed up under the leadership of a knight, Gaius Trebonius, and broke through the enemy, reaching the camp safely together with the cavalry and the servants who had joined them. The rest had formed up on a hill but could not maintain their position. They moved down on to unfavourable ground to try to fight their way back to the camp. Two of the cohorts were destroyed but the remaining three reached the safety of the camp. The Sugambri decided that they could not take the camp and retreated with their booty over the Rhine. Tension in the camp did not abate. Even the arrival of Caesar's cavalry did not at first quiet the men's minds. They were convinced that the cavalry had retreated after Caesar's force had been wiped out. Finally, the general's arrival put an end to their fears. His account censures Cicero indirectly by criticizing his decision to allow foraging outside the camp. However, he surely shares some of the blame for placing an inexperienced unit in such a vital position. It would have been better, given the general instability of the area, to have assigned a veteran legion to such an important post. The step was even more necessary, given the effect on the soldiers' morale of occupying a camp that had been the site of the disaster that had overwhelmed Sabinus and Cotta.

Following this incident Caesar once again turned his attention to the Eburones. Their eradication was to be an object lesson for all of the Gauls. He assembled a large cavalry force from the neighbouring tribes and turned them loose on the Eburones. Their livestock was driven off and the grain consumed or burned. Every dwelling that could be found was destroyed. Caesar's expectation was that even those of the tribe who escaped the marauders would die of hunger over the winter. Nevertheless, the pursuit of Ambiorix still remained Caesar's main concern. Despite what must have been a substantial reward offered for his capture the Gaul and his small cavalry guard remained elusive. Finished with devastating the lands of the Eburones he took his army, less the two lost cohorts, back to Durocortorum (Reims, but the identification is not certain) in the territory of his dependable allies the Remi.

Once again he called a council of Gallic chieftains and held an inquiry into the plot of the Senones and Carnutes and the attack of the Treveri on Labienus's camp. The instigator of the plot, Acco, the leader of the Senones, was condemned and executed. Others involved in it fled before they could be brought to trial and were outlawed. The execution of Acco was an unusual step for Caesar to take. Normally, he left such matters to the tribes themselves. It sent a clear message that he was in charge and that he would brook no opposition. It may have seemed appropriate after a prolonged series of revolts and it fits with this radical treatment of the Eburones as another sign of Roman control. This naked demonstration of Roman power was to have unanticipated and serious consequences as Caesar himself later acknowledged.[5]

Caesar now sent his legions into winter quarters in the north-east. Two legions were again stationed on the borders of the Treveri among the Remi as Labienus had been the year before. Two more were quartered on the Lingones and the remaining six were stationed at Agedincum (Sens) among the Senones. Agedincum was well-placed to serve as a general headquarters. It lay near an area rich in grain. Further, it gave easy access to Italy and the Lingones had been faithful allies. As he had in 57 Caesar once again claimed that all Gaul was now pacified and after seeing to the legions' grain supply he departed for Cisalpina to perform his judicial duties.[6]

Chapter Nine

52: Vercingetorix and the Great Rebellion

When he arrived in Cisalpina Caesar learned of the death of Publius Clodius on 18 January 52 on the Appian Way in a fight with a rival gang leader, Titus Annius Milo. Clodius's funeral had provoked an orgy of violence ending in the burning down of the Senate House. The violence led to anarchy as no consuls had been elected. The people demanded that Pompey either be appointed consul or dictator.[1] The Senate responded by declaring martial law and Pompey was empowered to use his authority as proconsul to levy troops throughout Italy. Caesar's enemies, led by Cato, saw an opportunity to both end the violence and to draw Pompey closer to them. They proposed that Pompey be appointed to the extraordinary position of sole consul. The Senate passed the motion and Pompey entered office in March. He acted swiftly to bring the situation under control, first by overawing troublemakers and then by having legislation passed, some of which alarmed Caesar's supporters. The most troubling legislation for Caesar was a law requiring that all candidates for office must appear in person. It presented Caesar with a serious problem. As long as he retained his *imperium* as proconsul he was immune to prosecution. His aim was to pass directly from his governorship to the consulate. As consul he would once again be protected by his *imperium*. It was crucial that there should be no gap between these offices, which would leave him vulnerable. If he had to cross into the city to canvass for office his *imperium* as proconsul would lapse.

Earlier in the year all of the tribunes had proposed and passed a law allowing Caesar to stand *in absentia*. Pompey's law did not supersede this. However, on his own initiative he added a note to the law allowing Caesar's exemption to stand. Caesar's exemption would have stood based on the law of the ten tribunes, but it is hard not to conclude that the passage of Pompey's law at this particular time would draw unfavourable attention to Caesar's exemption. Pompey's changed attitude towards Caesar is also apparent in another law passed at the same time. Instead of a province being assigned to magistrates at the end of the year in office, there now would be a five-year interval. This meant that a successor could be sent to replace Caesar before he could stand for election. This too would result in the lapse of Caesar's *imperium* and would then open him to prosecution. A five-year extension of Pompey's command in Spain without a parallel extension for Caesar in Gaul must have added to the latter's anxieties. Caesar's disquiet about where Pompey's loyalties lay could only have been increased by the marriage of Pompey to the daughter of Quintus Metellus Scipio, who was closely allied with Cato. Pompey had refused a match proposed by Caesar after the death of Julia. Scipio was an ardent opponent of Caesar's so the marriage could only be construed as further distancing the two men. The signal sent was even clearer by later in the summer when Pompey had Scipio elected as co-consul. At Rome the year 52 saw a progressive weakening in Caesar's position as Pompey drifted into the camp of his enemies. Caesar's achievements in Gaul and the wealth he had amassed there made him the rival of Pompey. That was the one thing that Pompey could not tolerate. The Gauls were well aware of these developments at Rome and they played a pivotal role in the unfolding of events in Gaul. Caesar reports that the troubles at Rome had led to rumours current among the Gauls that Caesar could not leave Cisalpine Gaul because of a revolt at Rome and so was unable to join his army in Gaul. Without him the legions would not dare to leave their winter quarters. His absence now provided the opportunity for them to rise up and strike a blow for Gallic freedom.[2]

The Gallic leaders opposed to Caesar held a secret meeting in a remote location to discuss their grievances and coordinate their plans. They were particularly incensed about the death of Acco. Earlier rebels such as Indutiomarus had been spared and it must have seemed that the execution of Acco represented a new phase of more direct and harsher intervention in tribal politics. Caesar's backing of his supporters, such as Cingetorix among the Treveri, implied that the traditional customs and institutions of the tribal elites were now under threat. But what especially angered the Gallic chiefs was a more fundamental issue. It is best expressed in a speech by the Arvernian noble Critognatus at a critical point of the revolt:

> What else do the Romans seek, what else do they wish for than driven by envy to take possession of the towns and fields of men they know enjoy both a high reputation and are powerful in war and to subject them to eternal servitude? In waging war this has always been their plan. But if you are unaware of this look what has happened to that part of Gaul that borders us which has been made a Roman province. There traditional laws and rights have been upended, it now lies subject to Roman rule, oppressed by perpetual slavery.[3]

These are Caesar's words but nonetheless there is no reason to doubt the substance of Critognatus's complaint. The imposition of Roman rule was perceived as more than a threat to the political position of these nobles. It represented a social and economic one as well. They were well aware of the experience of the tribes in southern Gaul. After the conquest Roman traders and landowners had moved in along with tribute payments to Rome. Debt to Romans and Rome had become a persistent problem that led to recurrent tribal revolts. Roman wars in Spain had led to incessant demands for supplies and for military service in a conflict in which they had no interests at stake.[4] The fate of southern Gaul made clear that more than a political position was at stake. Roman domination was a threat to a way of life in a way that inter-tribal warfare never was. It endangered the entire social, political and economic fabric. This was especially menacing to the elite who dominated it. Earlier attempts to oppose Caesar had been limited to individual tribes or small coalitions: the spreading realization of the magnitude of the threat united the Gauls as never before.

At the conference the Carnutes said that they were willing to run any risk to be rid of the Romans and promised to provide the necessary leadership for a revolt. Their willingness comes as no surprise; they had consistently opposed the Romans. In 54 they had assassinated Tasgetius, their king who had been appointed by Caesar.[5] In the same year they had been active in Indutiomarus's revolt, and in 53 they had refused to attend a general meeting of the Gauls called by Caesar. In addition, their territory was a centre for some of the most revered shrines in Gaul and the site of an annual assembly that elected the Druids.[6] Despite this there is no indication that the Druids as a body played any role in the rebellion.[7] To bind themselves together for the duration of the war and to keep their plans secret, the assembled chiefs swore an oath as they united their military standards. Before the meeting ended the date for beginning the rebellion was fixed.

On the appointed day, probably in February, the Carnutes under the leadership of Cotuatus and Conconnetodumnus attacked the main town Cenabum (Orléans), on the Loire. They slaughtered the Roman merchants and businessmen settled there. The attack must have yielded a great deal of booty and food supplies as Cenabum lay in an area rich in grain. The one victim named by Caesar is Gaius Fufius Cita, a Roman knight who functioned as controller of Caesar's grain supply. In addition, the attack had a symbolic value: the irrevocable commitment of the Carnutes to the rebellion. The news of the attack spread quickly. It reached the territory of the Arverni, probably their capital at Gergovia 160 miles (approximately 260km) to the south. It was situated on a mountain south-west of the River Allier. The site is probably to be identified with the modern town of la Roche-Blanche a few miles from Clermont-Ferrand.

The Arverni had so far played only a marginal role in the conquest. They had once controlled a large number of client tribes and enjoyed a primacy in Gaul but with their defeat by the Romans in the 120s they had lost it, although they still remained powerful.[8] In the first year of Caesar's proconsulship they and the Sequani had been at war with the Aedui and had called in German mercenaries, but with the defeat of Ariovistus they disappear from Caesar's narrative and seem to have played no part in either supporting or opposing the Romans. Once again, confrontation with the Romans intersected with local politics. One of the leading young nobles was Vercingetorix. His father, Celtillus, had been executed for attempting to establish a monarchy over the Arverni. Vercingetorix now hoped to succeed where his father had failed. He assembled his clients, who readily agreed to support him in a coup. The other nobles, including his uncle Gobannitio, united to oppose him and were successful in banishing him from Gergovia. This did not stop the young man; he gathered supporters in the countryside and returned in triumph. A key element in his success was to persuasively link his position among the Arverni to the cause of Gallic freedom. The additional supporters made him powerful enough to over-awe his opponents, who were banished in turn. He was then acclaimed king.

Vercingetorix immediately began to take control of the rebellion. He sent embassies everywhere and formed alliances with the Senones, Parisii, Pictones, Carducci, Turones, Aulerci, Lemovices, Andes, and all of the other tribes along the coast. These allies were centred in western Gaul and neighbours to the Arverni, except for the coastal tribes, and some of them shared a common border with the Carnutes. Vercingetorix was chosen as commander and quickly set about organizing the rebel army. In accordance with standard Gallic procedure he demanded and received hostages from each of his allies as pledges of good faith and issued orders to them to provide a specific number of soldiers for the allied army. He enforced his orders with ferocious punishments that included execution and torture. This was an extraordinary development. During his campaigns in Gaul Caesar had faced individual tribes or coalitions on the battlefield. Perhaps the largest was that of the Belgae in 57. However, in these conflicts there is no hint of any central organization among allied tribes. After Caesar's initial refusal to engage the Belgic army the tribes simply returned home to face Caesar individually. Vercingetorix represents an entirely new direction in Gallic resistance to the Romans. For the first time their opponent was a centrally organized and directed army that represented an alliance of a number of different tribes. Its creation was in part due to the extraordinary personality of Vercingetorix and also to the effects of the Roman conquest. The Gauls' repeated failures against Caesar had led to the realization that their traditional military methods were no longer adequate. The Roman army in Gaul was too large to be dealt with without a collective effort. Importantly, it provided a model of a highly organized and centralized army that Vercingetorix correctly saw was the only possibility of defeating the Romans. His tribe, unlike the peoples of northern Gaul, had had prolonged contact with the Romans and there is a statement in Dio, although not in Caesar, that Vercingetorix had once been on friendly terms with Caesar.[9] There is no mention of military service with the Romans, although other Gallic nobles served in the auxiliary cavalry. Nonetheless, it remains a possibility and either way he would have had the opportunity to observe the Roman army at close quarters.

The news of the rebellion reached Caesar while he was still in Italy. Pompey's apparent acquiesce to his remaining in command in Gaul had at least temporarily stabilized his position at Rome and left him free to rejoin his legions in Gaul. Once he reached Transalpine Gaul he was presented with a dilemma; his legions were in quarters at Agedincum perhaps 200 miles (320km) to the north. If he ordered them to meet him in the province and re-group there they risked being attacked on the march when they would be most vulnerable. On the other hand, he was too unsure of the loyalties of his Gallic allies to entrust himself to them. Given these difficulties the question remains as to why Labienus, whom Caesar must have placed in overall command as he did on earlier occasions, and was probably stationed with the six legions at Agedincum, did not act. It may be, as has been suggested, that Drappes, a chief of the Senones, had attacked Roman supply convoys and so had cut off Labienus's grain supply, rendering him unable to move.[10] Perhaps as important was the lack of information available to Caesar's legionary commanders. There had been rebellions before. Although the Romans had suffered losses they were relatively easily suppressed. It is not clear that in the opening phases of this rebellion the Romans realized its extent and seriousness.

In an attempt to expand the rebel alliance Vercingetorix divided his army. He took one part and marched to the lands of the Bituriges, while he sent Lucterius the Cadurcan to the Ruteni. The arrival of Vercingetorix and his army in their territory presented something of a dilemma for the Bituriges. They were clients of the Aedui, who were closely allied to the Romans. Nevertheless, there were elements in the tribe favourable to Vercingetorix. As clients they sent to the Aedui asking for additional forces to resist the rebels. Their patrons responded by sending a combined cavalry and infantry force to support them. When the Aedui reached the Loire, which formed the border between their lands and those of the Bituriges, they lingered for several days and then returned home. They later explained to the Roman legates that they had stopped because they had discovered a plan by the Bituriges and Arverni to surround them if they crossed the river. Caesar states that certainty on the subject was impossible. But their explanation gains some credence from the fact that the Bituriges joined Vercingetorix when the Aeduan force withdrew. Caesar's comments were probably written after the Aedui had defected and joined the rebels and his view on the matter may be coloured by this. The incident points to a more general problem: the disaffection that existed even among tribes allied to Rome.

Lucterius was equally successful and the Ruteni came over to the rebel side. He then advanced to the territory of the Nitobriges and the Gabali at the north-western foot of the Cevennes Mountains, who also joined. He then moved against the Roman province with the intention of attacking its major centre at Narbo. Whether he did this on Vercingetorix's orders or not is unclear. When he heard of Lucterius's movements, Caesar immediately made for Narbo to prepare its defence. He stationed an outpost among the Ruteni, who lived within the province and were a separate tribe from those who had joined Vercingetorix, and among other tribes near Narbo. He then ordered a portion of his forces stationed in the province and the reinforcements he had brought from Italy to assemble in the territory of the Helvii. Caesar's defensive measures were successful and Lucterius was forced to retire. After these events Caesar set out to join his forces in Helvian territory. Caesar had formed a daring plan to launch an attack on the Arverni with the small force he had assembled while Vercingetorix and his army were still far to the north among the Bituriges. It was in the midst of winter and the Cevennes at that time of the year were a formidable obstacle because of heavy snowfalls. Nevertheless, his soldiers were able to clear a path through the snow to the depth of 6 feet and successfully crossed the mountains. Caesar's force fell upon the unsuspecting Arverni who had thought that the Cevennes provided sufficient protection. He dispatched his cavalry in all directions to create as wide a swath of terror and destruction as possible. His troops, except for his German cavalry guard of 400 men, were composed of new recruits and local levies from the province.[11] They could pose no real threat to Vercingetorix and that was not Caesar's intention. The purpose was to draw the Gallic leader south and open a route to the two closest legions stationed among the Lingones to the north-east. For two days Caesar remained in Arvernian territory overseeing his cavalry's ravaging of the region. He then entrusted the command to one of his legates, the young Decimus Brutus who had commanded his fleet against the Veneti in 56. He could not trust the Gallic cavalry serving with him and so concealed his intentions, saying that he would collect reinforcements and additional cavalry and would do his best to return within three days. After departing he made his way as quickly as he could, probably accompanied by his German bodyguard, east over the mountains to Vienne, a city of the Allobroges. Picking up a local force of cavalry, he pushed up the valley of the Saône at full speed because he was unsure of the loyalty of the Aedui, and reached the legions among the Lemovices.

After his arrival he sent word to the rest of the legions to assemble before the Arverni learned of his presence. These included the six at his headquarters at

Agedincum and the two on the borders of the Treveri. Vercingetorix, now aware of Caesar's arrival, moved back to the lands of the Bituriges and then marched to attack Gorgobina (modern La Guerche/Nièvre east of the River Allier). The town belonged to the Boii, who Caesar had settled there as clients of the Aedui after his defeat of the Helvii in 58. Vercingetorix's attack presented Caesar with a problem: if he moved to defend Gorgobina he might face supply problems as it was still winter. On the other hand, if he did not come to its rescue he ran the risk of spreading the rebellion by appearing to be unable to protect his friends. As the Boii were clients of his most important ally this could be disastrous. He decided that the second alternative would lead to greater problems. Instructing the Aedui to bring up supplies, he set out from Agedincum leaving two legions behind to protect the baggage and his head-quarters. He did not take the direct route to Gorgobina but detoured to attack Cenabum. The fact that it was where the rebellion had begun and where a massacre of Roman citizens had taken place made its destruction imperative.

The next day he reached Vellaunodunum, a town of the Senones whose exact location is uncertain. The town surrendered after a siege of three days, the inhabitants turning over their weapons and horses and giving hostages to Caesar. After leaving Trebonius to complete the surrender Caesar set out for Cenabum. After a two-day march he reached it late in the day and decided to begin the siege on the next day. He instructed his men to gather what was necessary for the attack, and since he was afraid that the inhabitants would escape from the town during the night, as it was situated near a bridge over the Loire, he ordered two legions to stand to arms and to maintain a watch during the night. The townspeople did attempt an escape, trying to cross the bridge around midnight. The escape left the town vulnerable and after setting fire to the gates Caesar entered it, stationing two legions as a guard. Those who had tried to escape were unable to do so as the narrowness of the town's streets and of the bridge slowed their flight. The town was plundered and burnt and its inhabitants no doubt sold into slavery, although Caesar does not mention this. The cost of rebellion was now clear.

Caesar and his army then crossed over to the western bank of the Loire, moving towards the Bituriges in order to engage Vercingetorix. The Romans' arrival forced him to lift the siege of Gorgobina as he turned to meet Caesar. On his march Caesar had demonstrated the inability of rebel towns to resist Roman siege methods, and at Gorgobina he would show that he could pro-tect Rome's friends. Caesar decided to besiege Noviodunum (Pommiers near Soissons), a town of the Bituriges. The fate of Cenabum and Vellaunodunum persuaded the inhabitants to immediately ask for pardon for their part in the rebellion and to seek peace terms. As usual he required them to hand over their weapons and horses as well as to surrender hostages. While the terms were being implemented and Roman soldiers and their centurions had been sent into the town to look for weapons and horses, the cavalry of the Bituriges suddenly appeared. They had been serving with Vercingetorix and presumably because of their familiarity with the countryside had been riding ahead of the main column as scouts. Their appearance gave the townspeople renewed hope and they took up their weapons once more, closed the gates and manned their walls. The centurions inside the town realized what was happening, seized the gates and extricated their men.

Caesar ordered his cavalry to engage the Bituriges. His Gallic auxiliaries were unable to deal with them so Caesar sent out his 400 German cavalry. The Bituriges, unable to withstand the attack, turned and fled. This is the first time that the Germans are mentioned as fighting on the Roman side in a battle and it may be that it was only during this year that Caesar began using them. They were to play an important role at the crucial siege of Alesia later in the year. The repeated superiority of German to Gallic cavalry is a striking feature of these campaigns. The defeat of their cavalry caused consternation among the townspeople. They seized those responsible for the uprising and handed them over to Caesar and surrendered their town.

Vercingetorix's inability to prevent the capture of these three towns cast doubt on his leadership. He called an assembly of his supporters to bolster his position and to propose a new strategy. He was faced with an extremely difficult situation. Caesar's campaigns had once again shown that Gallic infantry and cavalry could not meet the Romans in open battle and win; neither could Gallic towns withstand Roman sieges. The only way the Gauls could defeat the Romans was to cut off their supplies and through attrition force them to retreat. This was not a new tactic but one that had never before been suggested on such a large scale. Given the time of year (it was now March) there was no grain or forage in the fields. The Romans would have to scatter widely to collect their supplies from Gallic settlements and farms. He proposed a scorched-earth policy. The settlements and farms must be burnt to the ground and their stockpiles of grain destroyed despite the suffering it might cause. The needs of the population must take second place to the successful prosecution of the war. In this way either the Romans would retreat because of lack of supplies or they would have to scatter and then be vulnerable to the rebels' large cavalry force. In addition, any towns that were not sufficiently protected by their natural strength or by fortifications must be destroyed so that they would not be a source of supply for the Romans. He then argued that supplies would not be a problem for their own forces as they would be able to draw on the territories of their allies in the rebellion. He admitted that his plan would entail severe hardship, but surely that was preferable to enslavement by the Romans.

The proposal received unanimous support. Twenty towns of the Bituriges were set alight in a single day. Other Gallic states followed suit. At a general assembly they debated the fate of Avaricum (Bourges). The Bituriges begged the others not to destroy it. They claimed that given its natural and man-made defences it could be successfully defended. The Gauls agreed to spare it. Vercingetorix at first opposed the plan but eventually gave way. Men were then selected to garrison the town.

The decision on the fate of Avaricum illustrates one of the serious weaknesses that hindered the rebel alliance. Vercingetorix's leadership had no institutional support. He could only make and enforce decisions that had been approved by a consensus of other leaders. That put severe limits on his ability to plan and to execute strategy. His leadership depended on his personality and his success in facing the Romans. Setbacks invariably weakened his position and his ability to be an effective leader.

Caesar now began to move his forces towards Avaricum. Vercingetorix shadowed him on the march and chose for his campsite a position about 15 miles (24km) from Avaricum that was protected by woods and marshes. He sent out scouts who kept him constantly informed of the Romans' movements. He then began to put his strategy of attrition into practice. Roman foraging parties were attacked and suffered serious harm. The Romans tried to counter this by changing the times that the parties were sent out and varying their direction, yet despite these measures the Gauls inflicted heavy losses.

Due to Avaricum's position a siege would be a formidable undertaking. The town lay at the confluence of the rivers Auron and Yèvre. It was surrounded by marshes and slow flowing streams except on the south. On the south-east there was an approach by a natural causeway which, approximately 100 yards from the town wall, sloped down and formed a huge moat. Caesar sited his camp at the bottom of the causeway to block the main route into the town, although given the marshes he could not construct a siege wall to completely isolate it. His solution to the problem was to approach the walls by building a siege ramp. He had his soldiers construct sheds to protect themselves while they built the ramp as well as two siege towers. The most immediate problem he faced was the army's food supply. The Aedui on whom he counted for the majority of his grain proved lukewarm and were slow to make deliveries, while the Boii although friendly were recently settled in the area and had almost no surplus grain. The army's situation soon became serious. For several days the soldiers had to do without grain and could only relieve their hunger by collecting cattle from a distant village. This passage has given rise to the fable that meat did not form part of the normal diet of the legionary. This is untrue. The normal soldier's diet consisted of vegetables, meat and grain, which formed the bulk of the food consumed. Meat made up a substantial part of the diet both in the

Republic and the Empire, with each soldier receiving about one-half pound per day.[12] Caesar spoke to each of the legions in turn as they constructed the siege works, offering to end the siege if they found they could not bear their hunger. The men answered that it would be a disgrace to break off the siege once they had begun it and that it would stain their honour not to avenge the Romans who had perished at Cenabum. The incident once again illustrates Caesar's masterful handling of his troops and why, when civil war broke out, they followed him without hesitation.

As the siege towers were approaching the walls Caesar learned that Vercingetorix had his own supply problems. He had moved his camp closer to Avaricum and with his cavalry and light-armed was planning to ambush the Romans as they went out to forage the next day. To counter him Caesar led out his forces at midnight and in the morning arrived before the enemy camp. The Gauls had learned of his coming and had hidden their wagons and heavy baggage in the woods and then drawn up their army on an unwooded hill. The open space where they were positioned on the crest was barely 50 feet wide and the hill was surrounded by a marsh that was virtually impenetrable. They had destroyed the causeways across it. Brigaded by tribe they had control of all the fords and routes across the marsh. Attacking such a position across the marsh and uphill would have been extremely costly, even if successful. Despite these difficulties the soldiers were eager to do so but Caesar explained to his men that the costs of an attack in such conditions would be extremely high and although he valued their enthusiasm and their concern for his personal honour he would deserve condemnation if he allowed an assault to take place. He then led his men back to camp and continued with preparations for the siege.

Vercingetorix had been out with his cavalry when Caesar had moved against his camp. On his return the Gauls accused him of treachery: he had moved the camp closer to the Romans, further he had not appointed a commander in his absence, and finally they were suspicious of the fact that he had been absent when the Romans had approached the camp. They claimed that he was aiming at the kingship of all Gaul and that he would rather be granted it by Caesar than win it through their support. Some of these accusations might have gained credence from the possible relationship between Caesar and Vercingetorix mentioned earlier. In addition, his unsuccessful conduct of the war to this point may have added further weight to the charges.

Vercingetorix mounted an able defence. The arrival of the Romans was pure accident which only showed how few Romans there were and their refusal to attack had marked them as cowards. He stated that he had no desire to win a command as the reward for treachery. Such a position could be his if he wanted it, now that they had begun a war that was bound to end victoriously. If they thought he did not deserve such a post he would gladly resign. He then brought forward Roman prisoners who had been coached to describe the desperate supply situation of their army. His speech had dispelled whatever doubts the Gauls had about his leadership and character. He was acclaimed by all and the army pledged their continuing fidelity to him. They then voted to send an additional 10,000 men to strengthen the town's defence. Caesar claims this was because the others were afraid that if the town held out the Bituriges alone would claim the credit for the victory. If this is true nothing could be a clearer indication of the difficulties faced by Vercingetorix. The attack on his leadership had no doubt been mounted by his rivals from both within his own tribe and by the leaders of other tribes. In addition, he had to deal with jealousies between rival tribes as they jockeyed for position among themselves. The decision to send the 10,000 appears to have been made with no reference to their usefulness in the siege. But their dispatch does highlight the inability of the Romans to cut off the town.

Caesar now resumed the siege. He remarks on the ingenious expedients that the Gauls employed to try to frustrate the besiegers. To counter the hooks that the Romans mounted on poles to pry loose stones from the fortifications they let down nooses to ensnare the hooks and drag them within the fortifications. They constructed towers on top of their walls and covered them with hides to increase their resistance to fire. As the Roman siege towers rose in height and as construction of their ramp continued, the Gauls raised the height of their own towers by adding additional scaffolding. They dug mines under the siege ramp to try to undermine it and countermines to attack those with which the Romans were attempting to undermine the walls. Their efforts considerably slowed the Romans' progress.

The construction of the town's walls created further problems for Caesar. As he remarks, almost all Gallic walls were constructed in the same manner. The wall consisted of a layered structure of horizontal and vertical beams built up in stages. On the wall's inner face the beams were securely joined to each other by large iron nails, while those beams that were laid transversely were fixed in the outer stone facing and protruded through it. After the framework was completed it was filled in with stones and earth. The inner face was either a vertical or a sloping ramp. Caesar mentions the difficulty of assaulting such a wall, the stone of its front face protected it from fire, while the timber framework with beams often 40 feet long was an effective defence against battering rams. Examples of this type of construction have been found at Basel in Switzerland and Manching in Bavaria.[13]

Despite the energetic defence and persistent rains the Romans had within twenty-five days constructed a ramp 330 feet (100m) wide and 80 feet (24m) high that almost touched the walls. About midnight, as the Romans were engaged in finishing the earthwork, smoke was seen coming from the ramp.

The Gauls had tunnelled under it and set fire to its wooden framework. At the same time they made a sortie from the two gates nearest the Roman towers and simultaneously the defenders on the walls began to hurl torches, pitch and other flammable materials on to the earthwork. In response, Caesar deployed the two legions he kept on watch and other men who were available because his troops were building the earthwork in shifts. He assigned these men to various tasks; some were given the job of repelling the sortie while others moved the towers out of harm's way and a large number poured out of the camp to extinguish the fire. The struggle continued into the next morning.

The Gauls, seeing the screens on the towers in flames and the difficulties the Romans had in moving forward now that they were exposed, sensed the possibility that victory might be theirs. The Romans fought in shifts. The legionaries battled with all their strength thinking that success in Gaul depended on this struggle.

In his narrative of the siege Caesar singles out one incident that he regards as an illustration of his opponents' courage and tenacity. A Gaul stood in front of the town's main gate and was throwing lumps of tallow and pitch onto the burning tower when he was struck by a bolt from a scorpion, a small and very accurate crossbow, and was killed. Another fighter stepped over his body and immediately resumed his work. He too was slain by a scorpion and replaced by a third and then a fourth man. All of them died in the same way. Despite the courage of the defenders they were eventually driven back and the fires extinguished.[14]

It was becoming clear that the siege was an unequal struggle and the Gauls at Vercingetorix's suggestion decided to abandon Avaricum to its fate. The decision was taken to start the flight at night to minimize casualties. The marshy ground and the nearness of Vercingetorix's camp made the prospect even more attractive. They were in the midst of preparations when the married women rushed out and threw themselves at the feet of their men pleading with them not to abandon them as they did not have the strength to join them in their flight. The men refused to listen and continued their preparations. In desperation they began to cry out to alert the Romans to what was going on. At this the men abandoned their plan. With the Romans now alerted they could easily be cut down by Roman cavalry as they fled.

The next day one of the siege towers was moved forward and the siege works were readied. Just at that point a severe rainstorm began which convinced the Gauls on the ramparts that the Romans would not attack immediately and they relaxed their guard. To lull the Gauls even further into a sense of security Caesar ordered his men to be less diligent than usual in carrying out their duties. The legions were concealed behind shelters and at a signal rushed out and gained control of the wall. The Gauls panicked at the sudden assault, abandoned their defences, and formed up in the squares and open spaces to fight the Romans. The latter began to occupy the whole circuit of the walls and did not come down to engage the Gauls directly. In fear that they would be encircled and have no chance of escape in a town that was unfamiliar to them the Gauls abandoned their weapons and fled as quickly as they could. Some were crushed as they attempted to force their way through the gates, others were killed by the Roman troops who had entered the town, and still others who made it outside the gates were cut down by the cavalry as they ran.

The Gauls suffered very heavy casualties. Usually troops who stormed a city would scatter in pursuit of booty. But at Avaricum the Romans' first thoughts were of revenge. The difficulty of the siege and the slaughter at Cenabum turned their minds to massacre. No quarter was given to old men, women or children. Caesar claims that out of 40,000 inhabitants only 800 safely reached Vercingetorix's camp.

Sieges were always the most difficult and dangerous of all military operations. Normally the attacking force sustained heavy casualties and often suffered, as in the case of Avaricum, from inadequate food and from epidemic diseases caused by their remaining in place and living in cramped conditions. Caesar only mentions the supply difficulties, but the heavy fighting must have resulted in many casualties. Added to this was the heavy and often dangerous labour necessary for constructing siege works and other equipment. Even in less difficult sieges than that of Avaricum, when a town was taken the men of military age were normally killed and the women and children enslaved. The troops enjoyed unrestricted license to rape, plunder and slaughter until their commander gave them the order to cease.[15]

As the survivors from Avaricum neared Vercingetorix's camp he took special precautions to conceal their flight and the fall of the town. He posted his own supporters as well as tribal leaders at some way from the camp to intercept the fugitives and secretly take them to their own tribes' quarters.

The next day Vercingetorix gathered his men and delivered a speech that was designed to minimize the impact of the fall of the towns on the Gauls' morale. He claimed that it had fallen due to superior Roman siege technology and trickery, not because of the bravery of the Romans. He disassociated himself from its fall by rightly claiming he had never been in favour of defending it but had yielded to the pleas of the Bituriges. He glossed over the prior defeats the Gauls had sustained at Cenabum and elsewhere, claiming that such reverses were a normal part of warfare. He promised to extend the alliance to those Gauls who had not yet joined. He then suggested that the best course at present was to fortify their camp.

The speech was well-received. The fall of Avaricum enhanced Vercingetorix's standing and weakened his opponents. The Gauls were well aware that he had advised against the attempt to hold the town and he had now been vindicated. There was also strong support for extending the war to as much of Gaul as possible. Doing so would not only add to the rebels' manpower but it would also create problems for the Romans who would find themselves overextended. The capture of Avaricum as well as the earlier victories at Vellaunodunum and Cenabum had brought Caesar no political benefit. They had only served to strengthen Vercingetorix's position and further unify the rebels.

Vercingetorix took immediate steps to implement his proposals. He sent out representatives to the tribes that had so far kept aloof from the rebellion, enticing them with gifts and promises. He then set about making up the losses suffered at Avaricum by instituting quotas from the tribes and requiring them to come to his camp on a set day. These actions soon made up for his losses. His diplomatic offensive also produced results. Teotomatus, a son of Ollovico, the king of the Nitiobriges who had been given the title of friend by the Senate, joined him with a large cavalry force and with mercenaries hired in Aquitania.

For a few days Caesar remained at Avaricum. The captured town provided him with an abundant supply of grain and the army needed to rest and refit after the strains of the siege. The winter was now almost over, which would make campaigning easier, and he set out in pursuit of the enemy in the hope of bringing them to battle or starving them out by a blockade. Before he could set out the leaders of the Aedui arrived to ask for Caesar's help. Once again, tribal politics created problems. The election to office of the *vergobret*, their supreme annual magistrate, was at issue. Two men were claiming that they had been legally elected while only one could hold office. One of them was Convictolitavis, a distinguished young man, while the other, Cotus, was an aristocrat with considerable connections and influence. Both men had strong support and the dispute threatened to tear the fabric of the state apart. The Aedui asked for Caesar's help to resolve the matter. The delay the request imposed was unwelcome. If he agreed to it, it would postpone the campaign against Vercingetorix and give Vercingetorix further time to prepare. But Caesar could hardly ignore such a request from the Aedui, Rome's oldest allies in the area. On occasion they had provided useful military support to him, but more importantly they had been a major source of supply. In addition, one side or the other might call in Vercingetorix as an ally. He had already seen some evidence of the tribe's less-than enthusiastic collaboration. Their negligence in delivering grain during the siege of Avaricum hinted at disaffection among the tribal elite.

To avoid breaking tribal laws which specified that *vergobret* could not leave Aeduan territory, Caesar summoned the two men involved as well as the entire council to Decetia, modern Decize, at the confluence of the Loire and the Aron, within their territory. After hearing the facts of the case Caesar awarded the office to Convictolitavis. It was a decision that stored up trouble for the future.

After a conciliatory speech calling on the Aedui to set aside their disputes he ordered them to send all of their cavalry and 10,000 infantry to serve as guards for his grain supply. Clearly Vercingetorix's strategy had had some effect. Caesar divided his army into two columns; four legions were assigned to Labienus to conduct operations against the Senones and the Parisii, while Caesar would take the remaining six legions along the valley of the Allier towards Gergovia, the capital of the Arverni.

Vercingetorix, learning of Caesar's arrangements, moved up the western bank of the river while Caesar made his way along the eastern side. He kept pace with the Romans, breaking down the bridges over which they might cross, and he posted scouts to deny the Romans the opportunity of constructing their own. This manoeuvre put Caesar in a difficult position. The Allier would not be fordable until the autumn. To wait until then would mean the loss of an entire campaigning season. The only course open to him was to trick Vercingetorix. He encamped in a wood opposite one of the bridges that had been torn down. The next day he hid two of the legions in the woods while he sent on the remainder, who were formed up so as to conceal the absence of the legions he had kept behind. When he estimated that those legions were now in camp he ordered his two legions to rapidly construct a bridge. The task was made easier because the piles of the original bridge had been left standing. He took his two legions across, encamped and summoned the other legions to him. Vercingetorix, realizing what had happened, moved on by forced marches to avoid a fight.

The march to Gergovia consumed five days and on the last day a minor cavalry skirmish occurred. Caesar then examined the site, which posed formidable problems. It was situated on a mountain rising 1,200 feet (367m) above the plain about 3.5 miles (6km) south of Clermont Ferrand. The northern side of the mountain was broken by precipitous cliffs, which made an attack impossible. An attack on the eastern side was equally out of the question. It was rugged, steep and dotted with ravines. Looked at from the south the town was situated on an oblong plateau that formed the mountain's summit, and the higher terraces were linked to an outlying height by a ridge on which the Gauls were encamped. Their tents were protected by a stone wall that ran for the entire length of the southern side of the mountain. There was no hope of taking Gergovia by storm. Even on the south side where the ascent was easiest the ground was steep and dangerous. The Gallic encampment on that side meant that such an attack could not succeed. The only possibility was to cut off the town's food supply with a siege. But Caesar could not start the operation until his own grain supply was secure.

Vercingetorix had seized control of a height close to the town and had placed various tribal contingents at intervals along the ridge. He was in constant contact with the tribal chiefs and did as much as possible to involve them in the planning as a way to cement their loyalty and maintain his army's cohesion. He constantly sent out his cavalry accompanied by archers to keep up his men's morale.

Opposite the town there was a hill with precipitous sides, the modern Roche Blanche, which was strongly fortified. The Gauls had also installed a garrison on it but only of moderate strength. If Caesar could gain control of it he would greatly ease the difficulties of besieging Gergovia, as he could cut the enemy off from their main water supply, the River Auzon, and prevent their forces from foraging. Caesar launched a night attack by which he was able to dislodge the garrison and seize control of the hill. He built a second smaller camp there with two legions, and linked it by a double ditch 12 feet (3.6m) wide to his main camp.

Despite this success Caesar was threatened by developments among the Aedui that remain difficult to explain. Convictolitavis, whom Caesar had recently installed in the tribe's chief magistracy, had begun a plot to end the Aedui's allegiance to Rome. Caesar claims he was bribed, but it is difficult to accept that this was the only reason for his change of heart. The money may have been an incentive, but even for the Aedui who had benefitted from Caesar's victories the Roman presence was a heavy burden. They had been under constant pressure to provide Caesar with supplies and troops, which must have created extensive unrest. The tribal elite had as much to fear from its Roman ally as the other Gallic states if the Romans established permanent control. The Roman alliance had been attractive when it could be used by the Aedui in their conflicts with their neighbours, but Caesar's campaigns had ended that possibility. The success of the Gallic revolt would once again open up the options that Caesar's campaigns had closed.

Convictolitavis seems to have been convinced of the success of that revolt and saw it as an opportunity to enhance his position. He began talks with younger members of the elite who had less to lose and more to expect from a radical change in the political and military situation. The most important faction among these young men was that of Litaviccus and his brothers. The conspirators came to an agreement and began to plan their strategy. They managed to have Litaviccus placed in charge of the 10,000 infantry that Caesar has requested to guard his supply lines to the Aedui. The Aeduan cavalry had already arrived at Caesar's camp before the infantry had set out. When the infantry had advanced within 27 miles (43km) of Gergovia Litaviccus called an assembly of the troops. With tears streaming from his eyes he addressed them as follows:

> Where are we going soldiers? Our entire cavalry force, all our nobility
> are dead. Eporedorix and Viridomarus without being allowed to offer

a defence have been executed. Know this from these men here who escaped the slaughter. I am overwhelmed by grief at the butchery of brothers and all my relations and am unable to speak.[16]

The men who came forward had been coached by Litaviccus and confirmed his version of events. The troops were convinced by the story and begged Litaviccus to tell them what to do. He pressed on them the urgent need to head for Gergovia and to join the Arverni in their struggle with the Romans to avenge the wrongs they had suffered. He then pointed to the Romans who had accompanied his force under his protection and urged the troops to take their revenge on them. Their goods were stolen and they were murdered. An act that he must have known would, as the massacre at Cenabum had done, irretrievably commit the Aedui to the rebel side. He then sent men back to Bibracte to rouse the Aedui to revolt with the same fabrications that had already proved so successful.

Meanwhile further trouble was brewing among the Aedui in Caesar's camp. Two young men, Eporedorix and Viridomarus, were disputing the leadership of their cavalry contingent. This quarrel was only a continuation of an earlier disagreement they had had over the appointment of the *vergobret*. After hearing of Litaviccus's plan Eporedorix had gone to Caesar during the night to inform him of it and to beg him to prevent the Aedui from defecting.

Caesar was clearly upset. Along with the Remi in Belgica the Aedui were his most important allies. His ability to carry on the siege of Gergovia depended on the Aedui provisioning him with grain and other supplies. If they rebelled his position there would become untenable. He immediately assembled a force of four legions and all of his cavalry and marched out of camp after issuing orders that Litaviccus's brothers should be arrested, but they had already fled. He left his legate Gaius Fabius in charge of the siege with two legions but had had no time to reduce the size of the camp to make it easier for the smaller number of troops to defend it. The Romans advanced 23 miles (37km) and came in sight of the Aeduan column. Caesar sent his cavalry ahead to slow the column's march but forbade his horsemen to kill any of the Aedui. He also commanded Eporedorix and Viridomarus to accompany them and show themselves to their fellow tribesmen. They rode up and called to them. When they were recognized the lies that Litaviccus had fed them were revealed. They immediately threw down their arms and begged for mercy. Finding himself exposed Litaviccus along with his clients fled to Gergovia. Caesar sent messengers to the Aedui to reassure them and to remind them that he could have put their infantry to death but had generously refrained doing so.

After resting his army for only three hours Caesar began his march back to Gergovia. As he advanced he was met by cavalry sent by Fabius to inform him that the camp was in danger. The small garrison that he had left behind was now under siege by a much larger force. The enemy had sufficient troops to fight in relays and the legions were on the point of exhaustion, since the size of the camp meant that no one could be spared in manning its defences. All of the camp's gates but two had been blocked and a screen had been erected on the ramparts as a defence against the Gauls' missiles. The threat to the camp spurred Caesar and his soldiers on. They reached the camp before sunrise.

Litaviccus's men reached the Aedui before Caesar's messengers. His accusations against the Romans were accepted as fact and they began to plunder the goods of the Roman citizens in Bibracte and then massacred or enslaved them. The ease with which his news was accepted points to how far the relationship with the Romans had deteriorated. Convictolitavis did all he could to support the uprising. Romans were expelled from Aeduan towns and then attacked and stripped of their baggage: among them was a military tribune, Marcus Aristeus, who was on his way to join his legion. However, once they had learned that their infantry was in Caesar's power they immediately halted their attacks and approached Aristeus claiming that what had taken place was not done publically but had been carried out by private individuals without community sanction. To give substance to this claim they set up an inquiry into the stolen goods and confiscated the property of Litaviccus and his brothers. An embassy was dispatched to Caesar to try to clear the tribe of any wrongdoing. Regardless of their pleas for forgiveness, the Aedui seem to have taken these steps to rescue their men from Caesar; in fact, they seem to have already decided to throw in their lot with the rebels.

Caesar claims to have been aware of all this and to have decided on a withdrawal from Gergovia. It is difficult to assess the truth of his statement. The fact that he later did so after suffering one of his few reverses suggests that he may be exaggerating his foresight as a way of at least partially excusing his failure at Gergovia. He claims that a chance opportunity arose that offered the possibility of success and that led to a change of plans.

On an inspection tour of the works at the smaller camp Caesar noticed a hill that had previously been fully occupied by the Gauls now appeared empty of defenders. He questioned Gallic deserters and his own scouts and learned that there was a crest along the ridge of high ground on the rear of the hill that gave access to the plateau on which Gergovia sat. To close off this approach Vercingetorix had withdrawn his men from the hill so that they could fortify the line of the ridge. The ridge was probably part of the heights of Risolles, north-west of la Roche Blanche, where Caesar's smaller camp was located. Questions have been raised as to whether such an action by the Gauls makes any military sense and if Caesar has altered the details to help excuse his failure at Gergovia. It is however perfectly plausible that after the loss of La Roche-

Blanche Vercingetorix had decided to create a fallback position from the hill along the ridge to prevent the Romans from reaching the plateau. Caesar, in claiming the hill was devoid of men, is probably exaggerating. Vercingetorix probably left a smaller than normal garrison while most of his men were engaged in fortifying the ridge.

Caesar now saw the possibility of drawing the Gauls off from their main camp below the town so that it could be attacked. He dispatched a number of cavalry to the hill around midnight, instructing them to create as much disruption as possible. The next morning at dawn he sent drovers mounted on their mules and pack-horses disguised as cavalry and interspersed with a small number of real cavalry to ride around the hill and create a diversion. Caesar then sent a legion towards the same high ground but it halted short of the hill and concealed itself in some woods nearby. All of these movements drew off the Gauls from their main camp to defend the height. In preparation for his real objective, the attack on this camp, Caesar began to move his legions to his smaller camp nearer the enemy camp in small detachments to conceal his intentions. He then instructed his legates, each in command of a legion, that it was especially important to keep their men under control. The ground was unfavourable and the speed of the advance was crucial. He reminded them that his plan was not for a full-scale battle but simply to seize an opportunity that had presented itself. He ordered the Aedui to make an ascent to his right to further draw off the defenders.

In a straight line the distance from the town wall to where the ascent began was just over a mile. Although there were paths that led up that were less precipitous, their turnings increased the distance to the walls. The Gallic camp, which was composed of a number of separate tribal encampments, lay halfway up the hill and was protected by a 6 foot stone wall that followed the contours of the mountain. Their tents filled the space between this fortification wall and the town walls. The area in front of the 6 foot wall was unoccupied.

At the signal for attack the Romans quickly reached the fortification wall, crossed it and captured three of the enemy encampments, including that of the Nitiobriges. Caesar claims that this was all he intended and now he ordered that the retreat signal should be sounded. Caesar was with his favourite Tenth Legion, which immediately halted. He says that the others, because of a wide gully, did not hear the call for retreat but were held in check by their officers, but apparently not very effectively. They continued their pursuit of the fleeing rebels. The town wall was reached, creating panic inside the town. Some of the soldiers of the Eighth Legion, led by their centurion Lucius Fabius, managed to scale the town wall. However, the Gauls employed in fortifying another part of the town heard the uproar. They sent their cavalry on ahead and followed with all of their infantry at full speed. The Romans were exhausted by their climb, fighting on disadvantageous ground and faced by a much larger enemy force. Caesar became anxious about the situation and sent to his legate Titus Sextius who was in charge of the smaller camp to bring up cohorts quickly and to station them at the bottom of the hill on the enemy's right flank. If the Romans were forced back Sextius's troops would deter the Gauls' pursuit. Caesar then advanced closer to the fighting with the Tenth and awaited its outcome. Although Caesar does not say so he presumably kept the Tenth as a reserve.

The Roman position deteriorated further when the Aedui, who had been ordered to ascend the hill, appeared and were mistaken for enemy reinforcements. Meanwhile Lucius Fabius and his men were killed and thrown headlong from the walls, while another centurion of the same legion Marcus Petronius, who was attempting to force the town's gates, saved his men at the expense of his own life by fighting back the enemy and giving his men time to escape. The Romans were overwhelmed and forced back down the hill. The Tenth, stationed on lower ground, served as a rally point while the cohorts of the Thirteenth that had been brought up from the smaller camp and stationed on higher ground moved down to the Tenth's former position. Once they had reached level ground the legions reformed and faced the Gauls, who now turned and made their way back to their own fortifications. The toll had been heavy, with the loss of 700 soldiers and forty-six centurions.

The next day Caesar assembled his troops and reprimanded them for their lack of discipline, although he made admiring remarks about their courage after so many tribulations. He then urged them not to despair. The defeat was due not to the Gauls' bravery but rather to their fighting at a disadvantage because of the uneven ground. Right after the assembly he led the legions out and deployed them for battle on level ground. Vercingetorix brought his own troops down but after a cavalry skirmish in which the Romans prevailed he led his men back to their fortifications. Caesar formed up once again the following day and again the Gauls refused battle. It is clear that Caesar did not expect the Gauls to fight. The manoeuvre was designed to restore his men's confidence rather than to threaten the enemy.

The fact that this was the gravest defeat that Caesar personally suffered in Gaul is indisputable but there has been much controversy over what Caesar intended at Gergovia.[17] It is clear that his string of successful sieges at Avaricum and elsewhere led him to underestimate the strength of the Gallic resistance. Gergovia was a tempting prize. If he had captured it along with Vercingetorix he would have been able to extinguish a tribal alliance that was by far the most dangerous threat to Roman control of Gaul. However given the natural strength of the site and the large number of Gallic troops he faced, his forces were inadequate. Once he realized that capturing it by storm was a near impossibility his only option was to starve it out but he simply did not have the manpower to do so. The attack on the Gauls' camp is mystifying. Did he simply intend a demonstration? If he did it is difficult to discern the purpose of it. Was it simply a demonstration to the Aedui and other tribes whose loyalty was ebbing away? It is hard to see what that would accomplish as long as he failed to take the town. It seems likely that Caesar intended to take Gergovia by drawing off the Gauls but that they responded too quickly and the Romans were defeated. Caesar has attempted to disguise his failure by obscuring the purpose of the attack and blaming his losses on his men's lack of discipline rather than on the failure of his gamble. In spite of Caesar's attempt to restore Roman prestige by offering battle to the Gauls, the failure to take Gergovia dealt a severe blow to his prestige. His legates had suffered reverses but Caesar had remained undefeated. Gergovia shattered any illusions the Gauls might have held about his invincibility and opened the way for a mass defection of the Gallic tribes now that they thought the Romans could be defeated.

After these attempts to restore morale Caesar decided to march to the lands of the Aedui. On the third day he reached the River Allier, rebuilt the bridges that had been destroyed and crossed over into Aeduan territory. While he had been at Gergovia the loyalty of the Aedui had become even more fragile. He was met by Eporedorix and Viridomarus who informed him that Litaviccus, accompanied by his cavalry, was approaching, trying to bring about a revolt before the Romans arrived. They claimed that it was vital that they be allowed to proceed to Bibracte so that they could forestall him and preserve their tribe's loyalty. The request put Caesar in a difficult position. He had strong suspicions that the two were trying to trick him into letting them go and that as soon as they returned home they too would join Litaviccus in inciting rebellion. To detain them would be to openly acknowledge that the Aedui had broken with him. Doing so would end any possibility that the situation could be resolved through negotiations rather than force. Before he knew the full extent of the danger it would be foolish to close down any option. He gave his permission for them to depart but as they were setting out he issued a pointed reminder of the many benefits he had conferred on the Aedui:

> He had found them deeply humbled, driven into their towns, deprived of their farmland, stripped of their resources and under tribute, and finally forced to deliver hostages under humiliating terms. He pointed out the great good fortune he had brought them so that they had not merely been restored to the former status but had attained a level of standing and influence beyond anything they had ever had.[18]

When Eporedorix and Viridomarus along with their cavalry reached Noviodunum at the confluence of the Loire and the Nièvre they learned that Litaviccus had been received favourably at Bibracte. They then met with the *vergobret* Convictolitavis and the Aeduan senate, which sent an embassy to Vercingetorix to negotiate peace terms and an alliance. Caesar had been right about the intentions of the two men. They had now openly joined the rebellion.

Noviodunum was a tempting target for the rebels. It functioned as the chief Roman grain depot. The army's heavy baggage was stored there, as well as its pay and archives. Its destruction would deprive Caesar of most of his grain supply, which might force him to retreat. The hostages Caesar had obtained from the various Gallic peoples were also kept there and their release might bring more tribes to join the rebellion, as well as store up gratitude for the future. The rebels killed the Roman soldiers and merchants they found there and divided the booty among themselves. Given the number of men they had available, they correctly judged that they would be unable to hold the town if Caesar laid siege to it so they set it ablaze to prevent the Romans from using it. The grain that they could manage to transport was shipped by river; the rest was either burned or spoiled by soaking in water. They then began to recruit local levies from the surrounding countryside and station guards along the Loire, which was swollen with water from melting snow. They hoped they could prevent the Romans from crossing it.

The loss of Noviodunum multiplied Caesar's difficulties. He was surrounded by hostile tribes, the Arverni to his rear, the Bituriges to his left and the Aedui to his front. He had lost the majority of his grain supply and this loss was compounded by the revolt of the Aedui, who had probably been his single most important source of supplies to this point. He could retreat to the Roman province which, without enough troops, was vulnerable. There at least he could regroup and resupply, but the route south was difficult. There was the substantial barrier of the Cevennes and he could not be sure of the loyalties of the tribes through whose territory he must pass. In addition, Labienus and his four legions that were operating against the Senones and Parisii would be cut off if he did so. He decided that the only course open to him was to reach the Loire before the bulk of Aeduan forces did. If he could cross it he could raid their granaries and make up for his lost supplies. By forced marches Caesar arrived at the Loire before anyone had anticipated. The speed of his marches is one of the most remarkable facets of his generalship.[19]

The cavalry discovered a difficult but useable ford. He posted them above and below the ford to break the force of the current while the legionaries crossed holding their equipment above the water. The Aedui were thrown into confusion by the rapid advance and the Romans crossed without opposition. The unspoiled countryside provided the Romans the grain and cattle they needed. Caesar paused only long enough to gather supplies and then marched on towards the lands of the Senones.

The news of Gergovia and the spread of the revolt placed Labienus in a difficult position. At the start of his campaign he had left his heavy baggage behind at Agedincum, guarded by a group of replacements recently levied in Italy, while he set out with four legions for Lutetia (Paris), the capital of the Parisii, located on the Ile de France in the middle of the Seine. At the news of Labienus's approach a coalition army composed of neighbouring peoples was raised and placed under the command of a member of the Aulerci, Camulogenus, known for his military expertise. To halt the Roman advance on Lutetia he encamped in the marshes about 20 miles (32km) south of Lutetia where he lay across Labienus's line of advance.

Labienus's immediate problem was to cross the marsh. He had wicker hurdles made and rubble brought up to construct a pathway over it. But this proved impractical. He retraced his steps to Metiosedum (modern Melun), a town of the Senones that also lay on an island in the Seine. He first seized fifty boats and used them to construct a pontoon bridge to the island, quickly gaining control of the town, as it had few defenders since many of the men had already been called up for service. He repaired the bridge over the Seine that the enemy had destroyed and brought his men across to the northern bank of the river and began to march downstream towards Lutetia. By crossing the river Labienus had turned the flank of Camulogenus's position in the marshes and rendered it useless. When the Gauls were informed of Labienus's manoeuvre they ordered Lutetia to be burned and all of the bridges across the Seine destroyed. They then moved to the river and took up a position opposite Lutetia on the southern bank.

Rumours of Caesar's retreat from Gergovia, the rising of the Aedui and the spread of the rebellion had began to reach the Gallic army. What appeared to be the growing success of the revolt upended Labienus's plans. The most important result was the revolt of the Belgic tribe of the Bellovaci to Labienus's north, whom Caesar had defeated in 57. They could field a large and powerful army. The Roman commander was now faced with the possibility of war on two fronts, and he was separated from his main base at Agedincum by the Seine. It would be dangerous to wait and he decided to return to Agedincum. Two problems presented themselves: crossing the Seine and the Gallic army facing him on its southern bank.

As dusk approached he called a council and gave instructions to his officers. He assigned each of the ships he had captured at Metiosedum to a knight with orders to move downstream silently for 4 miles (6.4km) and to wait for him there. He left five cohorts, about 2,000 men, behind at the camp, composed of those troops in whom he had least confidence. He instructed the legion's remaining five cohorts to leave camp at midnight with all of their baggage and march upstream as noisily as they could, and in addition collected as many small boats as possible, ordering their crews to make the loudest din they could as they rowed upstream. He then set out with his remaining three legions downstream to the spot where the boats had been ordered to halt. By chance, when Labienus arrived at the agreed upon spot a violent storm broke, which hid his forces from the enemy scouts who been posted along the river and he was able to quickly ship his cavalry and infantry across the river undiscovered. Labienus had used the same ruse as Caesar had done at the Allier, but this time the result was different. The Gauls misinterpreted his intentions, thinking that the Roman army had panicked and was now attempting to cross the river at three separate locations; at their camp, downstream and upstream from it. They detached a small force opposite the camp and another upstream to Metiosedum to advance as far as the Roman ships had gone, but they correctly divined that the main thrust would come at the point where Labienus had camped and sent the bulk of their forces there.

By dawn both sides had deployed and the battle had begun. On the Roman right the Seventh Legion routed the enemy forces opposite it, and on the other side of the battle line the Twelfth Legion launched their *pila* and inflicted heavy casualties, but the enemy line remained firm. The turning point came when the tribunes of the Seventh learned of the situation on their left wing. They brought their troops around behind the enemy and attacked his rear. Under attack from two directions the Gauls' situation was now hopeless, although they did not try to flee and most died fighting. The Gallic force that had been posted opposite the camp came up to help their comrades. They occupied a hill but were unable to withstand the Roman attack and fled along with the survivors of the main force. The cavalry cut down all of them except for a small number who found sanctuary among the surrounding woods or hills. After the battle Labienus returned to Agedincum, collected the baggage and then marched to join Caesar.

Labienus had extricated his army but had been unable to stop the revolt of the northern tribes. The general situation had worsened. Almost all of central and northern Gaul was in revolt. The rebellion of the Aedui was perhaps the most significant setback. Their wealth and prestige influenced the other tribes to rise. The Remi and Lingones alone remained loyal.

Once they had joined the revolt the Aedui sent to Vercingetorix to invite him to explain his plans. They agreed with his strategy but tried to take over the leadership, demanding the supreme command for themselves. Vercingetorix refused and to resolve the matter an assembly was set to meet at Bibracte. Almost all of the Gallic tribes attended except for the Remi, the Lingones and the Treveri. The latter were under attack by the Germans and were too preoccupied to support either side, while the first two remained firm in their alliance with the Romans. The success at Gergovia told in his favour and

Vercingetorix was confirmed as supreme commander. The Aedui resented the outcome but were too committed to the revolt to leave the coalition.

Vercingetorix immediately asserted his authority. He demanded hostages from his allies and set a date on which they were to be handed over. He then ordered an immediate assembly of his 15,000 cavalry but did not request any further levies of infantry apart from the 80,000 that had already been contributed. He did however demand an additional force of 10,000 infantry from his new allies the Aedui and their clients the Segusiavi, as well as 800 cavalry, and wisely put an Aeduan, the brother of Eporedorix, in charge. His strategy remained the same: to avoid open battle with the Romans and by depriving them of grain and forage to force their retreat. His forces were sufficient for his purpose. The fate of the Belgic coalition in 57 showed that too large a force was as useless as one that was too small. Once again Vercingetorix demanded a severe sacrifice from his followers. They must burn their grain stores and their property to prevent them from falling into Roman hands as his strategy would not permit them to be defended. What Caesar's text does not make clear is the effect of such a strategy on Gallic non-combatants. How could they survive without food and shelter? His next step was to threaten the Roman province. If he could foment a rebellion there he could threaten Caesar's most secure base and hinder the movement of reinforcements from Italy. He sent a delegation to the Allobroges, whose recent revolts indicated their unhappiness with Romans. Surprisingly, the Allobroges refused to join. As has been pointed out, during his time in Gaul Caesar had forged close ties with them. In 58 he had defended them from the depredations of the Helvetii and had done favours for several of their leading men. Instead the Allobroges posted a garrison along the Rhône and closed their borders. One of the tribes in the province, the Helvii, did rise but they were overwhelmed by their neighbours. Caesar's legate in the province, Lucius Caesar, his cousin who had held the consulate in 64, levied twenty-two cohorts, probably about 10,000 men, to defend the province as all of Caesar's legions were operating in the north.

The spread of the uprising had isolated Caesar and he could expect no reinforcements from Italy or the province. Germany still offered possibilities, so Caesar sent for German cavalry and for the light infantry who fought with them from those tribes that he had subdued. The reference is unclear but perhaps the Ubii are meant.[20] He must have been impressed by their effectiveness. In 55, 5,000 of his Gallic cavalry had been routed by 800 Germans despite the inferiority of their horses. He mounted the Germans on horses taken from his officers and veterans who normally rode when the legions marched.

Caesar had decided that the province had to be defended. He began marching south-east through the territory of the friendly Lingones to the lands of the Sequani, which were situated close to the province. While he was on the march Vercingetorix mustered his forces and marched to within 9 miles (14.5km) of the Roman camp and stopped there, dividing his men between three separate camps. He assembled his cavalry commanders and informed them of his plan to harass the Romans on the march since they were encumbered by their baggage. If the Romans halted to mount a defence they would be unable to continue on and if they abandoned their baggage to escape the Gallic attacks they would lose essential equipment and their morale would suffer greatly. With less credibility, he assured them that the Roman cavalry would not abandon the safety of the column to mount counterattacks. To strengthen the cavalry commanders' commitment to his plan he had them swear a solemn oath that any who failed to ride twice through the enemy column would be outlawed.[21] His plan received enthusiastic approval and preparations were begun for the attack.

The next day he divided his cavalry force into three groups. Two were to ride along the flanks of the Roman column while the third was to harass it from the front. Caesar seems to have been surprised by the attack. The rolling hills near the town of Montbard in the valley of the River Brenne where the attack took place offered concealment for Vercingetorix's forces. In response Caesar also divided his cavalry into thirds and ordered them to attack the enemy. Fighting now broke out all along the column. At this point the ten legions halted and brought their baggage inside the column. Normally each legion's baggage followed it on the march. In essence they formed a hollow square with the baggage placed inside. If the column was under pressure at any point Caesar gave orders that the troops there were to form a battle line and to support the cavalry if it was hard pressed. Finally, the German cavalry on the column's right seized a ridge of high ground after driving off the enemy cavalry. They drove the Gauls down to the stream where Vercingetorix and his infantry had taken up their position. The Germans killed a number of them, while the rest fled as they were afraid of being surrounded. In addition, a number of important rebels were captured. The infantry who had been stationed in front of the three camps was assembled and Vercingetorix immediately began moving his army to Alesia after having issued instructions for its baggage to follow as quickly as possible. The failure of his attack must have deeply discouraged him. His plan rested on the success of his cavalry: his infantry played no role in the battle and surely he never intended that it should. It could not face the Romans in battle. Its true function was to guard his camps and to make sure that the tribes who supplied it remained committed to the Gallic cause. The constant success of the Germans meant that the only possibility left at this point was to harry detachments and foragers as the Germans' limited numbers could not completely protect the supplies necessary for 40,000 legionaries or safeguard the widespread foraging parties necessary to sustain an army of this size.

Vercingetorix's march to Alesia resulted in additional casualties. Caesar gave orders that the legion's baggage was to be taken straight away to the nearest high ground. He placed it under the guard of two of his legions and with the rest began his pursuit of Vercingetorix. This lasted until darkness and according to Caesar the Gauls lost another 3,000 men before they finally reached the safety of Alesia.

Alesia was the capital of the Mandubii. The town was located at the present site of the commune of Alise-Sainte-Reine on Mount Auxois about 30 miles (50km) north-west of Dijon in Burgundy. The site was first investigated in the 1860s and excavations have continued to the present.[22] The town was located on a limestone plateau approximately 1,300ft (400m) high. The plateau itself is about 1.2 miles (2km) long and 650 yards (600m) wide. Its slopes are steep and difficult to access since they are interspersed with vertical bands of rock. Surrounding it is a series of hills, with Bussy to the north-east, Mount Pennevelle to the south-east, to which it is connected by a narrow ridge, Flavigny to the south and Mount Rea to the north-west. These major hills are roughly the same height as Auxois, and in the areas between them there are scattered heights. To the west of Mount Auxois lies the plain of Laumes through which the River Brenne flows, which is at this point joined by two tributaries, the Ozerain, which flows through the small valley to the south of Auxois and the Oze, which runs along Auxois' northern side. The plain ends in a series of heights to its north. As at Gergovia the natural strength of the site precluded a direct assault, which even if successful would have been extremely costly. The Gauls had positioned themselves on the eastern side of the hill. To strengthen their defences they had dug a ditch and built a 6 feet (1.8m) wall. These blocked the relatively easy access to the plateau from Mount Pennevelle.

Since a direct assault was precluded, the only alternative was to capture the town by siege, which required the construction of massive fortifications. One of the striking aspects of the Gallic war is the engineering skill the Romans displayed in constructing siege fortifications. This expertise was part of a wider development in the use of fortifications by the Romans. They were used extensively not only in sieges but also on the battlefield. The Romans constructed a continuous siege wall over 10 miles (16km) in length to close off Alesia. The construction of the wall varied from place to place, taking advantage of the local topography and lying along the slopes of the hills surrounding Auxois. Along the perimeter of the siege wall twenty-three forts were built to serve as garrison points to guard against unexpected sorties. In addition, at night sentries and reinforced patrols were added. The circumvallation was fronted by ditches that varied in type and depth, depending on the nature of the ground. The wall in the Plain of Laumes had the most elaborate system. It was fronted by an elaborate system of two ditches, one filled with water and the other V-shaped.

Eleven camps were constructed. Archaeologists have identified the one on Flavigny as Caesar's camp, while Labienus was located on Mount Bussy.

As the construction continued a cavalry battle broke out in the Plain of Laumes where Caesar's cavalry camps were situated. It was a fiercely-fought battle and it is probable that Caesar's cavalry numbered about 6,000 and faced a far larger Gallic force. They were hard pressed when Caesar once again sent his Germans to their aid and stationed the legions in front of the camps to deter a coordinated infantry attack. The appearance of the legions and the Germans proved too much for the Gauls, who turned in flight. At this point their superior numbers told against them. There was a crush at the gates of their camp as the Germans pursued them right up to the ditch that fronted it and many were crushed to death. As a further distraction for the defenders of the Gallic camp Caesar had the legions advance a little distance towards the town.

This action made it clear to Vercingetorix that he could not break the siege by himself. The only possibility that remained open to him was to collect a relief army of all available men of military age. Once it arrived he could either pin Caesar between it and his troops in the town and cut him off, or destroy the Romans with simultaneous attacks. He made a decision to send all of his cavalry back to their own tribes to collect the relieving force. Once the circumvallation had been completed the cavalry would not be able to operate effectively and with the lack of forage for its horses would become an unsustainable burden. This left his 80,000 infantry, but even with these reduced numbers he only had grain stocks for thirty days, which might last a little longer if he instituted rationing. The cavalry were sent away near midnight through a gap in the as yet uncompleted circumvallation. Once this was done Vercingetorix had all of the grain stocks in private hands brought in under penalty of death for anyone who refused to cooperate. He rationed the grain, but luckily there was a large number of livestock in the town; these he shared out among those inside Alesia. He then withdrew all of his forces within the town walls. In doing so he abandoned Pennevelle, which had provided the easiest route for a relief army and would have been costly to take if Caesar had mounted an attack to seize it. Allowing the Romans to occupy it was a serious error.

Learning that Vercingetorix had summoned a relief army Caesar now extended and strengthened his grip on the city. A contravallation was constructed against an attack from the outside. Since it was outside of the circumvallation it stretched for 13 miles (c.21km) and ran along the heights, except in the west where it crossed the plain. It was at that point where attack would be easiest that the defences were the strongest. He had a ditch 20 feet deep with vertical sides constructed between the Oze and the Ozerain. Using this as a base point he had the other fortifications constructed 400 paces (about 130 yards or 120 metres) behind the ditch. This would put the main lines of fortifications outside missile range. At this point two further ditches 15 feet wide were excavated. The inner one was filled with water from the river. Behind them an earthwork was constructed topped by a palisade surmounted by parapets and battlements with large pointed stakes attached where the palisade and earthwork met. Towers were built around the circumference of the palisade at 80-foot (24m) intervals. The defences at other points were far less elaborate, often taking advantage of the ground, and functioned more as a barrier than a defensive bastion. The larger camps were integrated into the contravallation while the smaller ones were placed between the two walls.

One of the most potent enemies of any large stationary army was the need for supplies, especially forage and grain. The 40,000 troops in Caesar's army would soon exhaust nearby sources, which meant that substantial numbers of troops had to be sent some distance to gather supplies. The troops that remained behind were subject to frequent attacks from the town. In addition, the extension of the fortifications must have further taxed his manpower. To lessen this problem Caesar decided to build additional defensive barriers in front of the defences on the vulnerable Plain of Laumes. These consisted of a series of lethal barriers and traps. Tree trunks and branches were cut down, stripped of their bark and sharpened at their ends. These were securely planted in ditches 5 feet deep in rows of five and firmly fastened to the ground. To increase the difficulty of pulling them up the branches were left above ground and intertwined with each together. In a fashion typical of soldiers' slang they were appropriately called 'gravestones'. Beyond them eight rows of pits were dug in a checkerboard fashion 3 feet (1m) deep and sloping inward from top to bottom. Sharpened stakes as thick as a man's thigh were inserted into them and then the earth around them was flattened to hold them firmly in place. The pits were then camouflaged with twigs and brushwood. The soldiers called them 'lilies' from their resemblance to that flower. Finally, in front of these another set of shallow pits were dug for logs that were laid horizontally, in a random fashion, and then covered with barbed iron hooks. These were nicknamed 'goads' or 'spurs'. These obstacles and traps could not stop a full-scale attack, but could slow it sufficiently to allow the Romans to bring up reinforcements to the threatened point. This would be especially true of attacking cavalry, which would have to dismount to make their way through them. The completion of the double line of fortifications was an amazing tribute to Roman military engineering.

Vercingetorix's request for aid found a ready response among the tribes. A conference was called to discuss how the troops should be levied and how large the levy should be. First, it was decided not to call up all men of military age as Vercingetorix requested. Such an army would have been too cumbersome, difficult to supply, and create problems of command. Quotas were assigned to the major tribes: the Aedui and their dependents were to supply 35,000 men;

the Arverni and their clients were to levy the same number; while the smaller tribes were grouped together and supplied anywhere from 2,000 to 12,000 troops. The Bellovaci refused to contribute the 10,000 men requested by the allies, but did for the sake of their ties to Commius, king of the Atrebati, send a token force of 2,000. In all Caesar claims the relief army consisted of 8,000 cavalry and nearly 250,000 infantry. Although these numbers are consistent with other tribal forces Caesar mentions, the figure seems far too large. It is difficult to see how the Gauls could have supplied or commanded a force of this size, which depended on the mutual cooperation of a myriad of tribal leaders. It is true that they were intent on lifting a siege and this would have simplified the problem of command and also that there would be less need to manoeuvre the entire force in the open. Despite these considerations it still seems an unwieldy force. It is safe to say that it was probably the largest army that the Gauls ever fielded. The tribes that were involved included almost all of Caesar's conquests since 58 and indicate the vast scope of the revolt. The only area that sent no troops was Aquitania, where the burden of Roman control was lightest. The most important commands were given to Commius, the Aeduans Viridomarus and Eporedorix, and to the Arvernian Vercassivellaunus, a cousin of Vercingetorix. All of these men, except for Commius, were drawn from those tribes that had supplied the largest contingents. Commius, the sole representative of the Belgae, may have been chosen for his widespread influence with them. The plan was for it to attack the Romans from the outside while Vercingetorix launched a simultaneous attack on the enemy's interior lines.

Raising an army of such size must have taken a considerable time and that intensified the strain on Vercingetorix's food supplies. The thirty days that Vercingetorix had counted on for the arrival of the relieving force had expired and the situation in Alesia had grown increasingly desperate. The grain was now gone and the Gauls were cut off from any news about the fate of the relieving army. An assembly was called and various proposals were put forward. Caesar quotes only one speech at length, that of Critognatus, an Arvernian. He proposed that the able-bodied make use of the old or those of no use in warfare as food.[23] It serves Caesar's purpose to underline the lack of humanity of his opponents and to enhance the magnitude of his victory over men determined never to yield. It was decided to adopt the proposal only as a last resort; meanwhile all those unfit for war were compelled to leave Alesia. This primarily affected the Mandubii, whose town it was. They along with their women and children made their way to the Roman lines. There they begged the Romans to admit them offering themselves as slaves, but Caesar had instructed the guards not to allow them in. Caesar does not state his reasons for this action but it seems likely that he hoped the Gauls would be forced to take them back and thereby increase the pressure on their food supply.

While these events were taking place the relief army finally arrived and took up a position, probably to the south-west on the hill of Mussy-la-Fosse, about a mile from the Roman siege works. The hill offered a base from which to launch an attack across the Plain of Laumes, which appeared to be the easiest approach to the Roman fortifications as well as the most suitable ground for cavalry operations. The day after their arrival the Gauls sent all of their cavalry down into the plain. The infantry were posted on the higher ground at the base of the hill. The Gauls in Alesia had a clear view of the plain and the appearance of the relief army was greeted with rejoicing. They led out their forces and positioned their infantry in front of their camp. They then filled in the trench that lay closest to the Roman lines and prepared an attack.

To counter these preparations Caesar posted his entire force along his inner- and outer-lines, in assigned positions so that his men would know what their post was when the attack came. He then ordered his cavalry out to engage the Gauls. This time, in accordance with the practise of some of their German adversaries who had defeated them numerous times, the Gauls interspersed a few light-armed archers and skirmishers among their cavalry. The light-armed proved their worth. They wounded a number of the Roman cavalry who then withdrew from the battle. This increased the numerical superiority that the Gauls enjoyed. Caesar had perhaps as many as 6,000 cavalry to the rebels' 8,000. The heights around the plain provided ideal viewpoints for both sides as they watched the course of the battle and cheered their own men on. The fighting went on from noon until the approach of darkness without a decisive victory by either side. Then Caesar's Germans massed their cavalry and delivered a decisive charge which routed the enemy. The retreat of the Gallic cavalry exposed their light-armed, who were ridden down. With their morale severely damaged Vercingetorix and his men abandoned their advanced positions and marched back to Alesia. The main result of the battle was to make an assault across the plain impossible. The Gauls would have to carry tools and siege equipment and would be especially vulnerable to a cavalry attack if they advanced in broad daylight.

The day after the cavalry battle the Gauls decided to launch a night attack on the defences in the plain. During the day they prepared ladders, bundles of branches to fill up the ditches, and poles with hooks attached to their ends to pull down the Roman rampart. When the darkness was complete they advanced over the plain and began their attack. As they approached the Roman fortifications they launched a hail of missiles to try to drive the defenders from the ramparts. The Romans took up their positions under the command of Gaius Trebonius and the young Mark Antony. The legionaries replied with a missile barrage of their own, augmented by artillery, and reserves were brought up. As the Gauls advanced they entered the zone of pits and traps. Many were impaled on the goads and others who fell into the unseen pits were skewered by stakes. Nonetheless, the Gallic missiles took their toll of the defenders and there were heavy casualties on both sides. Despite this the defences held. As dawn approached the Gauls became afraid of an attack on their exposed flank from the Roman camp on a nearby hill and retreated to their camp. Somehow, word of the planned attack had reached Alesia and Vercingetorix once again prepared a simultaneous assault on the Roman lines from the other direction. But his weakened force took too long to complete its preparations. They filled in the first line of trenches but before they could reach the circumvallation wall they learned that the attack had been called off. Once again the Gauls had failed to successfully coordinate their attacks. The attack failed in part because of the obstacles and traps the Romans had constructed. Their effectiveness was increased by the assault being launched at night, which multiplied the difficulties the attackers encountered. Defeat in the cavalry battle had made launching a daytime assault too risky so that the infantry attack had to be broken off at first light. They had also failed to sufficiently reconnoitre the ground in advance. An omission they would soon remedy.

The failure of the two attacks convinced the Gauls that a direct assault on the Roman lines from the plain was impossible. They held a meeting to discuss further plans. They summoned locals who knew the area well and had reconnoitred the Roman defences. These men revealed a weakness in the Roman fortifications. There was a hill north of Alesia that the Romans had been unable to include within their defensive ring because of the difficulty of fortifying it. Modern scholarly opinion is divided on the identification of the hill. It is usually taken to be Mont Réa but some scholars have suggested Mont Bussy.[24] Both are too large to be easily included in the Roman defences. The Roman camp, on whichever hill it was, was positioned on the slope below the crest so it could be attacked from above. The camp's two legions were under the command of the legates Gaius Caninius Reginus and Gaius Antistius. After carrying out a reconnaissance of the position the Gallic commanders assembled a picked force of 60,000 for the attack. Unlike the previous night attack, it was decided to assault the camp and its fortifications at midday as the ground was too broken for cavalry.

The attack was to be led by the Arvernian Vercassivellaunus, one of the four chief commanders. He led out his troops at night, marching to the north of the hill to escape detection. He completed the march around daybreak and rested his men behind the hill out of sight of the Romans. As the time for the attack drew near he led his men out and began to assault the fort on the lower slopes of the hill. At the same time the Gallic cavalry rode up to the Roman defences in the plain and the rest of the infantry marched out in front of their camp. Both of these manoeuvres were designed to distract the Romans from the impending attack on the hill. When he saw that the attack was in progress Vercingetorix once again brought his men out to storm the Roman circumvallation. This was the most dangerous attack so far. There was fighting all along the Roman fortifications, which made it difficult for reinforcements to be sent to where the attack seemed to pose the greatest danger.

Caesar took control of these reserves. However, the crucial struggle was focused on the camp on the hill. If the Gauls broke through here they could end the siege. But if the Romans held on it was likely that the relief army's morale would crack and it would then disintegrate. The Gauls had a decided advantage as they were attacking from uphill. Some hurled a continuous stream of missiles at the defenders while others formed a tortoise and advanced on the walls, and still others brought up earth to cover over and neutralize the outer defences. These traps and pits were similar to the ones that had taken a heavy toll in the night attack. The assault continued unabated as the Gauls rotated in fresh troops. The Romans, hard-pressed and without reinforcements, were beginning to exhaust their supply of missiles and heavy casualties were significantly reducing the number of defenders.

Realizing the seriousness of the situation Caesar sent Labienus and six cohorts (about 2,500 men) to the aid of the defenders. He instructed Labienus to sustain the defence as long as possible, but if he were forced back he should mass his troops and launch a counterattack.

The Gauls' attack in the plain was far less successful. It is difficult to know whether it was ever a serious assault rather than a diversion. The Gauls had already experienced the strength of the Roman defences at this point and although Caesar clearly believes this was a serious attack a diversion seems more likely. The attack from the men in Alesia on the Roman defences on level ground met with no success so they shifted their assault to a higher point. As they did so they were met with a hail of missiles from the defenders on the rampart's towers, but they regrouped and filled in the ditches and began to tear down the wall and its parapet with hooks. Caesar sent Decimus Brutus with some cohorts to shore up the defences there, but it was clearly not enough to halt the attack, so he soon committed more cohorts under the command of Gaius Fabius. Even this proved insufficient and Caesar personally brought up fresh troops, they finally turned the tide and the Gauls were driven back. He now turned his attention to the fighting at Labienus's position, collecting four cohorts from the nearest fort and ordering a unit of cavalry to follow, as well as sending another unit to ride around the outer wall of the fortifications to take the enemy in the rear. Labienus saw that the defences would not hold and had collected eleven cohorts to launch a counterattack. In all Labienus now had an impressive force consisting of the two legions stationed at the camp and seventeen cohorts, in all about 15,000 men. Caesar's description of the struggle from this point emphasizes the effect of his appearance on the course of the battle. His scarlet commander's cloak was immediately visible to the Gauls on the hill as well as his own men and his appearance spurred a final effort on both sides. Given the intense bond of loyalty that Caesar had developed with his own troops and the hatred the Gauls must have felt for him, there is no reason to doubt that his appearance had a profound effect on both sides. The battle was joined with renewed ferocity but it seems to have been the appearance of the cavalry in the Gauls' rear that finally broke up the attack. The Gauls fled and were pursued by the cavalry. The leader of the Gallic attack, Vercassivellaunus, was captured and other commanders were killed. Enemy losses were heavy as they fled back to the safety of their camp. The fate of Alesia had been decided. Its garrison, weakened by hunger and realizing that all their hopes had been dashed, retreated into the town while the relief army, equally disheartened, disbanded and fled. The Romans were too exhausted to pursue immediately but at midnight Caesar sent cavalry in pursuit. They caught up with the Gallic rearguard and inflicted additional casualties.

The situation inside the town was desperate and there was no longer any other prospect but that of slow starvation. The day after the climactic battle Vercingetorix called a meeting of tribal leaders and offered to surrender himself to Caesar or to be executed by his own followers in an attempt to placate the Romans. There were no other choices. The leaders sent a delegation to Caesar to discuss the terms of surrender. He ordered them to hand over their weapons and to bring the leaders of the revolt to him. Vercingetorix was handed over along with the weapons Caesar had demanded. Caesar's account of the surrender of the Gallic leader is as matter of fact as the rest of his narrative of the war. Vercingetorix was imprisoned at Rome until Caesar celebrated his triumph in 46, when he was finally executed. The execution had been delayed by the civil war. A highly romanticized version of Vercingetorix's surrender is preserved in an account written a century-and-a-half later in Plutarch's *Life of Caesar*. It is worth quoting in full:

> Vercingetorix the leader of the revolt putting on his most beautiful armour and decorating his horse rode out through the gates and then in a circle around Caesar who was seated on a tribunal. He dismounted from his horse and threw down his armour and sat himself at Caesar's feet not moving until he was handed over to those who would guard him until Caesar's triumph.[25]

Dio has an equally elaborate account of the surrender based on the fact that Vercingetorix hoped his prior relationship with Caesar would win him pardon. Both are rhetorical embellishments of what really happened. But it was an incident worthy of elaboration.[26]

Although the revolt was not over any hope of success had vanished. Vercingetorix was a remarkable man. He had achieved something that no earlier leader of the Gallic resistance had achieved. He had created and led a coalition of tribes that spanned almost all of the lands that Caesar had conquered. He had done so by force of personality alone. There were no existing institutions for him to use and only a vague sense of cultural similarity bound these various peoples. He had devised the only possible strategy that had a chance of success. He realized that the Gauls could not face the Romans in battle. This was certainly true of Gallic infantry but it was equally true of their cavalry, the Gauls' most effective arm. In the final instance it was the superiority of Caesar's auxiliary cavalry that defeated Vercingetorix, much of it composed of Gauls who bet their future on Rome's success. An indirect strategy of striking at the Romans' supply lines was the only viable option to defeat them. But Vercingetorix's demand for the Gauls to pursue a scorched earth proved impossible to implement. The fate of Avaricum provided ample evidence that he was right to ask the Gauls to abandon their towns and to strip their countryside of supplies, but it is not clear how practical such tactics would have been or what would have been its effect on the civilian population. It was probably impossible to continue with such a strategy in the long term given its heavy cost.

With the growth of nationalism in France and in other European countries in the nineteenth century, Vercingetorix became a national hero who epitomized the French will to resist external aggression, especially relevant after France's defeat by Prussia and its loss of Alsace and Lorraine in the war of 1870/1871. He surfaced again during the German occupation of the Second World War. The best known representations of him are the statue at Alise-St.-Remy, erected at the initiative of Napoleon III in 1865, and one at Clermont-Ferrand near Gergovia, completed in 1903 by Bartholdi, the sculptor of the Statue of Liberty.[27]

Caesar adopted a different policy with respect to the captured leaders of the Aedui and Arverni. The importance of these tribes suggested a more lenient approach. Vengeance was less important than reconciling them, so he had the option of detaining them, hoping to use them as bargaining chips or of releasing them unconditionally and thereby hoping to create potential allies bound to him by the favours. In a society as heavily dependent on patron–client relations as contemporary Gallic society was, this could be an effective political tactic. The more dispensable captives were distributed as booty to his men to be sold as slaves. Caesar then moved into the lands of the Aedui and won them back to their earlier allegiance. He was met by Arvernian envoys and they too surrendered unconditionally. He demanded a large number of hostages as a guarantee of good faith. Perhaps equally important in securing their loyalty was the return of 20,000 prisoners captured at Alesia to both of these tribes.

The legions were then sent to winter quarters (52/51). Labienus was posted with two legions in the lands of the Sequani with the legate Marcus Sempronius Rufus assigned to him. Another two legions were to winter among the friendly Remi under the command of the legates Gaius Fabius and Lucius Minucius Basilus, to protect them from the Bellovaci who had not yet been pacified. Gaius Antistius Reginus with one legion was sent to the Ambivareti who were clients of the Aedui and whose lands were probably adjacent to theirs and to those of the Bituriges. Titus Sextius was quartered among the Bituriges with a single legion while Gaius Caninius, also with a single legion, was to winter among the Ruteni, clients of the Arverni who bordered the Roman province. Cicero's brother Quintus and Publius Sulpicius were stationed at Cabillonum and Matisco respectively, both in Aeduan territory near the Saône to oversee the army's grain supply, each with a single legion. The last two postings once again point up the importance of the Aedui to the Roman war effort. Caesar prepared to winter at the Aeduan capital Bibracte with a single legion. The fact that he did not winter in Cisalpine Gaul, although the threat to his political position at Rome was growing more serious, is evidence that despite the defeat of Vercingetorix Roman control in Transalpine Gaul still faced significant dangers, despite the twenty-days thanksgiving he had been voted by the Senate on the news of his victory over Vercingetorix.

Chapter Ten

51: Caesar's Final Campaigns

Caesar's own narrative ends with the entry of the legions into winter quarters. This seems to imply that he meant to continue his narrative into the following year but the political chaos at Rome and then the civil war intervened and his narrative was never finished. The book covering his last campaign in Gaul is the work of Aulus Hirtius, one of Caesar's legates, who completed the work at the request of Caesar's close friend Balbus. Hirtius's narrative is our best source for the events of this year but does not have the scope or quality of the work of his former commander. This is most clearly visible in his assertion that the Gauls had an overall war plan at the beginning of 51. He claims that the Gallic tribes had decided that a strategy based on confronting the Romans with a single coalition army had failed and that they now adopted an approach in which the Roman army would be faced with too many simultaneous rebellions to respond to all of them. On the face of it this seems highly unlikely. It would demand a level of consultation and planning among the various tribes that seems impossible. It is much more likely that internal political calculations as well as a continuing underestimation of the threat posed by Caesar's army determined the war-making policy of the individual tribes.

Leaving his quaestor Mark Antony in charge at Bibracte, Caesar on the last day of 52 moved against the Bituriges who had already suffered heavily at Avaricum. He was accompanied by a guard of cavalry and made his way to the Thirteenth Legion under Titus Sextius, which was too small a force to keep the Bituriges under control, and combined it with the Eleventh under Reginus stationed nearby. After leaving two cohorts behind to guard the baggage Caesar advanced with his customary speed and appeared before the Bituriges were aware of his arrival. He sent his cavalry on a wide sweep, capturing many of the Bituriges who, unaware of his coming, were peacefully working in their fields. Those who were warned in time made their escape to neighbouring peoples but Caesar pursued them relentlessly. He cowed the neighbouring tribes, who abandoned their resistance and so deprived the fugitives of any hope of sanctuary. The Bituriges, unable to oppose Caesar, quickly surrendered. As he had in the case of the Arverni and Aedui Caesar treated them leniently. Once the campaign was over Caesar led his men back to their winter quarters after promising a bonus for their service and returned to Bibracte. He had only been there for eighteen days when a delegation from the Bituriges arrived to complain of an attack by the Carnutes. The attack may have been set in motion by Caesar's own expedition against them: the tribe, which was seriously weakened by his attack, would have been an attractive target for raiding. Caesar responded immediately. A campaign against the Carnutes would make clear the benefits of being a dependent of Rome and at the same time strike at an important centre of resistance in central Gaul. He took the Sixth and Fourteenth Legions, who were stationed near the Saône on logistical duties, and set out to punish the Carnutes.

The Carnutes were already weakened after having suffered severely during the rebellion. The fate of Cenabum and other towns that had fallen to Caesar had persuaded them to abandon a number of their own and seek safety in temporary shelters scattered over the countryside, even though it was winter. Instead of simply letting his soldiers loose to plunder and burn their lands as he had done with the Bituriges, to spare his men constant exposure to the harsh weather Caesar chose Cenabum as his base and sent out cavalry and auxiliary units to ravage the countryside. These raids were extremely effective and the soldiers returned to Cenabum loaded down with booty. The effects of the weather and the plundering expeditions proved too much for the Carnutes who fled to the neighbouring peoples after suffering greatly.

After these campaigns Caesar considered that there was little threat of any large-scale resistance except among the Belgae. The Bellovaci and their neighbours were planning an attack on the Suessiones, a client of the Remi who lived near modern Soissons. It was less the fate of the Suessiones that concerned him than that of their patrons the Remi. They had been consistently loyal to the Romans even during the rebellion of the year before and had been an important source of supplies for the army. In addition to practical considerations it was absolutely essential that he be seen to offer effective protection to those tribes that supported him. Leaving two legions at Cenabum to keep watch on the Carnutes under Trebonius, he assembled a force of four legions to confront the Bellovaci.

Once he arrived in their territory he sent out cavalry to reconnoitre and to collect prisoners to question about the Bellovaci's plans. They revealed that most of the tribe had fled except for a few scouts who were captured and brought back to camp. From them Caesar learned that the Bellovaci had assembled a coalition of tribes to oppose him including the Ambiani, the Aulerci, the Caletes, the Veliocasses and the Atrebates. The coalition army had chosen to camp in a naturally strong location on high ground covered with trees and surrounded by a marsh. Their heavy baggage had been hidden out of sight deep in the forests. The precise location is unknown but it was probably in the forest of Compiègne near the town of the same name close to the confluence of the Rivers Aisne and Oise.[1] The Belgae had several leaders but the most important were Correus of the Bellovaci who had earlier conducted successful guerrilla operations against the Romans, and Commius who had served Caesar well in Britain and had been made king of the Atrebates by him but who had joined the revolt and had been one of its major commanders. Commius had sought support from nearby German groups and brought back about 500 cavalry. The Bellovaci and their allies had developed a dual strategy depending on the number of troops Caesar brought against them. If he came with a force no larger than three legions (about 15,000 men) they would face him in battle, but if he had a larger army they would stay in their easily defended position and try to cut off his supplies as Vercingetorix had planned to do. The scarcity of grain and forage in winter would probably have made this an easier task than it had been in the summer of the previous year. Although Caesar does not specify the size of the enemy force, given their plans that might have been perhaps 30,000 men.

The strength of the confederates' position prompted Caesar to devise a plan to draw them out. If they would engage a force of three legions he would try to persuade them that that was the total of his forces. He placed his three most effective legions, the Seventh, Eighth and Ninth, at the head of the column preceding the baggage, while he positioned the Eleventh at the rear to give the enemy the impression that he only had three legions with him. Perhaps he remembered the attack launched by many of these tribes on his column nearly six years before. His marching formation could be easily reformed to repel an attack or deploy for battle. The Belgae at the approach of the legions, which seemed to be ready for battle, drew up in front of their camp but did not move down from higher ground. They did not engage nor did Caesar, who was surprised at the size of the Gallic force. His plan had failed. He pitched camp facing the enemy with a deep, narrow valley in between. His camp was heavily fortified, with a 12 feet (3.6m) rampart surmounted by a parapet and fronted by a double ditch 15 feet (4.5m) wide with perpendicular sides. These were far more impressive fortifications than the normal marching Roman camp in the field. In addition, towers were constructed on the ramparts with gangways running between them so that the troops would be able to throw missiles at the enemy from two different levels. These defences could be held by a comparatively small garrison, a necessity at this time of year since a number of soldiers were needed for foraging.

Both sides were active and there were often skirmishes between Roman auxiliaries and the Belgae. Nonetheless the Gallic strategy of attacking the foragers was effective. The scarcity of supplies meant that Roman foraging parties were widely spread and that left them vulnerable to attack. The only obvious solution for Caesar was a direct attack on the Gallic camp but the Gauls kept to their camp and the natural strength of the site meant that if he did attack the camp directly he might not succeed and suffer heavy losses. Clearly this was a much more difficult campaign than the relatively easy victories over the Bituriges and Carnutes. He summoned three more legions to join him as quickly as possible. In addition, to defend against the raids on his foraging parties he ordered the Remi, Lingones and other Gallic states to supply additional cavalry. The Belgae set up an ambush using one of the oldest of all tactical tricks. They lured the cavalry of the Remi into the trap by placing a few horsemen where the Remi would easily see them and when the Remi attacked these men they fled back to the much larger cavalry force posted in ambush. The Remi were encircled and sustained heavy casualties.

The attacks and the skirmishing continued until the Bellovaci learned of the approach of the additional legions. The siege of Alesia was still fresh in their minds. They began organizing an evacuation of their camp. The heavy baggage and non-combatants were to form the head of their column, to be followed by their troops. The column was originally scheduled to depart during the night but the need to organize the wagons delayed the column's departure until dawn, when their preparations were now visible to the Romans. To protect the rear of the column they formed up their infantry in front of their camp facing the Romans. Anxious to stop the enemy's withdrawal Caesar reconnoitred the marsh and discover a ridge that almost stretched across it to the enemy camp. Only a narrow depression separated it from the enemy's camp. It is not clear why the ridge had not been found earlier. It may be that the enemy had stationed troops there that hid it from the Romans. Caesar had boards laid over the marsh and quickly crossed it and moved up to the plateau at the top of the ridge. There he drew up the legions in battle formation and set up artillery, as the enemy was still in range.

The Gauls, confident in the natural strength of their position, were ready to give battle. Caesar was equally aware of it so instead of attacking he drew up a screen of twenty cohorts (two legions) and began to build a camp. Once this was completed he posted the cohorts and cavalry with their horses at the ready. Caesar's new camp created a serious problem for the Bellovaci. They had had to halt their withdrawal as they were afraid that if they began withdrawing the Romans would attack them as they did so. They hit upon a plan to disguise their withdrawal. They collected bundles of straw and piles of twigs and placed them in front of their camp facing the Romans. When they were ready to move they set them alight. Their movements were hidden by the fire and smoke. They withdrew as quickly as they could. The fire and smoke also held the Romans back. Their cavalry was uncertain about what was waiting for them on the other side of the blaze, fearing a possible ambush, and the smoke so obscured their vision that they could not move forward. The Gauls were able to withdraw ten miles in safety and pitched another camp in a second naturally strong position. Despite Caesar's claim that they retreated in disorder it is clear that they had executed a well thought out and successful plan. Once in place at their new position they renewed their attacks on Roman foraging parties.

Once again Caesar's intelligence gathering served him well. He learned that one of their leaders, Correus, had assembled a force 6,000 infantry and 1,000 cavalry to set an ambush near an area rich in grain and forage. Caesar hurried to the spot, sending his cavalry ahead with light-armed infantry dispersed among them, and then cautiously following with the legions. The cavalry and light-armed would screen his approach and would be taken by the enemy for a normal foraging party. The place that the Gauls had chosen for an ambush was an isolated valley that extended no more than a mile in any direction and was ringed by a river and forests. The Roman cavalry advanced into it and the Gauls sprung their trap. With the knowledge that the legions were coming up in support the cavalry fought well and for a long time both sides were evenly matched. Then the pendulum began to swing in the Romans' favour as both sides became aware of the legions' approach. Their arrival was decisive. The Bellovaci turned and fled, but the woods and river created a death trap. They prevented easy escape and more than half their force was lost during the flight, including Correus. After such a heavy defeat Caesar feared that the Gauls would once again retreat. Knowing that their camp lay only 7 miles (11.6km) away on the other side of the Oise he brought his troops across it and hurried to confront them.

The defeat proved too much for the Bellovaci, who opened negotiations for surrender. They argued that the loss of so many men had been punishment enough for them and they blamed the revolt on Correus, who was now conveniently dead. Caesar recognized the falsity of their second argument but decided that clemency was preferable to continued fighting. The Gauls persuaded the other rebel states to join in the surrender and spare Caesar the trouble of further campaigning. Commius had escaped and remained irreconcilable. Before the rebellion of the previous year he had been agitating among various tribes to restart the revolt. Labienus had discovered this and sent a unit of soldiers to assassinate him. The attempt failed but it ended any possibility of reconciliation. Later in 51, as winter approached, Commius and his men had fought a skirmish with Roman cavalry that was indecisive. But he had not given up hope of inciting his fellow Atrebates to rise in rebellion. Meanwhile, he used his cavalry to launch a number of raids on Roman supply convoys. Antony, the legate stationed in the area, dispatched a cavalry unit in pursuit and finally, after a number of skirmishes, Commius was defeated, although at some cost. Seeing no hope of success he entered into negotiations with the Romans. He handed over hostages and was ordered to remain where he was and follow orders in the future. Commius asked one thing in return: that he might never again have to look on another Roman, and Antony granted him his wish.

Major opposition was now crushed but many of the Gauls were still not reconciled to the new dispensation. To deal with the continuing resistance Caesar dispatched Fabius with twenty-five cohorts to support the two under-strength legions under the command of Rebilus in the land of the Pictones south of the Loire, in what later formed part of the province of Aquitania. The Fifteenth Legion, which had been with Labienus in winter quarters, was sent to Cisalpine Gaul to guard against attacks on the citizen colonies. Caesar feared a repeat of an attack launched in the previous summer against the settlement of Tergeste in Illyria (modern Trieste) and he remembered the attempt in 52 to invade the province.

Caesar now turned his attention to Ambiorix and the Eburones. Ambiorix had been one of his most consistent and unyielding opponents. He had been behind the destruction of Cotta and Sabinus in 54 and had sought to forge an alliance of Belgic tribes, including the Treveri, to oppose the Romans. A number of attempts to capture him had all ended in failure. This would seem to indicate that he could draw on substantial support from his own people. Unable to capture him, Caesar determined on a strategy that would make the price of supporting him too costly. He sent out columns consisting of legionaries and cavalry to ravage the lands of the tribe and to kill or capture as many of the Eburones as possible. Labienus was sent with two legions against the Treveri, who had as usual been unwilling to meet Roman demands and had operated with Ambiorix in 54. Labienus defeated the Treveri and their German allies in a cavalry battle. Despite the devastation inflicted on the Eburones and the defeat of the Treveri Ambiorix was never taken prisoner.

The subjugation of Aquitania in 57 by Crassus had been incomplete and events there were affected by the rebellion in central and the northern Gaul.[2] A large rebel force had gathered in the land of the Pictones and part of it under a leader of the Andes, Dumnacus, was laying siege to the town of Lemonum (Poitiers), held by the pro-Roman Duratius. Learning of the siege, Rebilus set out to bring help. Nearing the town and reluctant to face the enemy with a weak force he camped in a secure location. When Dumnacus learned of his arrival he broke off the siege and turned to attack the Romans. His assault ended in failure and resulted in heavy casualties; he abandoned the attack and turned back to renew his siege of the town.

While these events were taking place another legate, Fabius, had been in action nearby and had received the submission of a number of tribes. Rebilus informed Fabius of the attack on Lemonum and Fabius set out to lift the siege. As he approached, Dumnacus and his army withdrew over the Loire. Fabius, informed by locals about the route of Dumnacus's retreat, decided to follow the rebels. Reaching a bridge over the Loire they had used he crossed and sent out his cavalry in pursuit. They caught up with the enemy column while it was still in marching formation and inflicted a severe defeat on it, but despite the losses the Andes continued their withdrawal. The next night Fabius sent his cavalry on ahead to slow the progress of the column. They met stiff resistance as the Andes' cavalry knew that their infantry was coming up in support. The Romans began to also attack the infantry who had formed a battle line. This was not sound tactics as cavalry usually could not successfully break infantry in formation. Its main effect was to fix the enemy column, which was exactly what Fabius had intended. The battle was not going well for the Roman cavalry when the legions came into view. The Gauls had been unaware of their presence and their sudden appearance created a panic among them. Their formation dissolved and many were killed during the pursuit: 12,000 died and their baggage train fell into Roman hands.

Dumnacus survived the defeat and remained at large. There was still the possibility that he could cause further trouble among the tribes that had joined the rebellion but had not been defeated. Fabius moved quickly and the opposition collapsed. Even the Carnutes, who had caused the Roman so much trouble and had never yet surrendered, finally did so. Dumnacus had now become a liability to the Gauls and had to seek safety in flight.

Other problems remained. A Senonian chief named Drappes had mustered a small army of 2,000 survivors from Fabius's campaign and was moving on the province. He had already launched successful attacks on Roman supply convoys. He had been joined by Lucterius the Cadurcan, who had tried to launch a similar attack in 52 but had failed. Rebilus set out in pursuit with his two legions, which were more than sufficient to deal with the small enemy force. The arrival of Rebilus put an end to any hope of invading the province and the two Gallic chieftains halted in the territory of the Cadurci and seized control of the town of Uxellodunum in the modern Dordogne, its identification being uncertain.

Rebilus pursued them there but the capture of the town presented serious difficulties. It was perched on a sheer rock cliff with limited access. Storming it was impossible so that the only practical alternative was to starve it out. Rebilus, dividing his cohorts into three groups, constructed a camp for each of them and then as quickly as he could he began construction of a circumvallation linking the camps and enclosing the town. The sight of the construction of the siege wall stirred memories of Alesia and the other Gallic towns that the Romans had taken among the troops and townspeople. A plan was needed to maintain the town's grain supply. Two thousand troops remained to defend the town while light-armed infantry was sent out under the command of Drapes and Lucterius to bring in grain while this was still possible. Within a few days a large amount of grain had been collected and the Gauls set up camp about ten miles from the town. Meanwhile, they launched night attacks on various forts that brought the construction of the siege wall to a halt, as Rebilus had too few soldiers to adequately man it and defend against the attacks.

Drappes and Lucterius planned to send small grain convoys to the town in order to avoid detection. They divided their responsibilities between them; Drappes stayed to guard the camp while Lucterius took charge of conveying the grain. Lucterius set out at night to avoid detection but the noise of the wagons alerted the Romans, who sent out scouts who returned and informed Rebilus of what the enemy was doing. Cohorts were dispatched from the nearest forts at dawn and attacked the convoy. The unexpected assault threw the Gauls in the convoy into a panic and they fled back to the guard posts that Lucterius had established along the route. The Romans made short work of these and few of the enemy survived. Lucterius managed to escape with a few men but did not return to camp. This was a stroke of luck for Rebilus, as the Gauls in the camp were unaware of the fate of Lucterius and the convoy. He sent his cavalry ahead along with German infantry who advanced at full speed and followed up with one of his legions. He left the other to guard his own camp and the newly-constructed fortifications. The Germans and the rest of the cavalry launched a vigorous attack on the enemy camp and then the appearance of the legionaries completed the rout. The camp was taken and all of the Gauls were either killed or captured. Drappes was among the prisoners. No longer facing external threats, Rebilus now turned his full attention to the siege of the town.

While this was happening Caesar was making a progress among the rebellious tribes. He left Antony with fifteen cohorts among the Bellovaci to watch Belgica. At this point he received letters from Rebilus informing him of the fate of Lucterius and Drappes and the progress of the siege. He also informed Caesar that although the force in the town was small it was putting up a determined resistance.

Caesar now decided to put an end to all opposition. It was not the importance of Uxellodunum that mattered but the fact that in holding out against him it could serve as a potent symbol of continued Gallic resistance. His failure at Gergovia in 52 had helped ignite the great rebellion and he was determined that there should be no repetition of it. He decided to act immediately. He ordered his legate Calenus to follow him with two legions and raced ahead with all of his cavalry to Uxellodunum.

When Caesar arrived he found the town enclosed by the Roman siege works. The problem that confronted him was how to avoid a protracted siege that would set back other projects, especially as his political position at Rome was becoming more precarious and resistance elsewhere in Gaul had not yet been suppressed. Since the town was well-supplied with grain Caesar turned his attention to cutting off its water supply. A river ran around the base of the hill on which the town sat and served as its water supply. The obvious course was to divert the stream but the nature of the ground made that option impossible. The river also presented difficulties for the besieged. The way down to it was steep and exposed to missile attack. Archers and slingers and artillery were posted covering the easiest approaches to the river. It now became too dangerous to use.

There was another source of water, a spring beneath the town walls that was made use of now that access to the river was cut off. It flowed out at a point where there was an area of about 300 feet that the river did not enclose. Caesar now moved to deprive the Gauls of that water supply as well. Soldiers brought up moveable shelters to protect themselves and began to build an earthwork, although they were subject to constant attack during the construction. The Gauls' missiles often found their mark as they were thrown down from the town walls. The Romans also began digging mines towards the water channels that fed the spring and its source. Construction of the earthwork stopped when it had reached a height of 60 feet so that it now loomed over the spring. A ten-storey tower was mounted on it, as well as catapults to cover the spring. As it was now too dangerous for the townspeople to approach the spring they began to suffer from thirst.

Their only way to end their torment was to destroy the tower and ramp. They launched a fierce attack trying to set the tower on fire. They pressed the Romans hard and inflicted a number of casualties. To divert the attackers Caesar ordered his troops to climb the hill encircling the town and to pretend to mount a general attack on the walls. The ruse worked. The Gauls recalled their men to defend the walls and ended their attacks on the tower. The Roman mines had now reached the spring's sources and its flow was diverted. Resistance was now hopeless and the town surrendered. This time Caesar's clemency was hardly in evidence: he decided on judicious use of terror to deter those still holding out. He ordered that the hands of all those who had fought were to be cut off.

All that now remained in central and northern Gaul were mopping up operations. These were successfully carried out. Labienus won a cavalry engagement with the Treveri and their German allies. He captured the leaders of the revolt and all resistance ended.

Caesar then turned his attention to Aquitania in the south-west where he had never campaigned. His appearance had the desired effect; all of the tribes sent delegations and turned over hostages. All open resistance was now at an end.

He turned south to the province and to Narbo its administrative centre. There he heard cases arising from the rebellion and distributed rewards to those who had supported Rome. Caesar once more claims that Gaul had now been pacified and this time he was correct. He sent his legions into winter quarters; four were posted to Belgica to watch for unrest, two were quartered among the Aedui, another two among the Turones who bordered the Carnutes, and the final two on the borders of the Arverni. After completing his business in the province Caesar moved north-east to join his legions in Belgica and wintered at Nemetocenna (modern Arras in the Pas de Calais). Although Gaul was finally at peace the Roman conquest was so recent and the area so large that further revolts remained a possibility. Caesar was especially concerned about this as the situation at Rome grew worse. He adopted a policy of reconciliation with the Gauls and made a special effort to win over the nobles and chiefs who controlled Gallic society with large cash payments.

At the end of winter 51/50 Caesar headed to Cisalpine Gaul to canvass for his quaestor Antony, who was standing for a priesthood. By the time he reached the province he heard that Antony had been elected at the end of September. This was good news as Cato and his enemies were intensifying their attacks. With the problem of Antony's candidacy resolved Caesar spent his time making a circuit of the communities there to garner support for his own candidacy for the consulship of 49. In addition, Cisalpina was the most prolific recruiting area in Italy. If it came to civil war it was crucial for Caesar to have its support. He then returned to Nemetocenna and conducted a purification of his army, signalling the end of campaigning in Gaul.

The conquest of Gaul north of the old province and extending from the Atlantic to the Rhine was due solely to Caesar. His motivations were those of any other Roman noble in his position: wealth and military glory. The need for both was particularly pressing when Caesar arrived in Gaul in 58. He had obtained his command in Cisalpine Gaul and Illyricum in the face of intense opposition and hatred. His finances were in terrible shape and his creditors barely allowed him out of Rome. Without adequate funds he could not compete politically; Cato and his friends would, if given the chance, politically isolate and destroy him. The triumvirate on whose support he relied was unstable. There was the intense jealousy between Pompey and Crassus that constantly threatened to tear it apart. Pompey, whom Caesar's enemies found the most acceptable of the three and who eventually moved into the camp of Cato, remained a constant worry for Caesar. Pompey was the most intractable of all of Caesar's problems. His conquests in the east and his other military successes had given him a status that even his political ineptitude did little to undermine. Caesar needed an arena in which to equal Pompey's achievements and Gaul provided it.

The addition of Transalpine Gaul to Caesar's province was merely an afterthought brought about by the fortuitous death of the man who was to have governed the province. It is likely that Caesar had hoped to launch a campaign in Illyricum but the events of 58 changed that. The movements of the Helvetii and the threat of Ariovistus drew Caesar north. In both instances it could be argued that he was protecting Roman interests. The Helvetii did pose a threat to the province and the Aedui as Roman allies had to be protected for the sake of Rome's prestige if nothing else. The stationing of the legions in the north during the winter of 58/57 was a clear indication that Caesar had adopted a policy of conquest that probably even this early included all of continental Gaul. The area was large enough to allow for extensive campaigning and conquest. Just as importantly, it was agriculturally rich and would offer the prospect of immense amounts of booty. Imperial expansion was a virtue, as it had always been for the Roman ruling class, and here was a vast field in which to exercise it. Political and personal rewards that came with it exerted a magnetic attraction.[3] This explains the two British expeditions of 55 and 54, which were hardly serious attempts to subjugate Britain but brought Caesar a twenty-day thanksgiving and increased his popularity at Rome. The bridge over the Rhine in 55 was a similar undertaking as well as his raids into Germany, which yielded little of practical value. The conquest of all of Gaul north and west of the old province was not a strategic necessity but the product of Caesar's personality, his needs and desires.

Caesar's success resulted from a combination of superior Roman equipment, technique and logistics, and Caesar's individual qualities as a general. Perhaps the most important ingredient was his ability to win and then keep his men's loyalties. A noticeable feature of *Gallic War* is the frequent praise for the common soldier and in particular of centurions, who are often mentioned by name and whose individual exploits receive extensive narration. Caesar maintained his bonds with them by a judicious use of favours and rewards. But it is clear both from his own work and that of other writers that his personal bravery and willingness to share the hardships of his men were crucial ingredients in maintaining their loyalty.[4]

His speed of movement was astonishing and time and again he arrived earlier than his opponents thought possible. It was a virtue that could sometimes get him in to trouble, as it did during his first expedition to Britain and as it was later to do in 46 when he landed in Africa with an inadequate force during the civil war.[5] In addition, Caesar had a marvellous ability to discern the enemy's weaknesses and to devise tactics that capitalized on it. During the rebellion of 52 he deceived Vercingetorix, whom he misled by sending troops ahead who successfully convinced the Gallic commander that the Romans had moved up river and so was able to cross the Allier River without opposition.[6]

At Uxellodunum he saw that the water supply was the key to taking the town and devised tactics that cut off access to it. He personally suffered only one serious defeat, at Gergovia. The first British expedition was a minor failure but his other reverses such as the fifteen cohorts lost with Cotta and Sabinus during the winter of 54 or Galba's failure in the Alps in 57 were not primarily his fault. He possessed a military machine far more effective than any Gallic army he faced and he used it with great daring and skill.

The conquest of Gaul was more than the product of military force. Crucial to Caesar's success was his ability to forge ties with the Gallic elite. He built up links to the leading men in each of the Gallic communities. In return for their support he conferred benefits upon them and solidified their position within their own tribes. Perhaps the most striking example was Diviciacus among the Aedui who not only supported Caesar but gave him valuable military intelligence. There were others as well such as the Nervian Vertico or the two leading men among the Remi, Iccius and Andecomborius. Caesar was not always successful in his choices. The most striking example is that of Commius, who Caesar made king of the Atrebates in 57 but who later joined the great rebellion in 52 and then, when it failed, fled to Britain. Other men he supported were either unpopular or murdered by their political enemies, such as Tasgetius of the Carnutes who had loyally supported Caesar who raised him to the kingship. His unpopularity among his fellow tribesmen, as well as political rivalry with other nobles, led to Tasgetius's assassination. There are other cases as well. But one of the key ingredients of Caesar's success was his ability to often pick the right Gallic notables and establish lasting ties with them that endured after Caesar left Gaul.

The cost of the campaigns in human life and in the devastation of large areas of Gaul was high. We have little information about Roman losses. There are only occasional references such as the 700 legionaries and forty-six centurions killed in the siege of Gergovia, or the fifteen cohorts or approximately 6,000 men lost with Cotta and Sabinus in 54. Eight years of campaigning, often under difficult conditions, must have taken their toll. The ancient sources do preserve figures for Gallic losses but they vary greatly and their value is uncertain. Plutarch claims that Caesar took 800 towns and conquered 300 tribes. He adds that Caesar faced 3,000,000 men in battle and killed 1,000,000 while taking the same number prisoner.[7] Other sources give 400,000 and approximately 200,000. Probably the latter figures are nearer the truth, although in no case do we know how these writers arrived at their figures, which all refer to combatants. The higher figures may reflect at least in order of magnitude the total of civilian and military casualties including those sold into slavery. The only precise figure we have is for the 53,000 Atuatuci sold into slavery, but such sales are frequently mentioned in *Gallic War* and the numbers must have been substantial. The devastation certainly led to starvation, which was fatal for many, the Carnutes being an obvious example. It is likely that the total of civilian casualties greatly outnumbered those killed in the fighting.

Before January 49 when the civil war began and Caesar moved to confront his enemies in Italy, he had already begun the work of turning Gaul into a province. He set a relatively-low level of tribute for the new province, which probably reflected the loss and destruction that his years of campaigning had caused.[8] Gaul was a relatively unimportant backwater in the four years that the civil war lasted. No major battles were fought there and there were no major actions, except for the siege of the city of Massilia (Marseille), which chose to side with Pompey and which Caesar besieged on his march to Spain in 49. After a courageous and ingenious defence it fell to Caesar's legate Trebonius and was leniently treated. The major battles of the civil war took place in Spain, Africa and the East. What is striking is the lack of any large-scale resistance after Caesar's departure.

Chapter Eleven

Epilogue: After Caesar

The situation in Gaul remained relatively quiet after Caesar's departure. The number of legions he left behind is uncertain and their locations are for the most part unknown. There was some unrest in the north-east between 46 and 44.[1] The Bellovaci once again created difficulties and the Germans were a standing problem. But there was no serious resistance to the imposition of Roman rule. Caesar had done his job well.

After Caesar's assassination in March of 44 a two-way political and military contest developed.[2] Among his supporters a struggle developed between Mark Antony and Caesar's heir the eighteen year old Gaius Octavius, who quickly began styling himself Caesar's son and stressing his ties to the assassinated dictator. This played a crucial element in his political fortunes and makes clear how strong the bonds between Caesar and his soldiers had become. Their opponents were led by Cicero and included many of Caesar's assassins. It was a faction motivated by Republican ideology that stressed a return to the political situation before Caesar's domination, and was also fuelled by personal interests. Initially, an attempt was made by these men to split Caesar's followers but it ended in failure. By November of 43 the pressure of this Republican faction had forced a reconciliation between Antony and Octavius, who now called himself Gaius Julius Caesar Octavianus after his formal adoption in August of 43. The two men were preparing to face a Republican army raised in the east by Brutus and Cassius. Joined by the far less important Marcus Aemilius Lepidus, the three men divided the Roman provinces in the west among themselves. The Gallic provinces were divided between Lepidus and Antony, with Lepidus receiving the old province in the south while Antony obtained the area conquered by Caesar plus Cisalpine Gaul. In October of 42 Antony and Octavian met the forces of Brutus and Cassius at Philippi in Macedonia and crushed them. Brutus and Cassius committed suicide. The opposition had been totally defeated and the new masters of the Roman world reapportioned the provinces. Octavian, who had emerged from the struggle in an immensely strengthened position, now received all of the western provinces excluding Africa, which went to Lepidus, who was now marginalized, while Antony was given the provinces east of the Adriatic.

In 39 Octavian's most important lieutenant Marcus Agrippa was sent to Gaul. There was unrest in Aquitania and in some areas in the north and north-east, which he pacified, and he also conducted a campaign in the south-west. He began to lay out a road system with its nodal point at Lyon to link Gaul together and facilitate troop movements towards the Rhine. The building continued for at least a decade, which implies that legions were stationed in Gaul but their location and number are uncertain. Agrippa returned two decades later in response to problems caused by German raiding and the changes necessitated by the final Roman conquest of Spain. Despite Agrippa's campaigns, German pressure on Gaul continued to be a serious problem.[3] In 16, the year after Agrippa departed the province, Marcus Lollius, perhaps the governor of the province of Belgica, was defeated in the course of a raid by German tribes from across the Rhine. The defeat was serious enough to require the presence of Octavian, now the Emperor Augustus after the defeat of Antony. He arrived in Gaul in the same year and remained there until 13. In response to these pressures in the north-east and the relative quiet in Gaul, the legions and their auxiliary units were moved from the interior to their final position on the Rhine frontier, which served both to protect Gaul and acted as a springboard for campaigns to expand Roman control into Germany, a goal that eventually proved to be beyond the empire's resources.

It was Augustus who fixed the definitive political boundaries of the Gallic provinces. Under Caesar, and in the period before the young Octavian became Augustus, Caesar's Gallic conquests were administered as a single province. Perhaps in 27 or a decade later Augustus definitively divided it into three provinces, Belgica forming the north-east, Aquitania the south-west with Lugdunensis comprising central Gaul. The old province along the Mediterranean was renamed Narbonensis. All four were governed by the emperor's legates who were directly responsible to him. However in 22 Narbonensis, as customarily happened when provinces were thoroughly pacified and without substantial military forces, was turned over to senatorial administration.[4] These administrative changes were accompanied by a census to apportion taxation and by further road building projects. In 12 Augustus's stepson Drusus took a further census, which resulted in some unrest. Perhaps in an attempt to counter additional unrest he established an altar at Condate across the Rhône from Lugdunum (Lyon), dedicated to the cult of Rome and the emperor. It was the first provincial centre to be established in the western provinces; probably in imitation of cult existing institutions in the eastern provinces. An assembly of leading men from Belgica, Aquitania and Lugdunensis met there annually. Its main functions were connected to the maintenance of the imperial cult and also to provide an arena for peaceful competition between Gallic aristocrats for imperial favour.[5]

This was also a period in which Roman influence on political and social life in Gaul dramatically increased. Before his departure Caesar had given certain quasi-citizen rights to thirty Gallic communities and awarded Roman citizenship to a number of Gauls who had supported him. Three colonies were founded north of the old province: one, Noviodunum (Noyon), at the confluence of the Loire and Allier; the second Lugdunum (Lyon); and the third Augusta Raurica (Augst). These colonies were oriented towards the north-east and the German threat. Over the next decade a number of colonies for veterans were established but the pace of Romanization was noticeably quicker in the south; there was a much more rapid adoption of Roman institutions and social forms there.[6] By the mid-first century AD senators appear with origins in southern Gaul. The process had proceeded so far that by the end of the first century Pliny the Elder could describe southern Gaul as more truly Italy than a province.[7]

The presence of Rome also led to changes in living patterns in the Three Gauls, probably influenced by the presence of Italian and Spanish settlers. Another impetus was supplied by Gauls who had served as cavalry in Roman auxiliary forces and then returned home. Their wealth and prestige soon eclipsed the traditional tribal leaders. In Narbonensis the old tribal capitals were replaced by Mediterranean-style urban areas. Vienne on the Isere, the capital of the Allobroges, was refounded as a colony by Caesar in 47 BC and adorned with a Roman style forum and public buildings. The same process occurred at Nemausus (Nîmes). Vasio (Vaison-la-Romaine), the capital of the Vocontii, was originally located – as were most Gallic towns – on a high rock, on the east bank of the River Ouvèze. It was moved to the west bank and rebuilt there by Agrippa in 20–19 BC. There were parallel developments in the north as well. Augustus compelled the Aedui to move from their capital at Bibracte to a new settlement at Augustodunum (Autun) some 15 miles away, and Gergovia was replaced by Augustonemetum (Clermont-Ferrand). In these as in other instances Roman town planning replaced Gallic.

There were few disturbances during the first three centuries of Roman rule in Gaul. The local elites seem to have quickly come to terms with their new masters. In AD 21, during the reign of Augustus's successor Tiberius (AD 14–37), a short-lived revolt broke out. Its leaders were two Gallic noblemen who were also enfranchised Roman citizens, Julius Sacovir an Aeduan, and Julius Florus of the Treveri, both of whom had served as auxiliaries in the Roman army. The main impetus for the revolt was the pressure of debt, which had also motivated revolts in Narbonensis a century before. The Roman army stationed on the Rhine frontier and its campaigns in Germany were mainly supported by Gallic tax payers and this imposed a heavy financial burden. The revolt seems to have excited widespread sympathy, but was concentrated among the Aedui and Treveri. It was easily suppressed by a combination of local garrison troops and the legions.[8]

It was not until AD 68 that Gaul once again experienced turmoil but it had less to do with local grievances than with developments at Rome. The actions of the Emperor Nero had alienated wide sections of the senatorial aristocracy. The revolt against him began in Gaul under the leadership of Gaius Julius Vindex, whose family originated in Aquitania and who was the governor of Lugdunensis in March of AD 68. Vindex had only local levies available so the revolt was easily suppressed by Lucius Verginius Rufus the governor of Upper Germany in May. However, the revolt proved fatal for Nero as it set in motion other revolts that finally ended in the emperor's suicide on 9 June of the same year. Nero's death destabilized the empire and for a year a series of military conflicts erupted that finally resulted in the establishment of a new dynasty at Rome, the Flavians. Despite the revolt's origin in wider imperial politics it had important repercussions in Gaul. The preoccupation of the Romans with civil war allowed disaffection to spread among Gallic nobles. Julius Classicus and Julius Tutor raised the Treveri and the Lingones. All Roman military camps from Mainz to the sea were destroyed and the rebels proclaimed a separate Gallic empire. After a year of hard fighting the rebellion was put down and as the general situation stabilized Gaul returned to its Roman allegiance.[9]

Gaul remained at peace until it descended, along with the rest of the empire, into the general chaos of the second-half of the third century. Between AD 260 and 274, Gaul and the German provinces broke away and established an independent empire whose institutions mirrored those of Rome. As unstable as the Roman Empire was itself at this juncture, it was ruled by three emperors during its short life. It was finally re-conquered by the Emperor Aurelian in AD 274. The causes of the turmoil in Gaul were the same as in the rest of the Roman world: a weakening of imperial institutions and a struggle of various local army units to dominate the empire.[10]

In the fifth century Roman control in Gaul finally began to disintegrate, leading to the permanent loss of the Gallic provinces. By the beginning of that century Roman frontiers in the west and north had begun to collapse. On the last day of AD 406 a marauding band of Germanic tribes crossed the Rhine into Gaul, ravaging and raiding as far as Spain. By AD 418 a group of Visigoths had established a kingdom in Aquitania and had begun a process that saw all of Gaul pass under the domination of the Germanic Franks and their king Clovis (AD 481–511).

Roman domination of part or all of Gaul spanned a period of over six centuries. Even with its passing the Romans left an institutional, linguistic and cultural legacy, especially in the form of Christianity, that was to have profound consequences for centuries after Rome was only a distant memory.

Appendix: The Development of the Roman Army of the First Century BC

The Roman legions that fought in Gaul during the last century BC were the products of a long and for the most part obscure evolution. Roman historical writing shows little interest in technical military details and when historians portray the army in action their accounts are full of anachronistic details that complicate any attempt to reconstruct a pattern of development. Nevertheless, the broad outlines of that evolution are reasonably secure.

Rome's earliest military force consisted of a tribal levy of 3,000 infantry and 300 cavalry. By the middle of the sixth century BC this had been replaced by a legion moulded on contemporary Greek armies and heavily influenced by Rome's neighbours. The legion of this period had a nominal strength of 6,000 citizens, probably divided into units of 100 commanded by the precursor of the later legionary centurions. It consisted of heavily-armed infantry serving at their own expense arranged in a tight rectangular formation, the phalanx. The men at its front usually were protected by heavy armour and a large shield. Their main offensive weapon was a heavy thrusting spear. This dense formation, when closed up for battle, allowed the men to protect one another. Phalanx tactics were simple: a massed charge that was intended to break the enemy formation and allow the light-armed infantry and cavalry who accompanied the legion to cut down enemy troops as they fled. Such a formation had severe limitations. Since it needed to maintain cohesion to deliver a decisive charge, broken ground or obstacles could cause severe difficulties. It was clumsy in responding to attacks on its flanks or rear, as any attempt to have the men face about tended to create disorder at the phalanx's front. Despite its limitations, the Roman phalanx was successful in asserting the city's dominance in much of Italy by the mid-fourth century BC.

Some time in the late-fourth century BC the legions underwent a series of major tactical changes. The reasons for them and their timing are not known for certain but seem to have been completed by the mid-third century BC. In place of the massed phalanx the legion was now divided into three lines, recruited according to age and personal wealth. The first two lines were twice the strength of the third, with 1,200 men in each of the first two and 600 in the third line. The first two lines formed the main fighting force of the legion, while the third, composed of older men, acted as a reserve. In addition, the legion had attached light-armed infantry and cavalry. It was divided into sixty centuries whose size varied in accordance with the size of the legion, but normally had sixty men in the first two lines and thirty in the third. These centuries were now administrative units: the tactical unit was the maniple, consisting of two centuries. Each of the three lines consisted of ten maniples. In parallel with these tactical changes came a major transformation of the legion's offensive weaponry. In place of the heavy thrusting spear the main offensive weapon was now a deadly and effective short sword, about 2 feet in length, which could be used either for cutting or thrusting. The legionary also carried two *pila* (singular *pilum*) or javelins that were discharged before coming to grips with the enemy and were designed to blunt the enemy's charge and disorder his ranks.

In effect, the maniples were miniature phalanxes that were able to operate independently of one another, and with the change in weaponry were able to deal with threats from any direction, as well as operate on broken or uneven ground. Time and again they demonstrated their superiority over the phalanx armies of the eastern Mediterranean.

When the legion was deployed for battle the maniples of each line were separated by a gap equal to the maniple's width, with the maniples of the line behind covering the gaps on the line in front. The first two lines normally advanced against the enemy in succession. If the first line failed to break the enemy formation it retired through the gaps in the second, which then moved forward to engage the enemy. The third line, still armed with the heavy thrusting spear, only went into action in emergencies. Each legion had light-armed troops and cavalry assigned to it.

The legion's cavalry, totaling 300 men, was drawn from the wealthier class of citizens. It was divided into ten units called *turmae*, consisting of twenty-eight troopers and two officers each. There was no specific overall commander of the cavalry force. Normally the commander of the army delegated this task to one of his subordinates.

The size of the legion increased over time. In the mid-second century BC a normal legion included 3,000 heavy armed legionaries and 1,200 light-armed troops, primarily armed with javelins and the legionary sword. In case of emergency the number of heavy armed infantry could be increased so that the legion contained 5,000 men in all. In the course of the second century BC legionary size increased with 5,000–6,000 as the norm. But this was only a paper strength and legions varied considerably in size due to casualties and other factors. At Pharsalus in 48 BC, the climactic battle of the civil war of 49–45 BC, Pompey's legions numbered about 4,800 men, while those of Caesar, who had suffered a considerable number of casualties and had not been reinforced, contained about 2,800 men. The numbers of legions in service also increased as Rome acquired provinces that required garrisons and was engaged in almost continuous warfare. It has been estimated that between 167 and 50 BC there were twelve to fourteen in service each year. Almost all freeborn Romans would experience some military service in the course of their lives. All men between the ages of seventeen and forty-six were liable for service in the field, excluding those whose property ratings fell below the minimum necessary. Over time the minimum was lowered until by the end of the second century BC it ceased to have any significance. The obligation to serve continued until a man reached sixty, but men over forty-six were only liable to service at home.

New legions were levied almost every year. They were not permanent units, so that when a new levy was carried out the legions were numbered from 'I' (1) on. It was not until the imperial period that legions became permanent establishments. Existing legions would be brought up to strength by a supplementary levy.

Until the beginning of the first century BC the legions went into battle accompanied by a force drawn from Rome's Italian allies. These allies had bilateral treaties with Rome specifying their military obligations, which included supplying both infantry and cavalry at their own expense. The infantry was organized in units called cohorts, which normally numbered 400–600 men. These cohorts could operate independently, performing garrison duties, as detached battle groups, or for any other task. In battle ten cohorts were deployed on each wing of the two legions of a consular army and so were known as *alae* or wings. In the battle line they were organized in maniples like their Roman counterparts and certainly by 300 BC were armed in the same way. The number of allied infantry serving with Roman armies varied over time but at times it amounted to twice the number of legionaries. The allied cavalry usually numbered two to three times the number of Roman cavalry and was normally stationed on the opposite wing to the Roman cavalry, although it was under Roman commanders. One of the most important factors in Rome's military success was the number of troops it could put into the field despite suffering what appear to be crippling losses, as was the case during the Second Punic War, when despite a number of serious defeats in 212 BC Rome could raise twenty-five legions and at least an equal number of allies.

Rome's armies were commanded by annual magistrates possessing *imperium* or the power of command. The most important were the two annually elected consuls. On campaign, until the first century BC a normal consular army consisted of two legions and their cavalry as well as allies. Their *imperium* was superior to any other magistrates. When two consuls were operating jointly they alternated command, daily sometimes with disastrous results when they differed on strategy and tactics. Praetors were one step below the consuls in rank but they also possessed *imperium*, although of a lesser grade, and so could command military forces. They operated either as subordinates of the consul or as commanders of independent armies of one legion and its complement of allies. As Rome's military needs grew a new class of commanders was created. These were the 'promagistrates', including proconsuls and propraetors. They were normally magistrates whose term of office was over but who were still needed to command military forces. Unlike the normal magistrates, whose command ended with their year of office, promagistrates could serve for extended periods of time, as Caesar did in Gaul. In rank they were subordinate to the consul if operating jointly with him.

Each legion also had six junior officers, called military tribunes, who were just beginning their political careers. They carried out any duties assigned to them by their commander, and on occasion could command in battle. From 200 BC their role gradually diminished. They were superceded by legates; men who had held at least the lower magistracies and had been admitted to the Senate. They could command in battle alongside the general in charge or lead independent forces. Caesar made extensive use of them in Gaul and his legates sometimes exercised independent command of as many as three legions. Many of these men later went on to further office as beneficiaries of Caesar's patronage.

An impassable social barrier separated the non-commissioned officers from these men. Of these the most important were the centurions, who are frequently named and their exploits praised in *Gallic War*. Often they were soldiers who had come up through the ranks and had become centurions after years of hard service. Each centurion commanded a century and the sixty centurions of the legion occupied a hierarchy depending on the particular century they commanded. In battle the senior centurion in the maniple commanded the entire maniple, with his fellow centurion acting as his subordinate and replacing him if he were killed or wounded. Despite the centurion's social inferiority to the officers who ranked above him, he was probably the single most important officer on the field once battle had begun and his maniple was engaged. The Romans recognized this and senior centurions received many times the pay and booty awarded to a common soldier. A senior centurion could end his service as a very wealthy man. There were other non-commissioned officers in the maniple but the only other important position was that of *signifier*, the man who carried the maniple's standard. If the maniple's centurions were killed in battle he replaced them as commander of the unit.

The end of the second and the beginning of the first centuries were marked by a number of important developments. The heavy thrusting spear of the third line disappeared so that all of the legionaries now carried the *pilum* and the short sword. This change may be linked to a change of tactical organization on the battle field. The maniple was replaced by the cohort as the main tactical unit. Like its namesake the allied cohort, it was composed of 400–600 men consisting of a maniple from each of the three lines. The division into lines was retained but those lines were formed from the ten cohorts of the legion. Although circumstances dictated various arrangements, the most frequent was to have four cohorts each in the first and second line and two as a reserve in the third. The cohort had existed in the Roman army since at least the end of the third century BC. Its use is frequently attested in the west, especially in the wars against the Spanish tribes. In effect it was a miniature legion that could operate independently and was large enough to defend itself if attacked. The change simplified the chain of command, facilitated the movement of troops during battle and allowed the general to concentrate more powerful forces at crucial points in the battle. It also simplified the ordering of the battle line because cohorts drawn from different legions could be deployed together. Strangely, the sources do not specify who commanded the cohort but it is likely that it was the chief centurion of the most senior maniple.

The introduction of the cohort as the main tactical unit of the legion is probably tied to one of the most important political developments of the early first century, the extension of Roman citizenship to all of Italy south of the River Po. The change was the result of a bloody two year war from 90–88. The need to integrate their former Italian allies, who were already organized in cohorts, into the legion must have facilitated the transition to the cohort. The frequent success of the allied forces in the course of the war may have persuaded Roman commanders of the advantages of the cohort in combat.

Chronologically linked to the appearance of the cohort is the disappearance of Roman cavalry and light-armed troops. The sources are silent on these developments as on so much of Roman military history. It is likely that the disappearance of the light-armed is linked to the change in the minimum property rating required for service in the legions. By this period it was so low that in effect it no longer existed. Service as a legionary carried more prestige and higher monetary rewards than service as a light-armed soldier. Also, the need for additional legions to garrison the new provinces acquired in this period must have made the state more willing to enroll men in the legions who would previously have served as light-armed troops.

Roman and Italian cavalry also disappear. Why young upper-class Romans ceased to serve as cavalry is not clear, but it may be related to a number of new social developments. Men who ranked as knights had originally formed Rome's cavalry forces but by the late-second century the significance of the title had changed. It was no longer linked to military service but to personal wealth. All citizens above a certain property level were now knights, although many of them were long past the age when cavalry service was practical. Rather they formed a second class of the elite that ranked below senators. Cavalry service was now also less attractive to young members of the elite who had hopes for a political career. Other positions on the consuls' staff offered the same opportunities without the dangers or burdens of active service. Although the effectiveness of Roman cavalry has been questioned, the swift disappearance of Italian cavalry after the spread of Roman citizenship indicates that it was social rather than military considerations that led to the end of citizen cavalry service.

The legions were sustained in the field by an elaborate supply system, which their enemies could not match. Foraging parties appear constantly in Caesar's narrative, as well as the hardships of campaigning before the grain was ripe in the fields. But foraging was by itself usually insufficient to support a large army, especially if, as in the case of a siege, it was immobile for a long period. Either supplies were requisitioned from the local population or nearby allies, or brought in from outside the theatre of operations. Local supplies were either gathered by soldiers or brought to the army by the locals who had to bear the cost of transport. Procurement of this type was crucial to the operation of all pre-modern armies. To counter the limitations of local resources the Romans developed a logistical transport system. A convincing argument has been made that the system depended on two types of bases, an operational base, which served as a major conduit for supplies into a theatre of operations, and a tactical base in the area of actual operations that changed its position with army movements. The main base was usually located at a population centre on the coast or on a navigable river as moving massive amounts of material by water was the cheapest and easiest mode of transport. The tactical base had to be supplied by pack animals and wagons, but the Romans could normally rely on local transport for much of the work. This arrangement was supplemented by strategically-located magazines, at least from the end of the third century BC.

The army did more than fight. It built roads, bridges and other large-scale projects. In Gaul the most well-known was the Rhône canal that Marius's soldiers constructed in 104 BC to ease their supply problems before meeting the Teutones in battle. The legion's engineering skill is perhaps best seen in siege warfare. The elaborate fortifications extending over a considerable distance at Alesia were beyond the ability of any other contemporary western army. It is also visible in the Roman use of artillery, not only in sieges but also on the battle field.

The Roman army was hardly invincible; the Romans suffered stunning defeats in northern Europe and elsewhere. The string of victories by the Cimbri and Teutones over Roman armies is proof that in certain circumstances the peoples of northern Europe could defeat the Romans. Despite these victories, the Romans finally prevailed. Given competent commanders or, in Caesar's case a general of genius, the Roman army's organizational, technical superiority and its enormous manpower was bound to prevail. This continued to be the case for centuries after Caesar's conquest in Gaul. It was only in the fifth-century AD, when the organization of the Roman state was in terminal decay, that the peoples of northern Europe finally had their revenge.

Notes

Introduction

1 Cassius Dio, *History of Rome* 43.19.1–4; Suetonius, *Life of Caesar* 37.1–2.
2 Cunliffe (1997) 41.
3 Caesar, *Gallic War* 6.11–20, see also Diodorus Siculus *Library of History* 5.24–32.
4 Caesar, *Gallic War* 1.4.2.
5 On the Druids in general see Aldhouse-Green (2010).
6 Momigliano (1987) 124–26.
7 Nash (1978) 455–472.
8 Clemente (1974) 21–70 and Goudineau (1983) 76–86.
9 Wightman (1985) 24.
10 Harmand (1978) 702.
11 Caesar, *Gallic War* 1.37.1.
12 Todd (2004) 1–7.
13 Diodorus Siculus, *Library of History* 5.29–30.
14 On Celtic arms and equipment see: Ritchie and Ritchie (1985), Ritchie and Ritchie (1995) 37–5, and Goudineau (1990) 259–271.
15 Polybius, *Histories* 2.23.1.
16 Polybius, *Histories* 2.33.3.
17 Hannibal had used them extensively during the Second Punic War.
18 Caesar, *Gallic War* 7.75.5.
19 Sherwin White (1967), especially 20–29, Saddington (1961) and Rankin (1987) 45–72.
20 Diodorus Siculus, *Library of History* 5.29.
21 Livy, *History of Rome* 38.17.
22 *Caesar, Gallic War* 2.27.5.
23 Livy gives a highly rhetorical and inaccurate account at 5.38; see also Plutarch, *Life of Camillus* 18, which is more sensible. An excellent reconstruction can be found in Cornell (1995) 313–318. For the Gallic migrations before 400 see Cunliffe (1997) 72–78.
24 Nash (1985) 46–60.

25 Livy, *History of Rome* 5.41.3–4.
26 Cornell (1995) 313–325.
27 Livy, *History of Rome* 10.27–30.
28 Polybius, *Histories* 2.19.12.
29 Polybius, *Histories* 2.20.2–3.
30 Polybius, *Histories* 2.27–30.
31 Harris (1989) 107–118.
32 For a good general account of the Second Punic War see J.F. Lazenby (1998).
33 Polybius, *Histories* 1.88.5.
34 Polybius, *Histories* 2.13.7.
35 For the development of the Spanish provinces see J.S. Richardson (1996).
36 Rivet (1988) 10–26.
37 Cunliffe (1988) 38.
38 Livy, *History of Rome* 37.57.1–2.
39 Livy, *History of Rome* 40.26.8 and Plutarch, *Life of Aemilius Paulus* 6.1–7.
40 Polybius, *Histories* 33.7–11. On these events see Ebel (1976) 58 and Dyson (1985) 147–148.
41 Cicero, *The Republic* 3.16.
42 Hermon (1993) 81.
43 Diodorus Siculus, *Library of History* 5.26.

Chapter 1: First Steps

1 The Salluvii were a mixed Celtic and Ligurian tribe living in the area behind Massilia between the Rhône and the Maritime Alps.
2 The sources are fragmentary and sometimes contradict each other. Even the peoples that Flaccus conquered differ in different sources. For discussions of the problems involved see Hermon (1993) 61–64 and Soricelli (1995) 27–34.
3 Stevens (1980) 71–76 is a good discussion of the problems in understanding the relationship of Flaccus' campaigns to those of Sextius. Once again the sources offer little help. The rebellion of 90 is attested in Livy *Periochae* 73.
4 Braund (1980) 420–422.
5 Strabo, *Geography* 4.2.3.
6 Rivet (1988) 41.
7 Rivet (1988) 40–41 and Soricelli (1995) 34–40.
8 Goudineau (1978) 690–692.
9 Suetonius, *Life of Nero* 2.
10 Ebel (1973) 80–81 and Rivet (1988) 43.
11 Cunliffe (1988) 79–82. There has been a dispute over the date the colony was founded, some scholars place it as early as 125. The traditional date of 118 is more likely.

12 For a good general treatment of the Gracchi, see Stockton (1979).
13 Salmon (1969) 122.
14 Caesar, *Gallic War* 1.45.2.
15 Ebel (1973) 80.
16 For this argument see Badian (1966) 901–913.
17 Ebel (1973) 75–100.
18 For the details of the migration and the encounters of these tribes with Rome see Donnadieu (1954) and Evans (2005).
19 Todd (2004) 35–39.
20 Evans (1994) provides an excellent biography with a stress on Marius' political activities. For a short discussion of his military reforms see Sage (2008) 199–207.
21 The most detailed ancient account is in Plutarch, *Life of Marius* 13–21.
22 Lewis (1974) 96.
23 For Catulus' campaign see Lewis (1974).
24 Plutarch, *Life of Marius* 24.2.
25 25.6.
26 Orosius, *The Seven Books of History against the Pagans* 5.16.22.
27 Demougeot (1978) 937.
28 For the knights in this period see Badian (1972).
29 Sage (2008) 197–198.
30 Gabba (1994) 104–128.
31 For a recent biography of Sulla see Keaveney (2005).
32 Scullard (1982) 86–89.
33 Leach (1978) 45. Pompey is said to have erected a trophy in the Pyrenees listing the 876 cities he had conquered; Pliny the Elder, *Natural History* 3.18. A growing number of scholars date the formation of the province to Pompey, but the evidence is not compelling.
34 There is an important discussion of Cicero's speech in defense of Fonteius in Clemente (1974) 97–130.
35 Cicero, *On Behalf of Fonteius* 11.
36 Cunliffe (1988) 81–83.
37 Cunliffe (1997) 214 and 238.
38 Nash (1978) 460–461.
39 Livy, *Epitome* 69 and Appian *Civil Wars* 1.29.
40 Cicero, *On Behalf of Quinctius* 11 and 12.
41 Cicero, *On Behalf of Murena* 42. For the large number of Roman businessmen and merchants, see *On Behalf of Fonteius* 11.
42 Dio 37.47–48.
43 Caesar, *Gallic War* 1.31.4–6.
44 Caesar, *Gallic War* 1.31.12.

45 Cicero, *Letters to Atticus* 1.19.2.
46 Cicero, *Letters to Atticus* 1.20.5.

Chapter 2: Caesar and Gaul: the Prelude

1 Plutarch, *Life of Crassus* 2.4.
2 For Caesar's activities in Spain see Dio, *History of Rome* 37.52–53 and Plutarch, *Life of Caesar* 11–12. See also Gelzer (1968) 61–63.
3 Appian, *Civil Wars* 2.8.
4 See Wiseman (1994) 368–375 on the events of Caesar's consulship, as well as Meier (1982) 133–221.
5 Two important perspectives on the work are provided by Stevens (1952) and Seager (2003).
6 Cicero, *Letters to his Friends* 5.12.10.
7 For this argument see Wiseman (1998).
8 *Gallic War* 1.39–40.
9 *Gallic War* 2.25.
10 *Gallic War* 4.25.
11 Cicero, *Brutus* 262.
12 Suetonius, *Life of Caesar* 56.4.
13 Plutarch, *Life of Caesar* 18.2.
14 Ramage (1985).

Chapter 3: 58: The Helvetii and Ariovistus

1 *Gallic War* 1.2. Orgetorix advanced his plan in 61. On these events see Gerhard (1991).
2 *Gallic War* 1.10.1.
3 Note the importance of clients and other dependents to Vercingetorix's rise to power, *Gallic War* 7.4.
4 For Orgetorix's plotting see *Gallic War* 1.3.4–1.4.3.
5 Wightman (1985) 24.
6 *Letters to Atticus* 1.19.1.
7 Timpe (1965) 203–204 and Seager (2003) 19–21.
8 *Gallic War* 1.5.1–4. On Vully see Goudineau (1991) 642.
9 *Gallic War* 1.12.5–6.
10 Keppie (1984) 82.
11 Rice Holmes (1911) 47–48.
12 Dumnorix had a Helvetian wife, *Gallic War* 1.18.7.
13 *Gallic War* 1.12.7.
14 *Gallic War* 1.18.1.
15 Rice Holmes (1911) 51.

16 The Emperor Augustus moved the capital of the Aedui into the plain below Mount Beuvray and it was renamed Augustodunum, modern Autun.

17 Rice Holmes (1911, 54) thinks the initial uphill attack was a feint. There is nothing in Caesar's narrative to suggest this. Goldsworthy (2003) rightly sees it as an unplanned manoeuvre. The attack of the Boii and Tulingi seems to have been launched to relieve pressure on the Helvetii.

18 Ebel (1976) 30 for the use of the Greek alphabet to write Celtic.

19 Numbers are a problem in ancient sources. In general they are not reliable for large barbarian groups. Many consider the figure of 368,000 to be a gross exaggeration. As pointed out in the text the other figures given by Caesar are congruent with it. This is the only time Caesar mentions a list which lends further support to it although the list may have been inaccurate. Perhaps it is safer as Goldsworthy (2003, 209) to simply state there was a substantial number involved.

20 Rice Holmes (1911) 50.

21 *Gallic War* 7.75.2.

22 Caesar uses Gaul here to mean the tribes of central France.

23 Diviciacus appears in *Gallic War* as Caesar's trusted advisor. He had led an embassy in 61 to the Roman Senate to seek Roman protection against the Sequani and Ariovistus. He was awarded a favourable reception but it is clear that this was simply a gesture with no substance. For an appreciation of him see Jullian (1909) 162–164.

24 The need may have been exacerbated by the fact that Ariovistus had in the previous year been named a friend of the Roman people while Caesar had held the consulship. *Gallic War* 1.35.2.

25 *Gallic War* 1.36.

26 *Gallic War* 1.39.1–2 and Dio 38.35.2 suggest that men were complaining about the fact that the campaign was unauthorized. This seems doubtful, as such expeditions were nothing new. For the significance of these remarks see the works cited in n. 7 above.

27 Caesar's version is given at *Gallic War* 1.43–46.

28 Gaius Valerius Proculus.

29 *On Germany* 6.

30 For a discussion of German cavalry equipment and tactics see Todd (2004) 35.

31 Other German prophetesses are attested. The best known is Veleda mentioned by Tacitus (*Histories* 4.65) in connection with the events of 69 AD.

32 For a summary of the various arguments and conclusions about the location of the battle see Pelling (1981) 751–766.

33 *Gallic War* 1.54.

34 In 49 Caesar had a law passed that awarded the region full citizenship.
35 Goudineau (1990) 130 thinks that that Caesar's original intention was the conquest of Illyricum and Raetia, which included much of modern Austria. Sherwin White (1957) notes that as late as 57, when he thought that Gaul was pacified, Caesar turned to Illyricum as a possible theatre of operations.

Chapter 4: 57: Caesar and the Conquest of the North
1 On the Belgae and Belgica see Wightman (1985).
2 The site is not securely identified but the most popular candidate is Vieux-Laon in Picardy.
3 Keppie (1984) 84–85.
4 *Gallic War* 2.6.
5 For the Gallic stereotype found in Greek and Latin authors see Cunliffe (1997) 5–6.
6 It was later to be used as Caesar's main supply base and was destroyed during the revolt of 52.
7 On Caesar's use of hostages see Moscovich (1979/1980).
8 *Gallic War* 2.15.3–5. For the effect of their German origins see Tacitus *On Germany* 28 and Strabo *Geography* 4.4.5.
9 Pelling (1981) 742–751 and Le Bohec (2001) 184–185.
10 Cuff (1957, 31) claims that it was Labienus' attack that decided the battle in the Romans' favour. This seems to overstate Labienus's role. If one accepts Caesar's description, the battle had already been decided in the Romans' favour and his intervention led to a more decisive victory.
11 Sherwin White (1957) 45.
12 Plutarch, *Life of Aemilius Paullus* 17.
13 *Gallic War* 2.29.3.
14 Levick (1998) 68–69.
15 *Gallic War* 2.35.1.

Chapter 5: 56: Consolidation
1 2.19.2.
2 On Clodius and his tribunate, including his relations with Cicero, see Tatum (1999).
3 For a good biography of Pompey see Seager (2002).
4 For the conference at Luca see Lazenby (1959).
5 On the political situation in Rome see Gelzer (1968) 117–124 and Meier (1982) 272–275.
6 Goldsworthy (2006) 191–192. On legates in general see Sage (2008) 112–114.
7 Stevens (1952) 7–10.
8 Strabo, *Geography* 4.4.1.

9 *Gallic War* 3.13.1–4.

10 For the Roman navy see Rougé (1981).

11 39.42.2.

12 *Gallic War* 7.75.2.

13 For the relations of the Romans and Treveri in this period see Mensching (1979).

14 *Gallic War* 1.1 and Strabo, *Geography* 4.4.2

15 On guerilla warfare during the war in Gaul see Deyber (1987).

16 *Gallic War* 4.37.1–4.

Chapter 6: 55: Britain and Germany

1 For example Rice Holmes (1911) 99 and Pelling (1981) 749–751 who thinks the river is the Meuse and that the battle was fought near Gern or Kleve. The majority of scholars think the river was the Moselle.

2 *Life of Caesar* 22.3.

3 Plutarch, *Life of Cato* 22. The senatorial delegation is mentioned in Suetonius, *Life of Caesar* 24.

4 *Gallic War* 4.17. On this see Giles (1969) 359–385 and Goudineau (1990) 232–258.

5 Wightman (1985) 3–4.

6 *Gallic War* 4.20.1.

7 *Life of Caesar* 47.

8 Strabo, *Geography* 4.5.2.

9 *Letters to Atticus* 4.17.6.

10 *Gallic War* 5.12.

11 On developments in Britain before the invasion see Grainge (2005).

12 Rice Holmes (1911) 103.

13 Grainge (2005) 105.

14 *Gallic War* 4.33–34.

15 *Gallic War* 4.38.5.

Chapter 7: 54: Gallic Resistance Grows

1 *Gallic War* 5.6.1–2.

2 Goldsworthy (2006) 280.

3 Balsdon (1967) 84.

4 *Gallic War* 5.16.1.

5 Strabo, *Geography* 2.5.8 points out that although the Romans could conquer Britain (and later did) there was nothing to gain from doing so.

6 Strabo, *Geography* 4.5.3.

7 Lintott (1993) 43–69 has an excellent discussion of the governor's role and his duties.

8 *Gallic War* 5.27.
9 These were the usual members of the commanding officer's council. It was customary practice for all magistrates to hold a council and listen to advice before they made important decisions. It continued in the imperial period when membership of the emperor's council became a powerful position. The only literary account of one is the fourth satire of Juvenal.
10 This is a standard defensive formation used when a force is surrounded. See Vegetius, *Epitome of Military Matters* 1.26.
11 On this battle see Sage (2008) 258–263.

Chapter 8: 53: Troubles at Rome and growing Threats in Gaul
1 For political developments in Rome during this period see Wiseman (1994) 368–423.
2 The situation is best summed up by the poet Lucan (*Pharsalia* 1.125–6) writing over a century later: 'Caesar would not tolerate a superior and Pompey an equal'.
3 See p. 50 above.
4 Rice Holmes (1911) 105.
5 *Gallic War* 7.2.4–5.
6 *Gallic War* 7.1.1.

Chapter 9: 52: Vercingetorix and the Great Rebellion
1 On these events see Tatum (1999) 214–240.
2 *Gallic War* 7.1.
3 *Gallic War* 7.77.15–16.
4 See above p. 171.
5 See above p. 85.
6 *Gallic War* 6.13.10–11.
7 Le Bohec (2005) 886–887.
8 See p. 2 above.
9 40.41.1.
10 Rice Holmes (1911) 134.
11 On Caesar's use of German cavalry see Tausend (1988).
12 Roth (1998) 24–32.
13 Ralston (1995) 65–68 and Cunliffe (1997) 229–230.
14 *Gallic War* 7.25.2–4.
15 Sage (2008) 276–278.
16 *Gallic War* 7.38.5.
17 For example, see Stevens (1952) 116–117 and Goldsworthy (2006) 331–332 for opposing points of view.
18 *Gallic War* 7.54.

19 Keppie (1984) 101.
20 Le Bohec (2001) 87.
21 *Gallic War* 7.67.1.
22 For a history of the excavations and a detailed analysis of its topography see Harmand (1967).
23 *Gallic War* 7.77.
24 Harmand (1967, 308–311) thinks Bussy is the likelier candidate.
25 27.8.
26 40.41.1.
27 For the man and his career see Harmand (1984).

Chapter 10: 51: Caesar's Final Campaign
1 Wightman (1985) 51.
2 See above p. 59–60.
3 The best discussion of Roman imperialism is Harris (1985). Although his detailed treatment of events ends in 70 BC his discussion of the factors that motivated conquest and expansion are valid for the entire Republican period and beyond.
4 Cuff (1957) 33–34.
5 [Caesar] *The War in Africa* 1–2.
6 See above p. 119.
7 *Life of Caesar* 15.3.
8 Suetonius, *Life of Caesar* 25.1.

Chapter 11: Epilogue: After Caesar
1 Wightman (1977) 106.
2 On the events of this period see Pelling (1996) 1–69.
3 Rice Holmes (1931) 4 and Drinkwater (1983) 120–121.
4 Drinkwater (1983) 20–22 and 94–95.
5 Fishwick (1978) 1201–1253.
6 Salmon (1969, 137–141) and Drinkwater (1983) 18–20.
7 Pliny, *Natural History B* 3.31.
8 Drinkwater (1983) 27–29.
9 For a first-rate narrative of these events see Wellesley (2000).
10 Drinkwater (1987).

Bibliography

Primary Sources in Translation

Appian, *The Civil Wars*, translated by J. Carter (London and New York, 1996), Penguin Books.

Caesar, *The Gallic War*, translated by C. Hammond, revised ed. (Oxford, 2006), The Oxford University Press.

Cassius Dio, *Roman History* translated by E. Cary (Cambridge, MA, 1914–1927), Loeb Classical Library: Harvard University Press.

Cicero, *Brutus and Orator*, translated by G.L. Hendrickson and H.M. Hubble (Cambridge, MA, 1939), Loeb Classical Library: Harvard University Press.

Cicero, *Letters to Atticus*, translated by D.R. Shackleton Bailey (New York, 1978), Penguin Books.

Cicero, *Letters to His Friends*, edited and translated by D.R.Shackleton Bailey (Cambridge, MA, 2001), Loeb Classical Library: Harvard University Press.

Cicero, *Pro Fonteio (On behalf of Fonteius)* in Cicero, *Orations, Pro Milone, etc* translated by N.H. Watts (Cambridge, MA, 1931), Loeb Classical Library: Harvard University Press.

Cicero, *Pro Murena (On Behalf of Murena)*, in Cicero, *Orations, In Catilinam 1–4*, etc., translated by C. Macdonald (Cambridge, MA, 1976), Loeb Classical Library: Harvard University Press.

Cicero, *Pro Quinctio (On behalf of Quinctius)*, translated by J.H. Freeze (Cambridge, MA, 1930), Loeb Classical Library: Harvard University Press.

Cicero, *The Republic and the Laws*, translated by N. Rudd (New York, 1998), Oxford University Press.

Diodorus Siculus, *Library of History*, translated by C.H. Oldfather (Cambridge, MA, 1933–1967), Loeb Classical Library: Harvard University Press (Cambridge, MA, 1919–1959).

Livy, *History of Rome*, translated by B.O. Foster. The translation includes the *Periochae* and the *Epitome*. Loeb Classical Library: Harvard University Press.

Pliny, *Natural History*, translated by H. Rackham (Cambridge, MA, 1938–1952), Loeb Classical Library: Harvard University Press.

Orosius, *The Seven Books of History Against the Pagans*, translated by R.J. Deferrari (Washington, DC, 1964), Catholic University of America Press.

Plutarch, *Plutarch's Lives*, translated by B. Perrin (London and New York, 1914–1926), Macmillan.

Polybius, *The Histories*, translated by W.R. Paton (Cambridge, MA, 1922–1927), Loeb Classical Library: Harvard University Press.

Strabo, *The Geography of Strabo*, translated by H.L. Jones (Cambridge, MA, 1931–1954), Loeb Classical Library: Harvard University Press.

Suetonius, 'Life of Caesar' in *The Twelve Caesars*, edited and translated by R. Graves and J. Rives (London and New York, 2007), Penguin Books.

Tacitus, *Agricola and Germania*, translated by H. Mattingly, revised by J.B. Rives (London and New York, 2009), Penguin Books.

Tacitus, *The Histories*, translated by K. Wellesley, revised by R. Ash (New York and London, 2009), Penguin Books.

Secondary Works

Aldhouse-Green, M.J. (2010), *Caesar's Druids: Story of an Ancient Priesthood*, New Haven, CT: Yale University Press.

Antonucci. C. (1996), *L'Esercito di Cesare 54–44 a.c.*, Milan.

Badian, E. (1958), *Foreign Clientelae (264–70 BC)*, Oxford: Clarendon Press.

Badian, E. (1966), 'Notes on Provincia Gallia in the Late Republic', in *Mélanges d'archéologie et d'histoire offerts à André Piganiol*, edited by R. Chevallier: 901–918.

Badian, E. (1968), *Roman Imperialism in the Late Republic*, Oxford: Basil Blackwell.

Badian, E. (1972), *Publicans and Sinners*, Ithaca, NY: Cornell University Press.

Balsdon, J.P.V.D. (1967), *Julius Caesar and Rome*, London: English Universities Press Limited.

Benedict, C.H. (1942), 'The Romans in Southern Gaul', *American Journal of Philology*, 30: 38–50.

Billows, R.A. (2008), *Julius Caesar: The Colossus of Rome*, London and New York: Routledge.

Braund, D.C. (1980), 'Aedui, Troy, and the *Apocolocyntosis*', *Classical Quarterly*, 30: 420–425.

Brown, R.D. (1999), 'Two Caesarian battle-descriptions: a study in contrast', *Classical Journal*, 94: 329–357.

Brunt, P.A. (1971), *Italian Manpower 225 BC–AD 14*, Oxford: Oxford at the Clarendon Press.

Büchsenschütz, O. (1995), 'The Celts in France', in M.J. Green, ed. *The Celtic World*, London: Routledge 552–580.

Burns, T.S. (2003), *Rome and the Barbarians, 100 BC–AD 400*, Baltimore and London: Johns Hopkins University Press.

Bowman, A.K., Champlin, E. and Lintott, A. (eds) (1994), *The Cambridge Ancient History*[2]. *Volume X: The Augustan Empire, 43 BC–AD 69*, Cambridge: Cambridge University Press.

Carney, T.F. (1970), *A Biography of C. Marius*, Chicago: Argonaut Inc.

Clemente, G. (1974), *I Romani nella Gallia meridionale (II-I sec. a C.)*, Bologna: Patron.

Collins, J.H. (1972), 'Caesar as Political Propagandist', *Aufstieg und Niedergang der Römischen Welt*, 1.1: 922–966.

Conley, D.F. (1983), 'Causes of Roman victory presented in the *Bellum Gallicum*: Caesar the commander vs. other factors, *Helios* 10: 173–186.

Connolly, P. (1974), *The Roman Army*, London: Macdonald Educational.

Cornell, T.J. (1995), *The Beginnings of Rome*, London and New York: Routledge.

Crook, J.A., Lintott, A. and Rawson, E. (1994), *The Cambridge Ancient History*[2]. *Volume IX: The Last Age of the Roman Republic*, Cambridge: Cambridge University Press.

Cuff, P.J. (1957), 'Caesar the Soldier', *Greece & Rome* 4: 29–35.

Cunliffe, B. (1988), *Greeks, Romans and Barbarians:. Spheres of Interaction*, London: B.T. Batsford.

Cunliffe, B. (1997), *The Ancient Celts*, Oxford: Oxford University Press.

D'Amato, R. & G. Sumner (2009), *Arms and Armour of the Imperial Roman Soldier*, London: Frontline.

Delbrück, H. (1975), *History of the Art of War Within the Framework of Political History Vol. I: Warfare in Antiquity*, translated by W.J. Renfroe Jr, Lincoln and London: University of Nebraska Press.

Demougeot, E. (1978), 'L'invasion des Cimbres-Teutones-Ambrons et les Romains, *Latomus* 37: 911–938.

Deyber, A. (1987), 'La guérilla gauloise pendant la guerre des Gauls (58–50 avant J.-C.)', *Études Celtiques*, 24: 145–183.

Donnadieu, D.A. (1954), 'La campaigne de Marius dans Gaule Narbonnaise (104–102 av. Julio-Claudian): la bataille d' Aix-en-Provence (Aquae Sextiae) et ses deux épisodes', *Revue des Études* 56: 281–296.

Drinkwater, J.F. (1983), *Roman Gaul: The Three Provinces 58 BC–AD 260*, Ithaca, NY: Cornell University Press.

Drinkwater, J.F. (1987), *The Gallic Empire: Separatism and Continuity in the North-Western Provinces of the Roman Empire*, Stuttgart: Franz Steiner Verlag.

Dyson, S.L. (1968), 'Caesar and the Natives', *Classical Journal* 63: 341–346.

Dyson, S.L. (1971), 'Native Revolts in the Roman Empire', *Historia* 20: 239–274.

Dyson, S.L. (1976), 'L. Calpurnius Piso Caesoninus and Transalpine Gaul', *Latomus* 35: 356–362.

Dyson, S.L. (1985), *The Creation of the Roman Frontier*, Princeton, NJ: Princeton University Press.

Ebel, C. (1976), *Transalpine Gaul: The Emergence of a Roman Province* , Leiden: Brill.

Ebel, C. (1988), 'Southern Gaul in the Triumviral Period: a Critical Stage of Romanization', *American Journal of Philology* 109: 572–590.

Evans, R.J. (1994), *Gaius Marius a Political Biography*, Praetoria: University of South Africa.

Evans, R.J. (2005), 'Rome's Cimbric Wars (114–101 BC) and their Impact on the Iberian Peninsula', *Acta Classica* 48: 37–56.

Fischer, F. (2004), 'Caesars strategische Planung für Gallien : zum Verhältnis von Darstellung und Wirklichkeit', in *AD Fontes*, Festschrift G, Dobesch, Vienna: 305–315.

Fishwick, D. (1978), 'The Development of Provincial Ruler Worship in the Western Roman Empire', *Aufstieg und Niedergang der Römischen Welt* 2.16: 1201–53.

Freyberger, B. (1997), 'Die Entwicklung Südgalliens zwischen Eroberung und augusteischer Reorganisation (125/22 bis 27/22 v. Chr.)' *Gymnasium* 104: 319–343.

Gabba, E. (1994), 'Rome and Italy: The Social War', in *The Cambridge Ancient History*[2]. *Volume IX. The Last Age of the Republic*, Cambridge: Cambridge University Press: 104–128.

Gardner J.F. (1983), 'The 'Gallic Menace' in Caesar's Propaganda', *Greece & Rome* 30: 181–189.

Gelzer, M. (1968), *Caesar Politician and Statesman*, translated by P. Needham. Cambridge, MA: Harvard University Press.

Gerhard, Y. (1991), 'Orgétorix l'Helvète et le *Bellum Gallicum* de César', *Les Études Classiques* 59: 267–274.

Gilbert. F. (2004), *Le Soldat Romain: A la fin de la Republique et Sous le Haut-Empire*, Paris.

Gilbert. F. (2006), *Legionnaires et Auxiliaires: Sous le Haut-Empire Romain*, Paris.

Gilbert, F. and Vincent, F. (2011), *L'armée de César pendant la guerre des Gaules*, Paris.

Giles, R.C. (1969), 'How Caesar Bridged the Rhine', *Classical Journal* 64: 359–365.

Goldsworthy, A.K. (1996), *The Roman Army at War 100 BC–AD 200*, Oxford: Oxford University Press.

Goldsworthy, A. (2006), *Caesar: the Life of a Colossus*, London: Weidenfield and Nicolson.

Goudineau, C. (1978), 'la Gaule transalpine' in Nicolet, C., *Rome et la conquête du monde: 264–27 av. J.C.*, Paris: Presses Universitaires de France, 679–699.

Goudineau, C. (1983), 'Marseilles, Rome and Gaul from the Third to the First Century BC' in P. Garnsey, K. Hopkins and C.R. Whittaker (eds), *Trade in the Ancient Economy*, Berkeley: The University of California Press: 76–86.

Goudineau, C. (1990), *César et la Gaule*, Paris: Editions Errance.

Goudineau, C. (1991), 'La guerre des Gauls et l'archéologie', *Comptes rendus de l'Académie des Inscriptions et Belles-Lettres* 641–653.

Grainge, G. (2005), *The Roman Invasions of Britain*, Stroud, UK: Tempus Publishing Ltd.

Greenhalgh, P. (1981), *Pompey: the Roman Alexander*, Columbia MO: University of Missouri Press.

Hackl, U. (1988), 'Die Gründung der Provinz Gallia Narbonensis im Spiegel von Ciceros Rede für Fonteius', *Historia* 37: 253–6.

Harmand, J. (1967), *Une campaigne Césarienne: Alesia*, Paris: Éditions A. et J. Picard et Cie.

Harmand, J. (1978), 'La Gaul indépendente et la Conquête', in Nicolet, C., *Rome et la conquête du monde Méditerranéen* II, Paris: Presses Universitaires de France 700–726.

Harmand, J. (1982), 'La conquête césarienne des Gaules. Le bilan économique et humain', *RSA*, 85–130.

Harmand, J. (1984), *Vercingétorix*, Paris: Fayard.

Harris, W.V. (1985), *War and Imperialism in Republican Rome, 327–70 BC*, Oxford: Clarendon Press.

Harris, W.V. (1989), 'Roman Expansion in the West', in *The Cambridge Ancient History*[2]. *Vol. VII: The Rise of Rome to 220 BC*, Cambridge: The Cambridge University Press, 107–118.

Hermon, E. (1991) 'Modèles d'administration provinciale durant la République et son application en Gaule transalpine entre les années 125–59 av. J.-C.', *Cahiers des Études Anciennes* 26: 197–214.

Hermon, E. (1993), *Rome et la Gaule Transalpine avant César*, Naples: Loyene, Quebec: Presses de l'Université Laval.

Hoffman,W. (1952), 'Zur Vorgeschichte von Caesars Eingreifen in Gallien', *Der Altsprachliche Unterricht* 4: 5–22.

Holmes Rice, T. (1911), *Caesar's Conquest of Gaul*[2], Oxford: Clarendon Press.

Holmes Rice, T. (1928), *The Architect of the Roman Empire*, Oxford: The Clarendon Press.

Inker, P.A. (2008), *Caesar's Gallic Triumph: The battle of Alesia 52 BC*, Barnsley, UK: Pen & Sword Military.

Jullian, C. (1909), *Histoire de la Gaule III*, Paris: Librairie Hachette.

Keaveney, A. (2005), *Sulla the Last Republican*[2], London and New York: Routledge.

Keppie, L.J.F. (1984), *The Making of the Roman Army*, Totowa, NJ: Barns and Noble Books.

Kraus, C. (2009), 'Bellum Gallicum', in Griffin, M., *A Companion to Julius Caesar*, Chichester, UK and Malden MA: Wiley-Blackwell: 159–174.

Lazenby, J.F. (1959) 'The Conference at Luca and the Gallic War: a Study in Roman Politics 57–55 BC', *Latomus* 18: 67–76.

Lazenby J.F. (1998), *Hannibal's War*, Norman, OK: University of Oklahoma Press.

Le Bohec, Y. (2001), *César chef de guerre*, Monaco: Rocher.

Le Bohec, Y. (2001), 'Stratégie et tactique dans les livres V et VI du «De bello Gallico»', *Revue des Ëtudes Latines* 79: 70–92.

Le Bohec, Y. (2005), 'Le clergé celtique et la guerre des Gaules: historiographie et politique', *Latomus* 64: 871–881.

Le Bohec, Y. (2005), 'César et l'économie pendant la guerre des Gaules' in Meßner, B., Schmitt, O. and Somme, M. (eds), *Krieg-Gesellschaft-Institutionen: Beiträge zur einer vergleichenden Kriegsgeschichte*, Berlin: Akademie Verlag: 317–333.

Le Roux, P. (2006), 'Rome et le monde celtique à la veille de la conquête césarienne', in Paunier, D., *La romanisation et la question de l'héritage celtique, Actes de la table ronde de Lausanne 17–18 juin 2005*, Glux-en-Glenne: Centre Archéologique Européen.

Leach, J. (1978), *Pompey the Great*, London: Croom Helm Ltd.

Lendon, J.E. (1999), 'The Rhetoric of Combat: Greek Military Theory and Roman Culture in Julius Caesar's Battle Descriptions', *Classical Antiquity* 18: 273–329.

Levick, B. (1998), 'The Veneti Revisited: C.E. Stevens and the Tradition on Caesar the Propagandist', in Welch, K. and Powell, A. (eds), *Julius Caesar as Artful Reporter*. London: Duckworth and The Classical Press of Wales: 61–83.

Lewis, R.G. (1974), 'Catulus and the Cimbri', *Hermes* 102: 90–109.

Lieberg, G. (1998), *Caesars Politik in Gallien: Interpretationen zum Bellum Gallicum*, Bochum: Brockmeyer.

Lintott, A. (1993), *Imperium Romanum*, London and New York: Routledge.

Mathieu. F. (2007), *Le Guerrier Gaulois: Du Hallstatt a la Conquete Romaine*, Paris.

McDougall, I. (1991), 'Dio and his Sources for Caesar's Campaigns in Gaul', *Latomus* 50: 616–638.

Meier, Chr (1996), *Caesar: A Biography*, translated by D. McLintock, New York: Basic Books.

Mensching, E. (1979), 'Die Treverer im Jahr 57 v. Chr.', *Latomus* 38: 902–931.

Momigliano, A. (1987), *On Pagans, Jews and Christians*, Middletown, CT.: Wesleyan University Press.

Moscovich, M.J. (1979/1980), '*Obsidibus Traditis*: Hostages in Caesar's *De Bello Gallico*', *Classical Journal* 75: 122–128.

Nash, D. (1978), 'Territory and State Formation in Central Gaul', in Green, D., Haselgrove, C. and Spriggs, M, (eds), *Organization and Settlement BAR:* 455–472.

Nash, D. (1985), 'Celtic Territorial Expansion and the Mediterranean World', in Champion, T.C. and Megaw, J.V.S.D., *Settlement and Society: Aspects of West European Prehistory in the First Millennium*, New York: St. Martin's Press 45–67.

Pelling, C.B.R. (1981), 'Caesar's Battle-Descriptions and the Defeat of Ariovistus', *Latomus* 40: 741–766.

Pelling, C.B. (1996), 'The Triumviral Period', in *The Cambridge Ancient History²*. *Vol. X: The Augustan Empire* Cambridge: The Cambridge University Press: 1–69.

Raaflaub, K. (2009), 'Bellum Civile', in Griffin, M. (ed.), *A Companion to Julius Caesar*, Chichester, UK; Malden MA: Wiley-Blackwell: 175–191.

Ralston, I. (1995), 'Fortifications and Defence', in Green, M.J. (ed.), *The Celtic World*, London: Routledge. 59–81.

Ramage, E.S. (1985), 'Augustus' Treatment of Julius Caesar', *Historia* 34: 223–245.

Rambaud, M. (1958), 'L'ordre de bataille de l'armée des Gaules d'après les Commentaires de César', *REA* 60: 87–130.

Rankin, H.D. (1987), *Celts and the Classical World*, London and Sydney: Croom Helm Ltd.

Richardson, J.S. (1996), *The Romans in Spain*, Cambridge, MA: Blackwell.

Ritchie, J.N.G. and W.F. (1985), *Celtic Warriors*, Aylesbury Bucks: Shire Publications.

Ritchie, J.N.G. and W.F. (1995), 'The Army, Weapons and Fighting', in Green, M.J. (ed.), *The Celtic World*, London: Routledge: 37–58.

Rivet, A.L.F. (1988), *Gallia Narbonensis: Southern France in Roman Times*, London: B. JT. Batsford Ltd.

Roman, D. (1993), 'M. Fulvius Flaccus et la frontière transalpine', in Roman, Y. (ed.), *La Frontière*, Travaux de la Maison de l'Orient Méditerranéen 21: Lyon: GDR-Maison de l'Orient: 57–66.

Roman, D. and Roman, Y. (1993), 'Idéologie et chronologie: le cas de la conquête de la Transalpine', *Ktema* 18: 147–157.

Roman, Y. (1991), 'L'intervention romaine de 154 avant J.-C. en Gaule transalpine: essai d'analyse', *Revue de archéologique de Narbonnaise* 24: 35–38.

Rosenstein, N. (2009), 'General and Imperialist', in Griffin, M., *A Companion to Julius Caesar*, Chichester, UK, Malden MA: Wiley-Blackwell: 85–98.

Roth, J.P. (1998), *The Logistics of the Roman Army at War (264 BC–AD 235)*, Leiden: E.J. Brill.

Rougé, J. (1981), *Ships and Fleets of the Ancient Mediterranean*, translated by Frazier, S., Middletown CT: Weslyan University Press.

Saddington, D.B. (1961), 'Roman Attitudes to the *Externae Gentes* of the North', *Acta Classica* 1: 90–102.

Sage, M.M. (2008), *The Republican Roman Army: a Sourcebook*, New York and London: Routledge.

Salmon, T.T. (1969), *Roman Colonization under the Republic*, London: Thames and Hudson.

Scullard, H.H. (1982), *From the Gracchi to Nero*[5], London and New York: Methuen.

Seager, R. (2002), *Pompey the Great*[2]. *A Political Biography*, Oxford: Blackwell.

Seager, R. (2003), 'Caesar and Gaul: Some Perspectives on the «*Bellum Gallicum*»', in Fantham, E. (ed.), *Caesar Against Liberty*, Cambridge: Francis Cairns 19–34.

Sherwin-White, A.N. (1957), 'Caesar as an Imperialist', *Greece & Rome* 4: 36–45.

Sherwin White, A.N. (1967), *Racial Prejudice in Ancient Rome*, Cambridge: Cambridge University Press.

Soricelli, G. (1995), *La Gallia Transalpina tra la conquista e l'eta caesariana*, Como: Biblioteca di Athenaeum.

Stevens, C.E. (1952), 'The *Bellum Gallicum* as a Work of Propaganda', *Latomus* 11: 3–18.

Stevens, C.E. (1980), 'North-West Europe and Roman Politics (125–118)', in Deroux, C. (ed.), *Studies in Latin Literature and Roman History II*: 71–97.

Stockton, D.L. (1979), *The Gracchi*, Oxford: The Clarendon Press.

Sumner, G. (2009), *Roman Military Dress*, Stroud: History Press.

Tatum, J. (1999), *The Patrician Tribune: P. Clodius Pulcher*, Chapel Hill NC and London: University of North Carolina Press.

Tausend, K. (1988), 'Caesars germanische Reiter', *Historia* 37: 491–497.

Thorne, J. (2007), 'The Chronology of the Campaign Against the Helvetii: a Clue to Caesar's Intentions?', *Historia* 56: 27–36.

Timpe, D. (1965), 'Caesars gallischer Krieg und das Problem des römischen Imperialismus', *Historia* 14: 189–214.

Todd, M. (1987), *The Northern Barbarians (100 BC AD 300)* , rev. ed. Oxford: Basil Blackwell.

Todd, M. (2004), *The Early Germans*², Malden, MA: Blackwell.

Vitali, D. (1999), 'The Celts in Italy', in Kruta, V. et al., *The Celts*, New York: Rizzoli International 230–247.

Vogt, J. (1960), 'Caesar und seine Soldaten', in Vogt, J., *Orbis: ausgewählte Schriften zur Geschichte des Altertums*, Freiburg: Herder: 89–109.

Welles, C.M. (2009), 'The Events of the Summer of 56 BC: Caesar in Brittany and the Manche', in Hanson, W.S. (ed), *The Army and Frontiers of Rome, Papers Offered to David J. Breeze*, Portsmouth RI: Journal of Roman Archaeology: 153–162.

Wellesly, K. (2000), *The Year of the Four Emperors*, London and New York: Routledge.

Wightman, E.W. (1985), *Gallia Belgica*, Berkley and Los Angeles: University of California Press.

Wiseman, T.P. (1994), 'Caesar, Pompey and Rome 59–50 BC', in *The Cambridge Ancient History*². *Volume IX: The Last Age of the Roman Republic*, 368–423.

Wiseman, T.P. (1998), 'The Publication of the *De Bello Gallico*', in Welch, K. and Powell, A. (eds), *Julius Caesar as Artful Reporter*, London: Duckworth and The Classical Press of Wales: 1–9.

Index

Modern names of towns are in parentheses